MAKING BOARDS WORK

What Directors Must Do To Make Canadian Boards Effective

DAVID S.R. LEIGHTON
Nabisco Brands
Professor Emeritus

DONALD H. THAIN
Magna International
Professor Emeritus

The Richard Ivey School of Business
The University of Western Ontario

McGraw-Hill Ryerson Limited

Toronto Montréal New York Auckland Bogotá Caracas Lisbon
London Madrid Mexico Milan New Delhi San Juan
Singapore Sydney Tokyo

McGraw-Hill
Ryerson Limited

A Subsidiary of The ***McGraw-Hill*** *Companies*

MAKING BOARDS WORK: What Directors Must Do To Make Canadian Boards Effective

Care has been taken to trace ownership of copyright material contained in this text. However, the publishers welcome any information that will enable them to rectify any reference or credit in subsequent editions.

Note to Readers: Throughout the book we have used many cases to illustrate our points. Although all are based on actual situations, none of them happened in exactly the way described. We have disguised names, places, companies, industries, dates and other key elements to protect those involved, and no inference is warranted as to their actual identity.

McGraw-Hill Ryerson Limited
300 Water Street
Whitby, Ontario L1N 9B6
http://www.mcgrawhill.ca

1 2 3 4 5 6 7 8 9 0 TR1 6 5 4 3 2 1 0 9 8 7

Canadian Cataloguing in Publication Data

Leighton, David S.R.
Thain, Donald H.
Making boards work: what directors must do to make Canadian boards effective

Includes index.
ISBN 0-07-552834-7

1. Directors of corporations – Canada.
2. Corporate governance – Canada.

I. Thain, Donald H., Leighton, David S.R. II. Title.

HD2745.L44 1997 658.4'22'0971 C96-932493-6

Publisher: **Joan Homewood**
Editor: **Erin Moore**
Production Coordinator: **Sharon Hudson**
Cover Design: **ArtPlus Limited**
Interior Design/Composition: **Computer Composition of Canada, Inc.**
Editorial Services: **Allyson May**
Printed and bound in Canada.

To Peggy and Helen.

Contents

Detailed Table of Contents

Foreword

A number of significant events in the last decade, ultimately labelled as failures by corporate boards and their respective directors, gave rise to two major initiatives resulting in the (U.K.) Cadbury Report of 1992 and the (Canadian) Dey Report of 1994, *Where Were The Directors?* The term "Corporate Governance" became the descriptive title for a plethora of written prescriptions covering every aspect of the subject, from the legalistic interpretation of director responsibilities to check lists and guidelines listing the ingredients of good corporate governance. The Toronto Stock Exchange, following the recommendation of the Dey Report, which it had sponsored, introduced annual voluntary reporting on governance to shareholders by publicly-traded companies in Canada.

There is no question that the result of this collective effort has been the awakening of directors and their boards to a higher level of director responsibility. However, I am certain that the response across corporate Canada has been decidedly uneven. It is clear that some companies have put forth a valiant effort to become, and to be seen as having become, models of good corporate governance, while others have not.

It is therefore very timely that David Leighton and Donald Thain have come forward with *Making Boards Work: What Directors Must Do To Make Canadian Boards Effective*, a book which will substantially advance the practical understanding of effective governance. In a sense, this work picks up where earlier writings left off. It is not another report of academic research. It is an eminently practical guide to action by shareholders and boards to improve board performance.

Making Boards Work focuses on "best practices" by boards, and professional standards of directorship. It identifies some of the many barriers to change and outlines a program to overcome them. It advocates that shareholders, boards and management collaborate to improve board effectiveness from within — and not have regulations and legislation imposed on them from the outside. It dismisses more radical solutions, such as getting rid of boards altogether, and rejects further government interference in the process of board reform.

In writing this book, the authors draw not only on their own extensive and rigorous research, but on more than 30 years' experience as directors and collectively involving membership on 31 corporate boards. Both have been chairmen of significant publicly-traded companies. Their prescriptions for board reform are strong stuff and, though often provocative and controversial, their analysis "rings true" to anyone who has been there.

I strongly commend this book to anyone interested in the way our corporations are governed. It should be "must" reading for board members, shareholders, managers, lawyers, accountants, money managers, politicians and government officials interested in making the capitalist system in Canada work better.

Arden R. Haynes, O.C.
January 1997

During his time as Chairman, CEO and President of Imperial Oil Limited, Mr. Haynes was actively involved in advocating improved board effectiveness and was a frequent guest lecturer at various universities across Canada on the subjects of business ethics and related corporate behaviour. Since his retirement, his interest in corporate governance has extended to the various boards of which he is a member. He is currently chair of the Governance Committees at the Royal Bank of Canada and Rio Algom Limited, where substantial changes are being implemented. Mr. Haynes is the present Chancellor of York University in Toronto.

Preface

Back in 1987, confronted both personally and professionally by many issues of corporate governance, we began to research and write extensively on the problems and performance of Canadian corporate boards of directors, and to advocate reforms and improvements. We had each been fortunate in our careers to have served on a number of corporate boards. Comparing notes on that experience, we had individually concluded that boards were capable of making a substantial difference in the way in which companies worked, and that improving board performance was a necessary, challenging and worthwhile objective. We had each seen highly effective boards at first hand; we had also experienced situations where boards were ineffective, impotent and seriously underperforming. What made the difference?

It is important to understand the research problem we faced. The hard reality is that stereotypical academic research in management — posing hypotheses, gathering relevant data, and testing for validity — was not then, nor is it now, possible in much of the field of corporate governance.

There are several difficulties. One of them is conceptual: in the words of Jean-Claude Delorme, former CEO of the Caisse de Dépot, "we cannot establish a cause and effect relationship between corporate governance and corporate performance. As long as we do not show that a relationship exists between the two, the principles of corporate governance will be the object of polite attention or perhaps more often the object of generalized scepticism." Despite this caveat, the volume of research in corporate governance has, from a trickle less than ten years ago, become a veritable flood. When we began the research program in corporate governance at the National Centre for Management Research and Development in 1989, a review of the bibliography was short and simple, and courses on the subject, in North America at least, were few and far between. At the time of writing this book, the bibliography has grown many-fold, and most leading business schools, including Harvard, Northwestern, Wharton and

Stanford in the U.S., and Ivey and York in Canada, offer a variety of courses ranging from short executive-level programs to graduate seminars. New journals have sprung up, and the few that were in existence in 1989 (e.g., *Directors and Boards*, founded 1976) have expanded. A growing number of articles on governance have appeared in the traditional management journals and in the popular press; *The Economist*, for example, quite regularly reports on the results of academic research on the subject.

THE RESEARCH PROBLEM

To the would-be corporate governance researcher, the nature of the subject poses a number of significant problems. Although much of the research properly focuses on the key role of the board of directors, the fact that directors are part of a small but dynamic and complex social group is often overlooked. Equally, it is often forgotten that the board as a body is only one element in a much more complex political, social, and economic system of governance that includes not only shareholders, management and operating-level employees, but also a sometimes bewildering array of ''stakeholders'' — customers, suppliers, creditors, pensioners, communities, public interest groups, regulators, politicians, governments, and whole countries. Furthermore, it is a highly dynamic system, constantly changing and evolving.

The difficulty is compounded by the nature of the board of directors and the way most boards operate. Few aspects of business are so inaccessible to the outsider: boards operate with virtually complete confidentiality. Most boards today number two or at most three ''insiders'' — the CEO and perhaps the president and chief financial officer — among their ranks; the rest are, to varying degrees, ''independents''. Their deliberations are conducted behind closed doors, and their decisions are normally ratified by unanimous votes and reported when required through a single spokesman, very much like a cabinet in the political sphere. There are good reasons for this, not the least being the danger of giving away competitive advantage or disclosing premature or misleading information that could affect the decisions of investors. As a result, the board of directors remains a kind of ''black box'', whose internal workings can only be surmised from public information about decisions announced and actions taken.

This is a serious, insurmountable problem for most researchers. Having a model for understanding, if not controlling, the way in which the research subject behaves is usually a prerequisite for insightful research in social science, where the subjects are living human beings. Social science research — which is what governance research is — is difficult and tentative enough without the complications introduced by virtually complete confidentiality about the way the research subject works, and the consequent lack of knowledge on the part of the researcher.

TRADITIONAL RESEARCH METHODOLOGY

A great deal of the recent research on corporate governance follows a pattern of "scientific method" adapted to the social sciences from earlier work in the natural and physical sciences, where the subject can be to some extent isolated, controlled and measured. In most corporate governance research, a hypothetical relationship is posed between some measurable governance variable — such as the compensation of the CEO, the number of shares owned by directors and/or management, or the ratio of outside to inside directors in a given company — and the company's financial results. A sample of companies is then selected, data gathered on the two variables (i.e., outside/inside director ratio, and a measure of financial performance, such as annual return on investment over a period of years), and statistical correlations run to see if there is indeed any significant relationship. Although individual researchers may apply considerably more sophisticated mathematical tests, such as multivariate analysis, and the data used to measure financial performance may be considerably more complex, involving a number of lagging financial measures of varying sorts, this is essentially the methodology used in most governance research today. On the surface at least, it seems perfectly logical: if the objective of boards is primarily to maximize "shareholder value" over time, then the use of some measure of shareholder value should be used to determine how well the board is doing its job. And if we can isolate some characteristic of boards, such as the ratio of outside to inside directors, we can test whether and to what extent the outside/inside composition of boards seems to influence shareholder value.

Innumerable academic studies of these type have been conducted to evaluate the effectiveness of a company's board of directors, or some feature thereof. None, to our knowledge, has ever been wholly convincing, for two main reasons: the lack of any direct, measurable cause-effect relationship between the functioning of the board and the results of the company, and the inherent difficulties involved in using reported accounting data to measure company performance. These in turn stem from some of the unique characteristics of corporate boards, and the lack of understanding of the nature and contextual complexity of these characteristics on the part of researchers through no fault of their own, denied as they are access to the corporate boardroom and lacking the ability to see the board operate.

Furthermore, this lack of knowledge extends to how the board interacts with the other elements of the corporation to produce the end result — expressed as a set of numbers produced for a specific purpose, subject to all sorts of accounting rules and conventions that change from time to time, not necessarily comparable from firm to firm, and which may be quite misleading as any indicator of intrinsic ''shareholder value''. Directors who have served on audit committees know that there is a great deal more art and judgment to accounting presentations than most outsiders appreciate. Mathematical manipulation of these numbers gives an aura of false precision to such research: the measurement problem remains.

That this research has not resulted in any conclusions of practical value should not surprise us. Anyone who has served on a corporate board can tell you that board influence is subtle, indirect and long term. Many times its greatest contribution is in the avoidance of mistakes. Most boards spend their time analyzing, discussing and approving proposals that originate with and, flow from, management. Only occasionally do they reject such proposals outright. Even more rarely do they initiate action on their own — such as replacement of a CEO, or payment of a bonus, for example. The quality and nature of board decisions is determined by many things, visible and invisible, including to a large degree the quality of information that is given to directors by management. This is not to say that the way in which a board operates does not have, or cannot have, a major influence on how well a company performs over time. It *does* say that trying to isolate various aspects of the board and how it is run, and quantifying and attributing results to these aspects, is virtually impossible.

DO-ABLE GOVERNANCE RESEARCH

If conventional approaches to governance research are not fruitful, is there a better way? We think there is, and that it is grounded in field research, messy, imprecise, and difficult as it is.

The very problems we have outlined led the authors into the field in 1987. We had both started our academic careers in the mid 1950s in the field of marketing, coming from the Harvard Business School and its tradition of empirical, case-based research. For a period of nearly 15 years we collaborated and published material based on field research. Our paths diverged, leading both of us into both boards and management, and then converged again in the late 1980s. In the interim, we had each served as a chairman of a significant corporation. We had observed 31 diverse corporate boards at first hand — in some cases over a period of as much as 25 to 30 years. We each had strong observational and conceptual skills, honed by years of case-oriented field research.

At that time, the field had been all but ignored by the academic world. It seemed logical then, and even more so today, that we concentrate our research efforts on something we knew well and was important. We recognized that our ''sample'' had come about largely by happenstance, and not by plan. Furthermore, we had been both participants in as well as observers of the events that had taken place, but we also knew that if we had not been participants, we could never have become observers. While these were certainly limitations to the purity of our research, they seemed to us to be the only way in which the ''black box'' problem could be overcome. We could start with knowledge of how the system worked, and we were confident that we could look reasonably objectively at our own roles in the process. How should we start?

We were quickly drawn into areas such as defining the job of directors and boards, leadership, management of the board, board culture, and the qualities and selection of excellent directors. We realized early on that much of what we had learned about boards had come about in problem situations, and this dictated much of our approach. As we discussed and refined some of our concepts, we began to write a series of articles outlining our ideas. These drew an extraordinarily strong response from directors, managers, and investors, and a series of ''best article'' awards from juries of businessmen. At this point we began to recognize that we were on to something, and the subsequent airing of our generalizations at conferences and in further articles led to further reinforcement: what we were saying made sense to people in the field. The idea that this might lead to a volume such as this was born at that time.

The critical factor in this assessment was our business audience. We were talking from experience, tempered strongly by our academic training, on subjects that were considered important, and what we were saying met with a generally positive response. Our ''sample'' of boards was being tested against the universe and its validity was being confirmed.

Having said this, we hasten to add that many of our ideas and recommended courses of action have been, and will continue to be, controversial. We have challenged a great deal of conventional wisdom. Nevertheless, we believe that our underlying data is sound and extensive, and we see our prescriptive recommendations as flowing logically from that base. We accept that not all our readers will agree with us, and that some of our academic colleagues will be critical of our work as ''soft'', and dealing with nonquantifiable observation. So be it.

Acknowledgements

In a very real sense, we owe our education in corporate governance to the many directors, and especially to the many chairmen, of the boards on which we have been privileged to have served. That education spans 31 corporate boards, roughly 280 man-years of board service, and literally thousands of board and committee meetings.

This history has been a learning experience in many ways — exciting, stimulating, intellectually and personally rewarding in many cases; depressing, time-wasting and frustrating in many others. We have been led to exhilarating heights on some boards, and soul-searching depths on others. We have learned from them all, the good and the bad. It is from the lessons learned that we decided to write this book.

Two individuals have had a particularly profound influence on our growth and development as directors. We were fortunate early in this process to serve under Ralph Barford and Allyn Taylor, whose leadership, wisdom, integrity and judgment provided us with role models, and demonstrated that boards could be effective contributors to the process of corporate governance: the central theme of this book.

In the process of board service, we have rubbed shoulders with literally hundreds of fellow directors and dozens of chairmen. Many have become our closest friends and colleagues, and we owe them much. Some who have had a particularly strong influence include Jack Adams, Philippe de Gaspé Beaubien, Jim Black, Bob Butler, Mickey Cohen, Jack Cooper, Purdy Crawford, Bill Dimma, Peter Dey, Tony Fell, George Gardiner, Sam Gibara, Jim Gillies, Gordon Gray, Ken Harrigan, Arden Haynes, Ross Johnson, Peter Maurice, John McArthur, Ben Orenstein, Gordon Osbaldeston, Bruce Pearson, Larry Tapp, Ross Turner, and Ed Waitzer.

We were first introduced to the importance of boards of directors in our work at the Harvard Business School, particularly under the influence of Edmund P. Learned, Myles Mace and Kenneth Andrews. We owe much to Harvard for a thorough grounding in the case method and empiricism, which is reflected in our approach to research.

The University of Western Ontario Business School (now the Ivey Business School) was home to both of us for a considerable portion of our working lives, and has had a tradition of research and writing on the subject of corporate boards. Our colleague, the late Jack McDougall, hosted conferences and wrote insightfully on the topic some 30 years ago; his was a voice ahead of his time. His research and ours has been supported by a number of the school's deans, including F.W.P. Jones, Jack Wettlaufer, Bud Johnston, and today, Larry Tapp, as well as by Dave Leighton's successors as directors of the National Centre for Management Research and Development, Jim Hatch and Ken Hardy. The *Business Quarterly*, Canada's management journal, published by the Ivey Business School, has been particularly helpful over the years, and many of the ideas in this book first saw the light of day in articles by us in that publication. The strong positive response to our articles, and the forum discussions arranged by the editors, encouraged us to proceed further to the point where we realized that we had the makings of a full-scale book. We are indebted to the editors, Andy Grindlay, Doreen Sanders, and Angela Smith, for their encouragement.

Many of our colleagues, both at Western and elsewhere, have provided ongoing stimulation through their ideas, comments, criticisms and help. Foremost among them must be Jim Gillies, who exemplifies the best qualities of academic and practitioner, and who kept the flame of interest in governance alive when no one else seemed to care. Others who have contributed much include Larry Agranove, Paul Bergman, Bruce Buchan, Arthur Earle, Jeffrey Gandz, Garnet Garven, John Gordon, Michael Kennedy, Jonathon Kovacheff, Katy Leighton-Squires, Donald Lewis, the late Keith Louden, Kathryn Montgomery, Roger More, Paul Moynihan, Jerry Mulcahy, and Patrick O'Callaghan. Valuable and much-appreciated help in the production of the manuscript was provided by Pat Avery, Kym Hunt, Sue O'Driscoll, Jean Robertson, Karen (Belch) Scriven, Anna Showler, and Connie Zrini. The staff at McGraw-Hill Ryerson, who took it from there, included Joan Homewood, Erin Moore, Lynda Peckham-Walthert and Julia Woods. John Dill, president of McGraw-Hill Ryerson, helped speed things along on at least two occasions. Any shortcomings in the work are, of course, the responsibility of the authors.

One of the difficult stylistic issues with which we grappled in writing this book was that of gender-neutral language. We recognize that there is a growing use of such language in business generally, and in boards specifically. But a chairman is still referred to as chairman in most legislation and corporate by-laws. Moreover, to refer to ''chair'' or ''chairperson'' in parts of the text, but to use ''chairman'' when quoting other writings, would, in our view, have been awkward and confusing. So we agreed to stay with ''chairman''. By the same token, using ''him or her'', or ''his or hers'', every time we used the third person pronoun seemed unnecessarily fussy and complicated. The fact is that women are still, regrettably, a very minor force in corporate governance and boards, like it or not. And while we set out to change the world of governance, we just didn't feel ready to try to change the world of English usage as well.

Throughout the book we have used many cases to illustrate our points. Although all are based on actual situations, none of them happened in exactly the way described. We have disguised names, places, companies, industries, dates and other key elements to protect those involved, and no inference is warranted as to their actual identity.

David S.R. Leighton
Donald H. Thain
London, Ontario
January, 1997

About the Authors

David S.R. Leighton is Nabisco Brands Professor Emeritus at the Ivey Business School. He has an MBA and DBA from Harvard, LLD degrees from Windsor and Queen's. He has served as board chairman of Nabisco Brands Ltd., and as a board member of numerous corporations. He was president and CEO of the Banff Centre for 13 years.

Corporate Boards

Acres International Ltd. (consulting engineers) 1985-89
A.I.L.-Alberta Investments Ltd. (investment fund) 1978-82
The Blackburn Group, Inc. (media holding company) 1987-present
Cambridge Shopping Centres Ltd. 1984-present
Camco, Inc. (appliance manufacturer) 1979-92, 1994-96
CJRT-FM (radio broadcaster) 1990-95
GSW, Inc. (metal goods manufacturer) 1966-present
Gulf Canada Ltd. 1980-95
GW Utilities Ltd. (holding company) 1986-93
D.H. Howden Ltd. (hardware wholesaler) 1968-70
Lornex Mining Corporation 1980-89
Montreal Trustco 1982-89
Nabisco Brands Ltd. (food products) 1981-86, Chairman 1983-85
Rio Algom Ltd. (mining, metals distribution) 1980-present
Rogers and Partners Securities, Inc. 1996-present
Scott's Hospitality, Inc. (hotels, restaurants, transportation) 1979-91
Standard Brands Ltd. (food products) 1972-80
Telemedia, Inc. (publisher, broadcaster) 1978-95
John Wiley and Sons, Ltd. (publisher) 1979-88

Donald H. Thain is Magna International Professor Emeritus at the Ivey Business School. He has an MBA and DBA from Harvard Business School. He is a prolific author, lecturer, and consultant. He has served as board chairman of Lawson and Jones Ltd., and as a director of a number of Canadian publicly-listed companies.

Corporate Boards

BioProcess Technologies, Inc. (high technology) 1981-87
Canada Table Pak, Inc. (packaging — co-founder) 1973-77
Charterhouse Group Canada Ltd. (merchant bank) 1963-75
Cooper Canada Ltd. (sporting goods manufacturer) 1972-87
Denison Mines Ltd. 1987-90
Goodyear Canada Ltd. 1983-93
GW Utilities Ltd. (holding company) 1990-93
Home Oil Company Ltd. 1993
Jaeger Canada Equipment Ltd. (industrial machinery) 1982-87
Lawson Mardon Group Ltd. (printing and packaging) 1981-90, Chairman 1983-85
Seaforth Sewer Tile Co. Ltd. 1958-61
Silcorp Ltd. (retailer) 1971-93

Chapter 1

BOARDS IN TROUBLE

"Shareholders have little direct influence in the management of American companies because boards play little role in corporate governance."
(Michael E. Porter)[1]

"... the only conclusion that one can derive from reviewing the writings and observations about boards by both practitioners and scholars, regardless of their political or philosophical background, is that boards have been largely irrelevant throughout most of the twentieth century..."
(James Gillies)[2]

"In every single business failure of a large company in the last few decades, the board was the last to realize that things were going wrong."
(Peter Drucker)[3]

Never before have business leaders, investors, the media, securities commissions, regulators, the courts, legislators, lawyers, auditors, consultants, and academics been so concerned about corporate governance and boards of directors. The reasons are increasingly obvious. Boards are in trouble. Both in management theory and in law, boards of directors are at the apex of the corporate control system. Their legal duties are clear: to "manage or supervise the management of the business and affairs of a corporation."[4] If in reality, they have been "largely irrelevant," there has been a void of direction and accountability at the top of Canadian business. How can this be? Does it matter? What, if anything, should be done about it?

Various commentators have proposed a number of solutions, including doing away with boards altogether. Our purpose is to describe and analyze how corporate governance really works, identify its problems, and propose practical solutions for business leaders who want to get on with the job of making their boards — and the board system — work better.

Our approach is often critical of the *status quo*, sometimes harshly so. But we are friendly critics, and the reason for our approach should be obvious: only by understanding and frankly diagnosing the problems of governance practice can we begin to outline the remedies necessary to help make the board system work as it was intended — indeed, as it *must* work if our private enterprise system is to survive and prosper.

THE JOB OF THE BOARD

The growing literature on corporate governance suggests that corporate boards, as representatives of the owners of a business — the shareholders — are intended to do four things:

1. Optimize long-term shareholder value (increases in share prices plus dividends), with minimum acceptable performance being to earn a return on investment greater than the cost of capital;

2. Earn a profit that compares favourably to the long-term return on investment of businesses in the same or similar industries;

3. Lead a business that is strong and competitive relative to its challengers, actual and potential;

4. Add value to the company by guiding its strategic management, particularly by appointing, supporting, overseeing, and controlling the best available management team.

In other words, if the board is really doing its job a competent investment analyst would ordinarily rate the company a "buy" or "hold," and knowledgeable insiders would agree that the board is making a solid contribution to long-term success.

Judged by these four criteria, the boards of many, if not most, public companies in North America fall short of what they are supposed to deliver, many so badly that they should long since have been shaken up and turned around or replaced.

HOW BOARDS HAVE FAILED

Notwithstanding the successes of individual companies, it is now increasingly obvious that the corporate board *system* has generally failed on all counts:

- Boards have not controlled management so as to maximize efficiency and value for shareholders.[5]
- Relatively few boards have presided over companies that consistently delivered satisfactory increases in shareholder value. For example, over the five-year period of 1989-94, only one-third of U.S. firms and 10 percent of companies listed on the Toronto Stock Exchange returned more than 10 percent annually (the approximate cost of capital) to shareholders in dividends and stock price appreciation.[6]
- Boards have presided over the deterioration in performance and management that is largely responsible for the decline in world competitiveness rankings of many North American companies and industries.[7]
- Specifically, in countless individual companies, boards have stood by and approved widely-publicized mistakes that have led to staggering losses, painful layoffs, costly legal proceedings, and endless grief for countless thousands of investors, employees, creditors, and suppliers.

There is now overwhelming evidence that the board system is falling well short of adequately performing its assigned duties. Without fundamental improvement by individual boards, the entire board system will continue to be attacked as impotent and irrelevant and the boards of troubled and failing companies will, with good reason, increasingly become the targets of not only aggrieved and angry shareholders but also employees, creditors, suppliers, governments, and the public.

BOARDS HAVE LONG BEEN CRITICIZED

To those already aware of the unsatisfactory performance of most boards of directors it will not be surprising that the power and effectiveness of boards as the key element in corporate governance have long been questioned. The argument that boards have been coopted by management at the expense of shareholders was well established by the early 1930s, when Berle and Means published their classic work on *The Modern Corporation and Private Property*.[8] Although the fact was noted, little was done to change matters. Boards remained a mystery — seldom, if ever, observed by outsiders, little known, little studied, and little understood. They were regarded as serving like a royal family, a kind of historical anachronism that at one time had some purpose, but which had slipped into a largely ceremonial role. In recent years, some insiders began to lift the veil of secrecy. In *Up The Organization*,[9] one of the best-selling business books of the 1970s, former CEO Robert Townsend exposed boards as follows:

> Most big companies have turned their boards of directors into non-boards. The chief executive has put his back-seat drivers to sleep...
>
> In the years that I've spent on various boards I've never heard a single suggestion from a director (made as a director at a board meeting) that produced any result at all.
>
> While ostensibly the seat of all power and responsibility, directors are usually the friends of the chief executive put there to keep him safely in office. They meet once a month, gaze at the financial window dressing (never at the operating figures by which managers run the business), listen to the chief and his team talk superficially about the state of the operation, ask a couple of dutiful questions, make token suggestions (courteously recorded and subsequently ignored), and adjourn until next month...
>
> Directors...spend very little time studying and worrying about your company. Result: they know far less than you give them credit for. What they know you can get best by a phone call. It is dangerous to take their formal advice seriously, or be too earnest about their casual questions. If they can ask important questions that the chief executive hasn't already thought of, he ought to be replaced.
>
> Directors have one function, other than declaring dividends, which is theirs to perform: they can and must judge the chief executive officer, and throw him out when the time comes. Since

this task is painful, it is rarely performed even when all the directors know it is long overdue.

In 1984, the legendary Harold Geneen, in another best-seller, *Managing*, seconded what Townsend wrote on boards and added a few thunderbolts of his own:

> Is the company doing well? Fine and good. It is doing well because of the chief executive and his management team. You don't need a board of directors at all. It is a rubber stamp. But if the company is not doing well, or as well as it could, then what? What can the board of directors do about it? How do they know that the company is not living up to its potential? All they can learn is what they are taught from the selfsame management team; all they can get is what they are given. Perhaps that is the fundamental reason so many American companies of late have meandered on through a maze of mediocrity. Of the top five hundred American industrial companies, I would estimate that approximately 95 percent of the boards of directors are not fully doing what they are legally, morally, and ethically supposed to do. They are not doing their jobs. And they couldn't, even if they wanted to...
>
> The board was elected to act in the place of the owners. The board's responsibility is to sit in judgment on the management, especially on the performance of the chief executive, and to reward, punish, or replace the management as the board, in its wisdom, sees fit. That is what is supposed to happen. That is what may appear to happen. But it doesn't.[10]

A more recent write-off of boards was by current best-selling author and Harvard Business School professor Michael Porter, who in 1990 wrote:

> Shareholders have little direct influence in the management of American companies because boards play little role in corporate governance. In practice, the only effective way to remove underperforming management or affect corporate direction is through takeover.[11]

MANY OUTSTANDING YOUNG CEOs ARE SKEPTICAL

To make matters even worse, many boards are currently held in scarcely-concealed contempt by younger, well-educated, high-potential top managers who will be at the forefront of the next generation of business leaders. Their cynical attitudes and critical opinions of boards were summarized by one young and outstandingly successful CEO of a major corporation who has very frankly written his all-star board off as a bunch of redundant back-seat drivers:

> The key directors on our board all know what I have done to make our company perform. They made me the CEO because I was the best candidate they could find. I have worked my butt off at great sacrifice to my family and personal life to transform this company and make it perform better than it ever had before. I don't need any of their penetrating questions or second-guessing. Thanks to my own tough bargaining, I am financially secure and set for life. If they can get someone better than me to do the job, then that's what they should do. Until then let them back off and stay out of my way.

Another young CEO who was a "franchise player" with a similar attitude described the problem this way:

> Our board costs us over $750,000 a year, and now that times are tough, and there's no slack in the system, we all have to justify our existence. There's no good reason to waste this much money. If we applied cost-benefit analysis to our board everyone would be horrified.
>
> We've dedicated our careers to the company and are here working 60- to 70-hour weeks. They know little about the tough problems that we spend the real time on. For anything that's really controversial we organize internal task forces and hire consultants to find the best answers. Now you tell me what can outsiders, old dinosaurs, contribute? Their biggest problem is that they are outside our information loop. We have a comprehensive, updated, multi-million-dollar information and control system but they're not on it because they're not computer lit-

> erate. All they have is executive summaries that we give them from the information we use to run the business. They don't know what is really going on. We've got four really big name directors who are each on a dozen other boards. They wouldn't have the time even if they did understand.
>
> Theoretically, they're supposed to represent the shareholders, our so-called owners, but that's unnecessary. I know personally many of our biggest shareholders. I stay in touch...talk to them myself. I know all about what they want and it's very simple and obvious. I don't need directors to tell me that!

Many incriminating reports have surfaced about the incompetence and impotence of boards in once-supreme companies like General Motors (GM) and IBM. If that is the way it is with the best, questions the younger generation of rising leaders, what about the rest? Attitudes like this, widely implanted and encouraged by professors at many leading business schools, challenge and undermine all the tradition-based, old-school conventional wisdom on which the board system rests.

While the validity of this criticism of boards can be questioned and important exceptions noted by credible insiders, no one can make a convincing general rebuttal because the evidence necessary to do so does not exist. The bottom line is that, no matter how supportive of the board system of governance one may be, problems do indeed exist. Moreover, there is much evidence that many in the know — especially institutional shareholders, regulators, and legislators — believe the problems are serious and that drastic improvement is long overdue.

DO BOARDS MATTER?

For most of the last 50 years, at least, the "irrelevance" of boards didn't seem to matter much. From time to time individual corporations faced fiascos or failed, and occasionally critics noted that the board was nowhere to be seen, but in general the absence of boards was regarded as perfectly normal: after all, if boards were irrelevant, failures of companies were failures of management, not of the governance system. The token role of boards came to be regarded as part of the natural, immutable order of things. Management ran the company, and boards were at best window-dressing, and at worst a necessary evil required by law.

The rationale was simple and compelling. With the development of stock markets and the broadening of the base of ownership, shareholders had become faceless, transient, and interested primarily in short-term market performance. Shrewd investors were quick to take "the Wall Street walk" and bail out of "sell" situations, by dumping their shares at the first sign of trouble. With this sort of volatile shareholder base, who were the "owners" that the directors were supposed to represent, and to whom the management was supposed to be accountable? Couple this with a system of shareholder democracy that was closer to farce than reality, and management or a major shareholder controlled the system — selecting the board, censoring and rationing its information, and effectively managing its operations. Management in many companies became a self-perpetuating autocracy, seeking its own security, determining its own succession, and setting its own compensation. Not surprisingly, this point of view became justified and taught as the gospel at most leading business schools.

There were, inevitably perhaps, attempts to articulate and rationalize this system. As early as the 1920s, Owen Young, head of the General Electric Company, was quoted to the effect that "managers are no longer attorneys for stockholders; they are becoming trustees of an institution."[12] One of his successors, Ralph Cordiner, picked up this idea and spoke of management being the "trustee for the balanced best interest of stockholders, employees, customers, suppliers and plant communities."[13] The concept of the corporation having responsibility to a wide range of stakeholders had, and still has, a certain superficial appeal, and indeed has been written into some state legislation in the United States.

Commenting on this development 30 years later, Peter Drucker stated:

> Because Ralph Cordiner and his contemporaries never even tried to ground management power in institutional arrangements, their assertion very rapidly became enlightened despotism. In the 1950s and 1960s it became *corporate capitalism*, in which an enlightened "professional" management has absolute power within its corporation, controlled only by itself and irremovable except in the event of a catastrophe. Stock ownership, it was argued, had come to be so widely dispersed that shareholders no longer could interfere, let alone exercise control... Within ten years after it had announced the independence of management in the large, publicly owned corporation, 'corporate capitalism' began to collapse. For one, stock ownership came to be concentrated again, in the hands of the pension funds."[14]

THE RISE OF CORPORATE GOVERNANCE

"Corporate governance" — a term almost unheard of until then — came to the fore in the 1980s. Businessmen, shareholders, scholars, regulators, and financial institutions suddenly came to the realization that something was wrong with the system. "Corporate capitalism" wasn't working, and the finger seemed to be pointing at the way America's corporations were being governed and, more specifically, to their "irrelevant" and "impotent" boards of directors. Informed commentators described their problem as follows:

> Megamergers, hostile takeovers, leveraged buyouts, and corporate restructurings have radically transformed the directors' role in the power structure of the American corporation. This transformation has evolved in the financial and legal dynamics of several struggles for control of major U.S. corporations. In the competition for control of our corporations, the boardroom is where the battles are fought and concluded.[15]

Indeed, a number of challenging forces converged on American business at that time. Boards of directors, still legally responsible, were thrust into key decision-making roles. And many, if not most, were found wanting. Shareholders, increasingly large pension funds and institutions, began to take a great deal of interest in the quality of the governance of companies in whom their funds were invested, and to challenge both boards and management in regard to many of their actions. Regulatory bodies, concerned with apparent abuses, began to crack down on delinquent organizations. Consulting firms added expertise in director search, compensation, and board operations. Books, journals, and seminars began to appear from a few leading academic institutions. What had long been virtually a non-issue suddenly became a "hot" topic.

THE REGULATORS MOVE IN

The precursors to this burst of activity were several reports in the late 1980's focusing on the role of boards and board audit committees in improving the quality of financial reporting emanating from corporations. In the United States, the Treadway Commission made a series of recommendations to the Securities and Exchange Commission in 1987. This was followed a year later in Canada with the publication of the MacDonald Committee report to the Canadian Institute of Chartered Accountants. The main recommendations in these reports, commissioned in response to the widening concern about governance, accountability and financial reporting, have been largely implemented, and despite some management opposition, have had a major impact in opening up the entire process of board governance.

In the U.K., the London Stock Exchange and the accountancy profession jointly established a committee to address the financial aspects of corporate governance. The report, known generally as the Cadbury Report (after its chairman, Sir Adrian Cadbury) was published in 1992. Somewhat broader than the Treadway and MacDonald reports, Cadbury looked beyond the audit function to a code of best practice for boards of directors, and the rights and responsibilities of shareholders. No doubt influenced by the publicity and early positive response generated by Cadbury in the U.K., the Toronto Stock Exchange in 1993 appointed a committee chaired by Peter Dey, former head of the Ontario Securities Commission, to survey corporate governance in Canada and to make recommendations for improvement. The committee reported in late 1994.

These various reports have generated a great deal of interest in their respective business communities, and have no doubt raised the level of awareness of governance issues. Concentrating on the form and structure of corporate boards, they represent an attempt to define and codify recommended acceptable practice. Each report stressed the importance of improved governance, of better board operating practice, and of the independence of boards from management. And they have all stressed voluntary action by businesses, rather than attempting to lay out a program of mandatory action by regulation.

Setting out voluntary codes of best practice is a worthwhile first step in attempting to improve the level of corporate governance. However, it assumes both a high degree of motivation on the part of the business community and the ability to make change expeditiously within the system. Our observation and experience lead us to challenge these assumptions. Defense of the *status quo* is powerful and ingrained, and few of the worst offenders will be moved by mere exhortation to do better voluntarily. Much of the text which follows is intended to focus on the reality of the obstacles that exist, and to outline a practical program for implementing the changes necessary to make boards more effective.

ALTERNATIVES TO SELF-MOTIVATED BOARD IMPROVEMENT

Internally-generated and led change is clearly the most desirable route. This is possible where there is consensus at the existing power centre, where a significant shareholder and/or the chairman and CEO agree that change is necessary and that the change should take a certain form. Under these circumstances the issue becomes, how best do we make it happen?

Externally-initiated change imposed on a reluctant or resistant board and management is a different matter. There are several options:

(1) takeovers;

(2) proxy contests;

(3) "power investing";

(4) shareholder activism; and

(5) legal action.

Generally speaking, the prospective costs and benefits of these change methods make the option of internally-initiated improvement stand out as the preferred approach.

Takeovers use the market for corporate control to throw out boards and managers who are allegedly not doing the job. They pit raiders, characterized as either "quick-buck" artists or corporate saviours, against existing management — characterized as either entrenched, sub-optimizing job-protectors or community defenders. Takeovers are often based on complex legal and financial manoeuvring that is immensely expensive and all-consuming. The mere potential for a takeover attempt is usually enough to galvanize management into self-improvement.

In proxy contests, shareholders use the corporate ballot box against the board and management in attempts to protect their rights, oppose unwise management initiatives, and elect their own directors. Although shareholder groups do occasionally win proxy contests, this tactic is difficult, costly, fraught with legal difficulties, and generally puts the shareholder at a severe disadvantage to management and the incumbent board, who have company resources at their disposal.

The third option, "power investing", is practised primarily by investment bankers, who pool their own money with pension funds and other institutions to take control of major corporations, often selling assets to finance the deal. Power investors control boards and focus on improving working capital management, cutting costs, and building competitive strength. Limitations in funding, management and organization, and antitrust laws restrict the extent to which this conglomerate-like approach can be applied in Canada.

Shareholders' collective actions rely primarily on associations of institutional investors to monitor and influence management either by various forms of persuasion, by joint action in voting against management-sponsored resolutions, or by boycotting security issues. Recent regulatory changes have made it easier for groups of shareholders to collaborate in this manner. Large institutional shareholders acting on their own can also exert a great deal of influence over management actions.

A last resort form of shareholder activism is litigation, possibly a class action, seeking the "oppression remedy" from the courts, which may order the directors to rectify any act or omission that harms any security holder. Although recent class action legislation makes this kind of action easier than ever before, it usually comes too late in the process to prevent damage, and is extremely time-consuming, cumbersome, and costly.

The existence of these external change agents provides a powerful impetus to corporate management and existing boards to get their acts together and improve their system of corporate governance before they find change imposed on them. Our efforts in the balance of this book will be devoted to addressing how to do it.

BOARDS IN TROUBLE

Despite significant differences in the two countries, there can surely be little doubt that Canada's corporate boards, like those in the United States, are in trouble — some more than others. Decades of neglect have left a rigidly-entrenched structure in which the locus of power has fallen almost completely either in the hands of management or a few major shareholders, who have little, if any, motivation for real change. The need to revitalize and empower corporate boards will inevitably mean a diminution in the power of management and/or major shareholders. It would be naive to think that either will give up its power without a fight. Moves to reassert general ownership (and through it, board) rights will be resisted at many levels and in many ways; progress will be incremental, and it will be slow. But the balance must be reasserted.

The stakes are high: nothing less than the legitimacy of capitalism and the competitiveness of Canadian industry itself. Failures of governance have been the root cause of many of the business failures of recent years. When the board of GM finally asserted itself after nearly 15 years of accumulating problems, it did so at an incredible opportunity cost and loss of shareholder value, competitive position, disastrous investments, and loss of jobs. In Canada there were the Royal Trust, Confederation Life, Olympic & York, and a long list of other corporate catastrophes. Many reasons were given, but at root they all represent a failure of governance. Governance does matter, and it matters that we get it right.

The essence of the governance issue is ownership and power to control. Ownership conveys legal power, and when the owners of the business are not able to exert their power over managers, or when large shareholders abuse the rights of others, trouble lies ahead. What has happened is that ownership and power have become disconnected: we have had ownership without power, and power without ownership. The balance must be redressed, and the principal vehicle for redressing that balance is the board of directors. The issue at stake here is how good a job the board does in representing the owners' — *all* the owners' — interests, and what can be done to ensure that they do that job well.

We begin our description, evaluation and analysis of the board system in Chapter 2, with an overview of the historical evolution of corporate governance and its most important features. In Chapter 3, we describe the board system and how it works, while Chapter 4 points out its strengths and weaknesses. Chapter 5 looks at the unique problems arising from the Canadian pattern of ownership; Chapters 6 and 7 review the key roles that boards are intended to play. Chapter 8 describes the ways in which boards have failed, and outlines the six key factors that determine the success or failure of boards; Chapters 9 through 15 present our analysis of each of the key success factors for developing an effective board. In Chapter 16, we describe how one company went about turning around a board that was in trouble, and in Chapter 17 we conclude with a look at governance changes that will likely evolve in the future in response to forces presently at work.

NOTES

1. Michael E. Porter, *The Competitive Advantage of Nations* (New York: The Free Press, 1990), p. 111. In none of his voluminous and highly-influential writings on corporate strategy does Porter give more than a passing nod to the role of boards of directors.

2. James Gillies, *Boardroom Renaissance* (Toronto: McGraw-Hill Ryerson and The National Centre for Management Research and Development, 1992), p. 3. Gillies gives a broad, historical diagnosis of the ills of corporate governance in North America.

3. Peter F. Drucker, *Managing for the Future* (New York: Truman Talley Books/Dutton, 1992), p. 208.

4. This is pretty well standard wording in the many federal and state corporation acts in North America. Variations are minor.

5. Michael C. Jensen, "The Modern Industrial Revolution, Exit and The

Failure of Internal Control Systems,'' *Journal of Finance* (July, 1993), pp. 852-855.

6. As reported in the Toronto *Globe and Mail*, April 12, 1995, p. 39.

7. See the annual World Competitiveness rankings published by the International Institute for Management Development (IMD) and the World Economic Forum both based in Switzerland. See also Peter Brimelow, ''The 'greed' myth'', *Forbes*, June 3, 1996, pp. 42, 43.

8. Adolph A. Berle and Gardiner C. Means, *The Modern Corporation and Private Property*, rev. ed. (New York: Harcourt Brace and World, 1970). Originally published in 1932, this study of the ownership of U.S. corporations is arguably the single most important work in the field of corporate governance.

9. Robert Townsend, *Up the Organization* (New York: Alfred A. Knopf, 1970), pp. 49-52. Townsend was at one time CEO of Avis Car Rentals. His book was a best-seller in the early 1970s.

10. Harold Geneen, *Management* (New York: Avon Books, 1984), p. 260. This widely-read work was the distillation of Geneen's many years' experience at the head of International Telephone and Telegraph (I.T.T.), where he led in introducing many of today's widely-accepted management techniques.

11. Porter, *The Competitive Advantage of Nations.*

12. Quoted in William T. Allen, ''A Glimpse at the Struggle for Board Autonomy'', Speech at Stanford Law School, April, 1990 (unpublished).

13. Quoted in Peter F. Drucker, *The Frontiers of Management* (New York: Harper & Row, 1986), p. 183.

14. Drucker, *The Frontiers of Management*, p. 184. This is a theme in several of Drucker's writings, including *Managing for the Future*, Chapter 31, pp. 235-50.

15. Arthur Fleischer, Jr., Geoffrey C. Hazard, Jr., and Miriam Z. Klipper, *Board Games: The Changing Shape of Corporate Power* (New York: Little Brown, 1988), p. 3.

Chapter 2

CORPORATE GOVERNANCE:
Power and Accountability in Business

"The need for an effective board has been stressed by every student of the public corporation in the last 40 years. To run a business enterprise, especially a large and complex enterprise, management needs considerable power. But power without accountability always becomes flabby or tyrannical and usually both. Surely we know how to make boards effective as an organ of effective governance." (Peter Drucker)[1]

To begin, we need to understand what corporate governance problems are all about. A look below the surface in the Janzen group provides an introduction to typical, commonly encountered issues that confront many boards and directors. These are the kinds of situations, hidden from public view, that exist even in many companies that to the outside observer may appear to be successful and well managed.

THE CASE OF THE JANZEN GROUP

When he died in 1991, Fred Janzen, an immigrant who arrived in Halifax in 1937 with $35 in his pocket, was a wealthy and powerful man who had built and firmly controlled a three billion dollar industrial empire. His widely publicized story was regarded as the triumph of hard work, brains, ability and aggressive, opportunistic deal-making over poverty, hardships, and set-backs. Beginning as a machinist, the trade for which he had apprenticed as a teenager in his native Germany, Janzen launched a career that went from becoming a partner with his first employer, taking control of a fast-growing auto parts company when his partner died, expansion and profitability in wartime, successful entry into oil and gas in the 1940s, and major acquisitions in the newspaper, radio and TV businesses in the 1950s. While his companies were not without their problems, they had been, on the whole, highly successful. Janzen had accumulated large debts with three major banks, but these had been offset somewhat by going four times to the equity market with public offerings. He was strongly positioned as the controlling shareholder in his group of companies and ruled them with an iron hand.

Following his death, Janzen's estate (administered by three trustees) became the controlling shareholder with 40 percent of Janzen Industries, essentially a holding company that was in turn the controlling shareholder of the manufacturing company (30 percent), the oil and gas company (35 percent), and the media company (37 percent). All four companies were individually listed, actively traded, and owned in part by institutional investors. Each had its own board. About half the directors were Janzen group managers and affiliated directors and the other half outsiders. Fred Janzen had been firmly in control as chairman and CEO of all four companies; his second-in-command was Ken Krug, vice-chairman and president of the holding company. Krug was Janzen's relatively young, long-time, trusted and indispensable trouble-shooter and right hand man. As Janzen's deputy, he served on the boards of the three operating companies, often speaking for Janzen and chairing board and management meetings in his absence. He was highly regarded and respected throughout the group and in related industry circles, and it was widely assumed that he would succeed Janzen if Janzen ever wanted to slow down and delegate more of his job. While Janzen, with Krug's support and assistance, master-minded the strategies of the operating companies, they were all headed by competent and hard-working presidents.

Janzen's will left everything to his family, church, and four charities. The trustees of his estate — a lawyer, an auditor and an investment banker, were all long-time cronies. While he regarded them as his closest friends and confidants, the family (particularly the younger members who were agitating for more money to support extravagant lifestyles) saw them as old, stuffy, officious hangers-on who had often taken advantage of their father's friendship in overcharging for their firms' services, and who jealously guarded their power and the allegedly exorbitant fees they were being paid.

On his death, Janzen's family was pushed, cautiously and reluctantly, to the centre of the stage. His wife, shy but forceful, had focused her attention on family and home and remained in the background of his business life. The children, three girls and two boys ranging from 32 to 45 years of age, were viewed with apprehension by the boards of the companies. The boys both had management jobs in operating companies, but were viewed by their father as disappointments. Neither got along well with Ken Krug, in part it was thought because of jealousy over Krug's close relationship with their father. Ben, the younger son, had dropped out of university and had not done well in the company; nevertheless, he was the only child with any apparent ambition to succeed his father. Two of the daughters were married to professionals with no occupational interest in the business. The other was married to a lawyer, who was perceived as a potential trouble maker: it was rumoured that he was about to commence a legal action challenging two clauses in his father-in-law's will.

Immediately after Janzen's death his companies were thrown into a state of confusion in regard to management succession, the role his family would play, and the possible sale of control *en bloc* to several interested buyers. Nearly all of his senior managers and directors gathered at his funeral and the main topic of hushed and guarded discussion before and after the service was: who will take over? and what happens now? In the days following the funeral, many off-the-record telephone calls crossed the network of worried directors and top managers. The consensus was that the next move was up to the trustees and the family. No one else seemed to know what would happen.

Ten days later, at the first regularly-scheduled Janzen board meeting after the funeral, the situation began to be clarified. To the shock of just about everyone in the room, Ben Janzen came in, sat down at the head of the table in his father's old chair and with his head down, not looking anyone in the eye, mumbled: "The family decided that I should take over from father as chairman and CEO, so let's get started. Ken, would you explain this first item on the agenda." With most of the directors looking on in puzzlement and dismay, the board seemed to switch to automatic pilot and, carried by tradition and routine, went through the motions of a perfunctory, short meeting in which Ben seemed to rely heavily on Ken. At the end of the meeting, after Ben and the lawyer who was chairman of the trustees had retired to Ben's office, the remainder of the board broke up into small groups to speculate about "what happened?" — the question on everyone's mind. Slowly the story emerged. Acting against the strong advice of several respected advisors, Fred Janzen had specified in his will that one of his children should succeed him and carry on in his place. In a meeting with the trustees, the family, led by Mrs. Janzen, had nominated Ben. End of discussion.

Over the next six months, business conditions worsened and two of the operating companies suffered serious setbacks. Ben's inexperience, willfulness, and seeming inability to take advice from management teams and Ken Krug exacerbated the situation. Ben, backed by the trustees because of their loyalty to his father and the family, inserted himself at the centre of the action. On three major decisions he opposed and overruled the recommendations of the managers involved. As a result, mistakes were made and problems neglected. Ostensibly because of Ben's heavy-handed reversal of a major strategic decision that was backed unanimously by his management team, the president of the most successful operating company resigned and was soon hired as the CEO of a competitor.

A year later, to the astonishment and great disappointment of most directors and senior managers in the group, Ben summarily fired Ken Krug, who had been giving invaluable service in attempting to cover for Ben's ineptitude and who had worked hard to maintain a semblance of sensible management. Although no reason was ever given, it was widely suspected that Ben made the move primarily to prove that he really was the boss. More and more Ben relied for advice and support on his father's former cronies, who manipulated him for their own political advantage. In the process, boardroom politics and expediencies superseded substantive concerns and rational management. A close observer, deeply upset and bitterly disappointed by Ben's "disloyalty and back-stabbing", reflected on the psychodynamics involved: "Ben and Ken are so different that we should have known that their chemistry would never mix. Ben was a university drop-out who owes everything he has to a birth accident. Ken worked hard in his family's business, beginning when he was still in grade school, and graduated near the top of his class both in science and in a well-known MBA program. He was pragmatic and demanding, but outstanding in his respect for people and ability to inspire loyalty. He was the son Fred probably wished for. Fred's obvious respect and regard for Ken intimidated Ben and, unfortunately, did not endear Ken to the rest of the family, who felt sorry for Ben." On the day Ken was fired he redeemed stock options at a gain of over $3,000,000, and Janzen shares, which had fallen from $27 to $21 on Fred's death, hit another new low of $15. Within two months Ken was appointed CEO of another company. Over this period, three different investment bankers, who had tried various approaches to the family and the trustees with possibly good offers to arrange the sale of family shares, were all repulsed out of hand by Ben. These offers were never properly reported to the boards. Nevertheless, the senior lawyer-trustee sold the family and the board on installing a "shareholders' rights" plan, or "poison pill", designed to discourage takeover attempts. His firm's bill for the work, which many felt was unnecessary and undesirable, was $300,000, judged by several members of the board to be exorbitant.

At the same time that problems were proliferating and results deteriorating, the board, largely at the family's insistence, raised the dividend. To pay, it was necessary to increase bank debt. In order to back his position and increase his comfort with the board, Ben unilaterally appointed two unqualified but supportive friends as directors. Two months before the 1993 annual meeting, in a meeting called by Ben, two highly competent veteran directors, who had opposed several of his decisions and who were fed up, either resigned or were fired.

In 1993, after the decline and reorganization of a money-losing subsidiary, one of the main banks notified the CFO that they did not intend to renew a major loan coming due in four months. Soon after, a leading institutional shareholder, thought to be speaking also for three other investment fund managers, notified the trustees and the board of his concern and disapproval of the way things were going, and asked that a governance committee of five long-serving outside directors be named to assess the competence, independence and performance of the board. He demanded that the poison pill be cancelled, and that the compensation and expenses of Ben Janzen and two of his newly appointed presidents be reduced and brought back into line with company results. In the meantime, with several investment analysts issuing unfavourable reports and putting Janzen Industries on their sell lists, the share price fell to $12. The company seemed to be self-destructing.

* * * * *

POWER AND ACCOUNTABILITY

The Janzen case, typical in many aspects of numerous situations, illustrates several of the basic issues of power and accountability in corporate governance. It is a classic story of chaos resulting from the disintegration of the power structure and the checks and balances needed to keep the system in equilibrium. It highlights the illegitimacy of power and authority without the necessary counterbalancing of accountability and responsibility; debilitating conflict among shareholders, management, and stakeholders because of the impotence and incompetence of the board of directors; and a clash of egos, self-interest and personalities, political and legal infighting; the influence of Rasputin-like behind-the-scene advisors; and the deep, conflicting emotions of family relationships — all bound together in a tragic destruction of capital. The board, emasculated by an autocratic leader like Fred Janzen, was powerless to govern. Reduced to a ratification mode for so many years, it was incapable of rising to the challenge and governing with authority and wisdom. A competent but weakened management group stood by helplessly, neutralized by the morally illegitimate power vested in Ben Janzen. Thousands of shareholders ended up losing heavily on their investments as the company slid into decline. Employees, creditors, suppliers, and entire communities saw their careers, savings, and hopes put in jeopardy.

Power arises ultimately from control over resources, and authority comes from the moral, legal and political right to command. Power and authority give directors and top managers the strength they need to decide and act, to run the company and allocate the wealth it produces. Today no one would dispute the power for good or evil of our corporations. Many are larger, better financed and better managed than some of the countries within which they operate. Their ability to marshall resources and solve problems is truly awesome.

With power goes accountability. Corporations are fictitious legal entities created by government on behalf of society, and accountable ultimately to society for their performance. Accountability and responsibility require that they answer to, satisfy, and maintain the support of the shareholders and major stakeholders who explicitly or implicitly grant them their mandates. Society's interest is in fostering their power to benefit, and limiting their power to harm, the public interest. Society therefore, no less than the owners, has an interest in seeing that businesses are well run.

Whatever else corporations may be — economic, technological, social, human — they are political organizations. This being so, corporate governance is the political science of business. It is the theory and practice of activities concerned with the election and/or appointment of those who rule the corporation and their planning and implementation of purpose, strategy, decisions, policies and action programs. It focuses on activities involving acquiring, defending or divesting ownership, and from it the power to appoint or elect directors and officers to represent the owners. It involves planning and controlling the purpose, strategy, and operations of the firm. And it involves accounting to the owners and to the broader public for the authority and responsibility which has been delegated.

THE SOURCES OF POWER

The concept of the modern corporation is built on the foundation of private property and ownership rights: the company is the property of whoever owns it. The owners can do with it as they like, subject to markets, social and political pressures and the laws of the land. Except as the laws and associated regulations dictate, they have no further legal responsibility to employees, pensioners, customers, creditors, suppliers, communities, or nations. But corporations derive their power through government from society. Laws and regulations change: if we are to understand the governance of corporations it is important to understand the evolving nature of the environment of business and the legal framework that both empowers and circumscribes all their decisions and actions.

The influence of corporations today is so pervasive that it is hard to think back to a time when there were no corporations. Yet in the sweep of time, the concept of a corporation is relatively recent. For most of recorded history, business was conducted by individuals: revenues, profits and losses were personal, and liabilities incurred were liabilities of the individual. When principals banded together in partnerships, the "joint and several" liabilities were still assumed by each member individually and the group collectively. The failure of the business would leave each member's personal assets fully exposed, a serious impediment to the collective accumulation and investment of capital. With these limitations and risks, most businesses remained small.

As ventures grew larger and required more capital from more contributors, the "joint stock" company was created, in which contributors of capital received "shares" in proportion to their contribution. In Europe, where the concept originated, these companies were chartered by the Crown to perform certain specified tasks, often tied to a ruler's political purpose. The "Company of Adventurers Trading Into Hudson's Bay", for example, was incorporated by royal charter in Great Britain in 1670 as part of a strategy for colonizing parts of North America; the company is still in existence. The Virginia Company of London, the first corporation in the United States, was given its Royal Charter in 1606 to develop the Virginia Colony. These and other companies of the era were run by a governor and a committee of the owners — the forerunner of today's board of directors.

The joint stock company was a vehicle for raising large sums of money for risky ventures; it provided a means of sharing the risk and providing some liquidity for the investor by making it possible to buy and sell an interest in the venture. The problem of liability remained, to be solved in time by the development of the legal right of limited liability — where the investor's liability for the debts of the enterprise was limited to the amount of capital put into the business, and no more. The corporation came to be regarded in law as a fictitious "person," one who could be sued, charged, convicted, and penalized as could any natural person, but whose owners' liability for the business was limited to the amount invested.

The limited liability corporation became a highly attractive device for doing business, and in time spread to embrace businesses of all types and sizes. The desire of investors for greater liquidity for their shares led to the development of stock markets, which in turn enabled financiers to tap the savings of an increasingly-prosperous population to finance such emerging industries as textiles and railroads. Corporate structures grew and evolved from single-unit enterprises operating in limited geographic areas with a single product line, to what Chandler calls the "modern business enterprise,"[2] characterized by a decentralized divisional organization and managed by a head office hierarchy of salaried executives. This modern enterprise is little more than 100 years old.

THE LIMITS OF POWER

In the checks and balances built into the corporate governance system, a number of factors limit the power of corporations and protect society from the abuse of that power. Corporations, even those normally thought of as monopolies, are constrained in their use of power by markets — markets for equity shares, corporate control and capital, markets for inputs (human resources, factors of production), and markets for outputs (products and services). Abuse or misuse of corporate power can and does bring about a response from these markets, imperfect as they may be. The wave of corporate takeovers in the late 1980s, for example, represented a market reaction to what was seen as undervalued assets, mismanagement, and underperformance by many companies.

Accepting market realities, and the very real limits they impose on corporations, companies are in fact creations of governments. Governments, too, limit corporate power.

> Although it is often forgotten, the modern corporation is formally governed not by one but by two entities — the board of directors, which is empowered by the shareholders to manage or to supervise the management of the enterprise, and by the government, which through legislation and regulation sets the rules under which companies may be chartered and operated.[3]

Governments have, in effect, through granting a legal charter of incorporation, made a contract with the company owners which allows them to operate their businesses with limited liability within prescribed rules. In the words of former U.S. Chief Justice Marshall, corporations are "artificial..., invisible, intangible, and existing only in the contemplation of the law".[4] What the law gives, the law can take away.

The power (and responsibility) to manage the modern corporation is vested by law in a board of directors elected by shareholders. Little more is said about governance in any of the host of federal and provincial Acts under which Canadian companies are incorporated, most of which are much as they were a century ago. The corporation is the private property of the owners, the owners elect the directors, and the directors are agents responsible to them for the management of their property, within the limits set by laws and regulations promulgated by government. In this strict sense, directors are accountable only to the owners, the shareholders, and can be removed if the owners are unhappy with their performance.

In the exercise of power, companies have a major and growing impact on the lives of employees, pensioners, customers, suppliers, debt and security holders, neighbouring communities and, in some cases, entire countries. This group, the "stakeholders" of the business, have no direct legal claim on the directors in the exercise of power. They do not elect them, and they cannot remove them. But they influence and limit the power of directors in a number of ways: they can strike, withdraw their business and boycott the company, and they can work through the political process to change the laws and regulations governing the business. Indeed, in the U.S., a number of states have passed community laws that require directors to consider the interests of all stakeholders in making decisions.

The recognition of wider stakeholder interests is also heavily influenced by the personal values of directors and shareholders who, as well as being directors or shareholders, are part of the community too. Most are members of some stature in the community and few are comfortable ignoring community attitudes, values, and perceptions. The result is the acknowledgement by most directors that recognition of stakeholder concerns is not only good business, but politically expedient and morally and ethically just, even if in a strict legal sense they remain directly accountable only to shareholders.

GOVERNANCE: FAD OR FUNDAMENTAL CHANGE?

Long a neglected aspect of organizational study, the division of power and accountability among shareholders, stakeholders, managers, and directors of business corporations has come to the fore in the last decade. Spectacular problems in Canada (Royal Trust, Confederation Life, Olympia & York); the United States (GM, IBM, American Express, Eastman Kodak); United Kingdom (Barings, Maxwell, Polly Peck); and Germany (Metallgesellschaft, Schneider) have been traced in large part to breakdowns in the system of governance. Predictably, these events have triggered concern, controversy, commissions of inquiry, new laws and regulations, and a flood of articles, books, conferences and speeches describing and debating solutions to the breakdown. Some of the "solutions" have substantially increased the liability of directors and added to the regulatory morass facing management and boards, with negative side effects in increased bureaucracy and operating costs and decreased competitiveness.

There is little doubt that a redefinition and realignment of power and accountability are required in our system of governance. The failure of major corporate generators of wealth is a high price to pay for shortcomings and failures in governance. The faults in the existing structure were identified years ago, but were largely ignored in the era of high growth and strong returns to investors. It took a major recession, the collapse of real estate markets, and the increasing globalization of competition to expose the weaknesses in the system. Society and corporations themselves have a major stake in seeing that the issue is addressed. The attention now paid corporate governance is a belated recognition and response to something seriously wrong in our society, and to the extent that the response is inadequate, society will suffer.

The problem is that due in part to the long neglect of the subject, not many people know how boards work. Boards of directors, necessarily for competitive and other reasons, operate in secretive ways behind closed doors: their meetings are off-limits to outsiders, their deliberations are largely unreported, they work on the basis of confidentiality, consensus, and solidarity. Only rarely does the public get a look at any aspect of their inner workings. Even senior managers, with the exception of CEOs and CFOs, seldom see a board at work from the inside. Only those who have been directors really know much about the process, and, as it differs widely from company to company, experience on one board may not tell much about other boards. On company organization charts, which usually show the directors on top, the board is a "black box" whose workings are unknown to all outsiders, including the shareholders who, theoretically, are required to elect it.

The broad nature of the board's mandate and its indirect involvement in operations makes it extremely difficult, if not impossible, to measure the effect of its actions (and inactions). Control of the nomination and proxy voting process by the board and/or management exacerbates the problem, and leads to the lack of effective accountability. Coupled with the astounding growth in recent years of shareholdings of large institutional investors such as pension and mutual funds, many of whom have avoided voting their shares or otherwise exercising their ownership rights, and it is little wonder that there has been a breakdown of governance. Power without accountability is always a formula for trouble. Commenting on this fundamental problem two widely respected authorities have written:

> Although difficult to believe in today's world, it is from the premise that shareholders can respond effectively to ineffective boards that much of corporate decision making gets its legitimacy. It is directors, after all, who appoint the officers and determine their level of compensation, and who set the long-term goals and make sure that management takes appropriate steps to carry them out. The fiduciary standard is supposed to ensure that they take all of these actions on behalf of the shareholders. But this is little more than a vestigial notion in modern times. As the creation of instruments to finance takeovers of any company, of virtually any size, has presented directors with the most demanding challenges in corporate history, they have found, as have the shareholders, that the traditional notion of a director's duty — and authority — was more myth than reality.[5]

Contributing to the breakdown in accountability in many companies has been the coopting of the board by management, a trend identified as early as 1932 by Berle and Means. In their authoritative, ground-breaking study, the authors argued that ownership and management had become separated, with the power devolving to management.

> In its new aspect the corporation is a means whereby the wealth of innumerable individuals has been concentrated into huge aggregates and whereby control over this wealth has been surrendered to a unified direction. The power attendant upon such concentration has brought forth princes of industry, whose position in the community is yet to be defined. The surrender of control over their wealth by investors has effectively broken the old property relationships and has raised the problem of defining these relationships anew. The direction of industry by persons other than those who have ventured their wealth has raised the question of the motive force back of such direction and the elective distribution of the returns from business enterprise.[6]

Presciently, they pointed out that: ''We are examining this institution probably before it has attained its zenith''.

The key institution linking ownership to management is the board of directors. If there is a breakdown in that linkage, the first place to look in seeking solutions is the board. And indeed, we find huge differences between theory and practice, between the expectations of the law, and the reality of today's corporate operations. This growing gap has led some to advocate the elimination of boards as outdated and ineffectual.[7] But the board system, however imperfect it may be in individual companies, can work. Many examples exist; we have served on several. Eliminating boards would solve nothing because their governing function would soon have to be restored. The challenge is to make the existing system work better.

> The business enterprise needs a government, and it needs a government that has power, has continuity and can perform. In other words it needs a government that has legitimacy. How can legitimacy be restored to the management of America's large, publicly-owned companies?[8]

Legitimacy derives from satisfactory economic and social performance, accountability, a democratic, merit-based process for gaining and holding office, and demonstrated leadership, effectiveness, morality, and service to all stakeholders. If legitimacy is to be restored to the system, the chain of accountability must be made more effective. And this, in turn, means restoring the rights and responsibilities of ownership to shareholders, *all* shareholders, and empowering directors to fulfill their role as agents of the shareholders. That is what this book is about: restoring accountability, and through it legitimacy, to the management of Canada's large, publicly-owned companies. Our purpose is to explain how good governance should work and what directors must do to make the board system more effective. Since this task obviously calls for a diagnosis of the problems of the board system and prescription of the remedies for its improvement, we must begin with a description of the board system as it now stands, what it is and how it works, the base from which its future development must be managed.

NOTES

1. Peter F. Drucker, *The Frontiers of Management* (New York: Harper & Row, 1986), p. 249.

2. Alfred D. Chandler Jr., *The Visible Hand: The Managerial Revolution in American Business* (Cambridge, Mass: Harvard University Press 1977).

3. James Gillies, *Boardroom Renaissance: Power, Morality and Performance in the Modern Corporation* (Toronto: McGraw-Hill Ryerson, 1992).

4. Quoted from *Dartmouth College v. Woodward* (1819) 4, Wheat, 518.

5. Robert A.G. Monks and Nell Minow, *Power and Accountability* (New York: Harper Collins Publishers Inc., 1993), pp. 76-77.

6. Adolph A. Berle and Gardiner C. Means, *The Modern Corporation and Private Property*, rev. ed. (New York: Harcourt Brace and World, 1970), p. 2.

7. "Get rid of company boards, Zimmerman says," *Globe and Mail*, Toronto, February 22, 1996, p. 131. Report of testimony to a Senate Banking committee to the effect that directors face huge legal liabilities but have little power to control the corporation.

8. Drucker, *The Frontiers of Management*, p. 252.

Chapter 3

HOW BOARDS WORK: Describing the Board System

All boards are in a dynamic process of transition from what they are to what they will become. The logical beginning point in understanding this process and its future development is to agree on a description of the board system as it now stands. Since there is no existing generally-agreed description, theory or model of the board system, the purpose of this chapter is to describe our view of the system as it is today.

All boards are unique: they vary widely depending on company size, ownership, environment and a host of other factors. Consider the cases of two fairly typical boards of widely held companies with vividly contrasting patterns of development, functions, structures, and processes.

CASE STUDIES: TWO TYPICAL BOARDS

Company A was a very large, successful transportation company whose share price had for many years been a component of a widely-used industrial stock price index. Its large, dark, woodpanelled boardroom reeked of tradition and understated luxury. The two lengthwise walls were dominated by seven spotlighted oil portraits of former chairmen/CEOs.

The board numbered 19. Following tradition, it was led by the chairman/CEO and included the president and the CFO. The other members were outsiders, seven being CEOs or former CEOs of major companies, three partners of large law firms, two retired heads of major investment banks with close ties to the company, three well-known public figures and an academic. The incumbent chairman/CEO, 64 years old and six years on the job, had personally chosen seven of the outside directors. Although the board had a nominating committee, it was heavily influenced by the chairman/CEO, who was an ex-officio member. His criteria for selecting directors were demonstrated business leadership, unquestioning support of management, and friendship and compatibility with incumbent directors. Each owed his or her presence to a leadership position elsewhere and was invited by a process that guaranteed exclusion of the "wrong" type of person.

The board-management balance of control and power followed a regular, planned cycle initiated by a far-sighted CEO/chairman in the 1960s. Anticipating his own retirement, he set up a management succession pattern under which the manager who would ultimately become the heir-apparent was carefully groomed and tested by being promoted sequentially from division manager to chief operating officer (COO); president and appointment to the board; CEO and vice-chairman of the board; CEO and chairman; chairman; and then retirement from the company and the board.

Boardroom seating arrangements were rigidly controlled by the placement of gold monogrammed leather agenda binders carefully laid out before each meeting. The president sat to the chairman's immediate right and the secretary to his immediate left. Other outside directors were seated down the table in strict order of seniority in service. The remaining inside directors sat at the far end.

As directors gathered, they settled around the table for the usual 10 to 15 minutes of friendly pre-meeting chat. However, once the meeting started, sharp at 10 o'clock, the mood changed to one of formality and adherence to ceremonial ritual and process. Meetings were routine and carefully planned to proceed at a rapid pace. Discussion was, by implicit mutual consent, very limited. Questions and answers were generally short and superficial. Board suggestions were always made with diffidence as advice to be considered by management when they made decisions, which would be reported back as finished business. At noon the meeting was adjourned to the sitting room next door for drinks. Five or six other top managers, invited by the chairman in careful rotation from a group totalling about 30, always joined the board for an elaborate and leisurely lunch.

Outside of board meetings there was very little interaction among directors, and none between directors and management other than the chairman. For example, one new director, in discussing with the chairman his appointment to the board, offered to spend two or three days visiting divisions, meeting managers, and sizing up the company in order to prepare himself to make a more informed contribution. The embarrassed chairman assured the new director that this would not be necessary. "You won't need any special preparation", he was told, "just come to the meetings and you'll fit in."

The well-attended annual shareholders' meeting was prepared, rehearsed and staged like a military exercise. The tightly-scripted legal formalities were quickly covered and the question period was rushed through and concluded summarily. Directors knew that they were highly honoured members of a super-exclusive club of the business elite, whose every board-related need was catered to. They were clearly there to support management as required. Social activities of the board centred on golf games two or three times per year at exclusive courses near the head office city or an out-of-town meeting site.

Long-time observation of the board confirmed directors' personal priorities: prestige and the related personal rewards for service. They aimed to be shrewdly and openly politically correct and proper in all they said and did. They were always discreetly compliant to management, reacting to initiatives and proposals put to them for approval and seldom initiating questions or suggestions. They invariably bowed to precedent and traditional process. The other CEOs in particular deferred to the chairman, clearly indicating that this was the kind of behaviour they expected from their own boards. Several of the foremost directors were wealthy, powerful and well-known, and they respected and associated primarily with peers who were similar in friendships, behaviour, political bent, social activities and contacts.

* * * * *

The board of Company B, a large but newly-reorganized manufacturing company, differed greatly from that of Company A.

Over a period of 17 years, the board of Company B had gone through four fundamental changes, all internally generated. At its inception as a private company, a five-person board was appointed, consisting of the owner-manager and four of his most trusted friends and supporters who served as advisors, held no shares and had virtually no legal power or responsibility. Four years later the owner sold 20 percent of the equity in a private placement to raise capital and finance growth; the new investor insisted on a detailed shareholders' agreement governing the division of rights, authority and responsibility, and a seat on the board. After two more years of rapid growth and profits, the company made an initial public offering (IPO) of 29 percent of the shares, leaving the original owner with 51 percent of the shares and control; three new directors were added to represent the new minority shareholders, and the major shareholder remained as chairman and CEO. Later, when the controlling shareholder died, his estate made a widely-distributed secondary offering of its shares and the board was again reorganized to put control firmly in the hands of independent directors representing the now widely-held ownership, which included several mutual and pension funds. Over this period, the company had been completely transformed, and the board evolved from a token advisory committee to being in control of a widely-held public company.

The boardroom of Company B was basically a multi-purpose, functional but comfortable, conference room, used almost continuously for management and staff meetings. The only decorations on the off-white, painted walls were framed proofs of company institutional advertisements.

The board numbered 11. The chairman was a senior outside director, and the CEO and CFO were the only members of management. Outsiders included three CEOs, an investment banker and lawyer for whom the company was a major client, a retired audit firm partner, a retired banker, and an academic. The chairman was 43 years of age and the rest of the board averaged below 50. Each had been chosen for specific strengths deemed important to the board's job. Several had young families and wives who had significant careers of their own. Five were highly computer-literate and were completely integrated into the company's information system, which they frequently accessed on-line from their homes.

Except for the CEO, who sat at the end of the table nearest the door, where his secretary occasionally slipped in to have a brief word or hand him a note, there were no fixed seating places. Agenda support material was distributed around the room in standard black three-ring binders. The atmosphere in the meetings was comfortably relaxed and informal. Meetings, which started around 9 o'clock and usually concluded sometime from slightly before noon to after 1 o'clock, were anything but tightly organized and formal. Animated discussion, penetrating questions, frank exchanges, and even mild arguments were the *modus operandi*. For lunch the group usually adjourned to the office cafeteria for a light meal picked up on a tray in a lineup with other employees.

All except two of the directors were, or represented, substantially committed shareholders. Together with the chairman, who was heavily invested in the company, they owned about 5 percent of the shares. There was no doubt that they were all consciously managing one of their own important investments. They openly supervised and guided management. Major problems were raised and, not infrequently, decisions were made on the spot with management directors leaving the meeting to advise their support people to get on with making some change. A "take-charge" atmosphere was palpable in the meetings. The board's behaviour and interactions were marked by openness and collegiality. The obligation to take responsibility and get at the tough issues was implicit; cooperation and team effort were notable. Dialogue was problem-and-solution oriented, and interchanges were frank, direct, and interesting. An outside observer would have judged most of them to be consultants or other professionals working together through group discussions as in an MBA class, not only under the leadership of the chairman but, more importantly, governed by their own expertise, self-discipline and commitment to an important shared enterprise.

* * * * *

These two case descriptions of typical but contrasting boards point out some of the many differences to be found in the development, traditions, function, structure, and process of the endless variety of boards of public companies. Any observer without an insider's longer term, intimate knowledge of the development and *modus operandi* of these boards would be limited to superficial and incomplete understanding of the complex, sensitive, and evolving internal dynamics and relationships. In company A, for example, only by understanding the "passing-the-baton" sequence and the resulting ebb and flow of individual power could an outside observer make accurate judgments of how this board really worked and why the combination of CEO and chairman was a planned, limited appointment. The evolution of company B is typical of the growth pattern of many startup businesses. The corporate world consists of many thousands of individual corporations, most of them small, at different stages of growth and decline, and all having a body called a board of directors. Describing a board "system" under these circumstances can be highly misleading. Boards come in all shapes and sizes, perform widely varying functions and are in a continuous state of transition.

THE EVOLUTION OF THE BOARD SYSTEM

Each individual board is a man-made open system which must be understood in both static (snapshots of the current operation as in the introductory cases) and dynamic (a moving picture of the longer term sequence of changes) terms. In this system, the complex interplay of powerful internal and external variables, change forces that drive creative and innovative adjustments, interact to maintain an equilibrium that is stable and functional yet, at the same time, dynamic and evolving. Similarly the overall general governance system, the sum of individual company governance systems, is changing, largely in response to the rising and undeniable demand from stakeholders for better performance and more accountability. Our analytical framework for explaining this evolutionary process is outlined in the Appendix at page 49.

The most important advance in corporate governance over the last few decades has been the regulatory requirement and empowerment of an audit committee with a majority of outside directors. A direct and effective response to stakeholder demands, it arose in part from financial debacles and irregularities, particularly the failure of banks and trust companies in the 1950s and 1960s. This major change in the board system began in Ontario in 1970 and became a Canada-wide law with the 1975 amendment of the Canada Business Corporations Act. While this change in the balance of power in favour of the board, and particularly outside directors, was vociferously opposed by the managements of many companies at the time, it is now taken for granted and widely acknowledged as contributing to the effectiveness of corporate governance.

Approaching the 21st century, the development of other significant changes can be observed. Although "the really tough issues are still being avoided...public disclosure of corporate governance policies compared with recommended standards of behavior has already forced many companies to improve the independence and effectiveness of their boards".[1] Many boards are taking their responsibilities more seriously; many companies have more independent directors on the board; most have set up independent nominating committees and compensation committees; some have appointed a "lead" director, and many have cut the board down in size. Another notable new development, discussed in Chapter 7, is that corporate governance seems headed in the direction of a strategic management audit committee of outside directors that would evaluate and report on company results and management performance in the same manner that the audit committee evaluates and reports on the integrity of financial statements.

This dynamic process, continuous and unstoppable, raises many fundamental questions for business leaders and corporations:

- How satisfied are our shareholders, and other stakeholders, with the performance and accountability of the company and its board?
- How effective is the board?
- What are the governance risks and problems we face?
- What exactly should we be doing to anticipate and avoid the embarrassing and costly mistakes in governance that have plagued so many other companies?
- What should we be doing to make our board more effective and how should we do it?

The answers to such questions inevitably require a sound understanding of the board system and the major forces and trends that drive the direction and rate of its change.

It is true that much of the power in the modern corporate world is concentrated in a relatively few large companies — generally described as the "Financial Post 300" in Canada, the "Fortune 500" in the U.S., or by some similar name in other countries. These are the huge corporate powerhouses, well-known companies that dominate the economies of the countries in which they are incorporated. They are the organizations that are of most concern in discussions of corporate governance, boards of directors, and accountability. But it should be kept in mind that the corporate world, and hence the board system in general, is much broader and all-encompassing, and solutions that are appropriate for the giants are not necessarily those that will work for the larger body of smaller organizations.

GOVERNANCE AS A SYSTEM

The first step in coming to grips with governance issues is to understand how companies and their boards work. In all the discussion of corporate governance there has been a tendency to focus solely on boards of directors, as if governance and boards of directors are synonymous. This is a mistake. Corporate boards are part of an overall governance system, in which they share authority and responsibility with other critical subunits of the corporation, and where the relationships with those other parts are often crucial to their effective operation. To understand the role and functioning of boards, we have to understand how the total governance system works. We need a model, or theory, of the firm, and the environment within which it operates.

The theoretical basis that best fits the governance model is that of the *system.* Through research and observation, we have come to know a good deal about systems, both physical and human. Company systems comprise a *structure,* a number of related component parts, and a *process*, the interactions through which the parts work together to perform a *function*, the purpose of the organization. These parts interact and are interdependent with each other. Not only is it important to understand the functioning of the components; it is necessary to understand their interrelationships as well. Changing one component will affect other components in the system; there is an optimum *balance* if the system is to work most effectively. Focusing on improving the functioning of one component without considering the effects on other components of the system is called *suboptimizing*, and the result may be that the performance of the total system becomes worse than before. It is *the results or output of the system as a whole* that we are interested in optimizing over time, and to do that we must understand how the whole system works.

The corporation is a man-made system with complex physical, human and economic dimensions. For purposes of governance, the human subsystem interests us most: the system of individuals and groups that is tied together by human exchange and the communications and information systems necessary to make it work. Physical systems may be quite complex, but human systems with their constantly-changing internal personal and social interactions and dynamic interplay with their environments — customers, competitors, unions, suppliers, governments and so on — are infinitely more so.

Within a corporation, one way of understanding the system is to break it into its governing elements (see Exhibit 3.1):

1. Its charter (government permission for, and restrictions on, the scope of operations),
2. The shareholders (i.e., the owners),
3. The board of directors, elected by the owners as their representatives,
4. The officers and top management employees appointed by the board to run the operations, and
5. The operating employees, hired and supervised by management, who carry out the front-line work.

These are not discrete, independent elements; they are an assemblage of overlapping and interdependent subunits that cannot be put in neat boxes. Rather the four groups which together make up the company, can best be seen as a series of interlinked or overlapping circles, each representing a delegation of power and authority beginning with the government and flowing from the owners down to the operating levels, with accountability flowing backup through management and the board to the owners and eventually to the government. The overlapping nature of the components means they are interdependent, and must function together for the same purpose for the system to work well. Superior performance by one component, for example the board, is of little use if other elements are functioning badly. The output of the system depends on a subtle balance between the elements and their interaction, and the whole is much greater than the sum of its parts.

The corporate system clearly does not operate in a vacuum. The environment in which it operates (see Exhibit 3.2) may also be seen as a system comprising many groups and individuals who are linked by direct and indirect exchanges with the corporation and thus have a stake in its success. The suppliers of materials, equipment, or services depend on it for revenues. The communities in which the company operates depend on it for jobs and tax revenues. Customers, local service groups, distributors, creditors, governments at all levels, and the public — collectively, the stakeholders in the business — all have an interest in the company's well-

Exhibit 3.1

THE COMPANY AND ITS CONSTITUENT PARTS

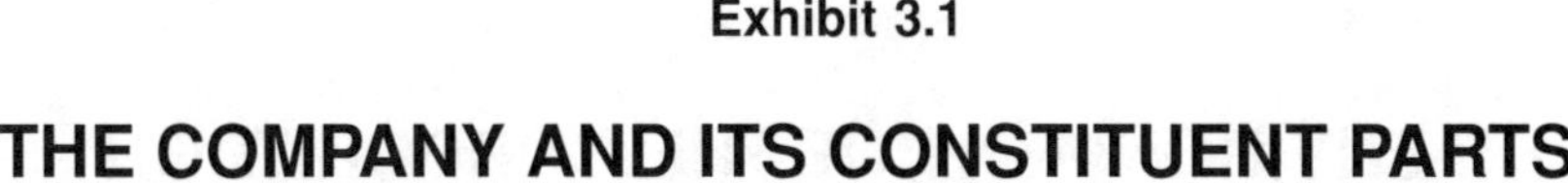

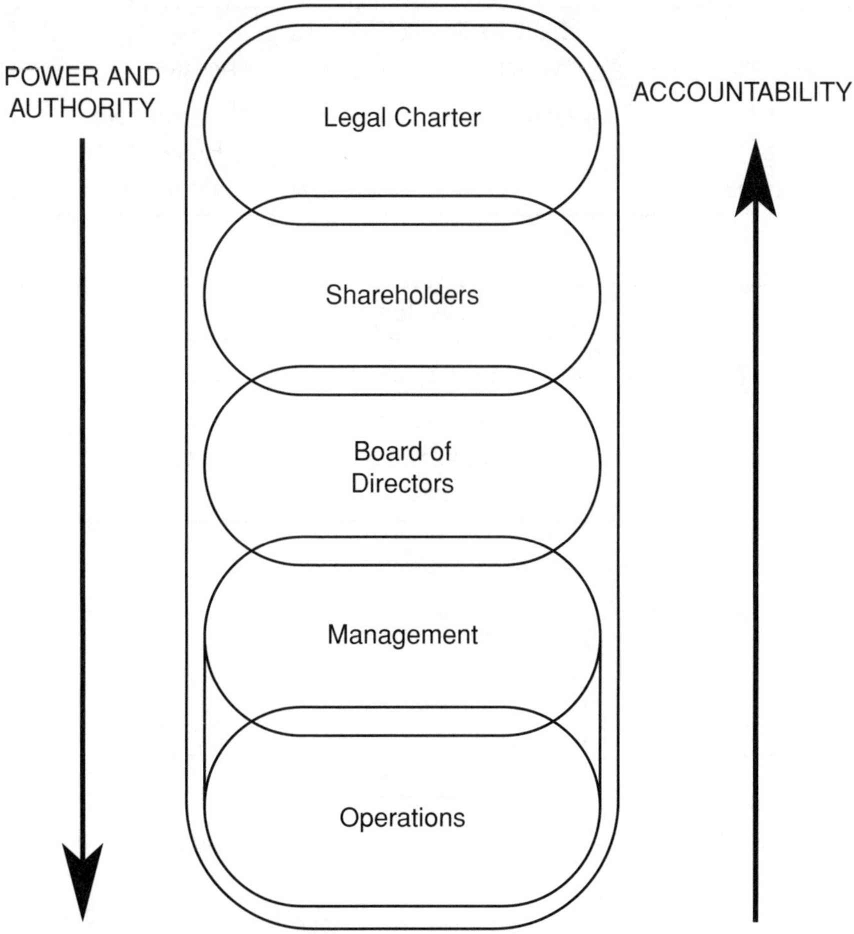

being. They form a constantly-changing group whose interests shift over time. The corporation needs to be sensitive to these interests and maintain a balance in its relationships with them.

THE BOARD AND ACCOUNTABILITY

In *theory*, the board is elected by the shareholders. Its job is to provide its best judgment, independent of management, so as to add value to the shareholders' investment over time. Its concern is primarily long term, and it must take a broad view of adding value. As agent, it intervenes between

Exhibit 3.2

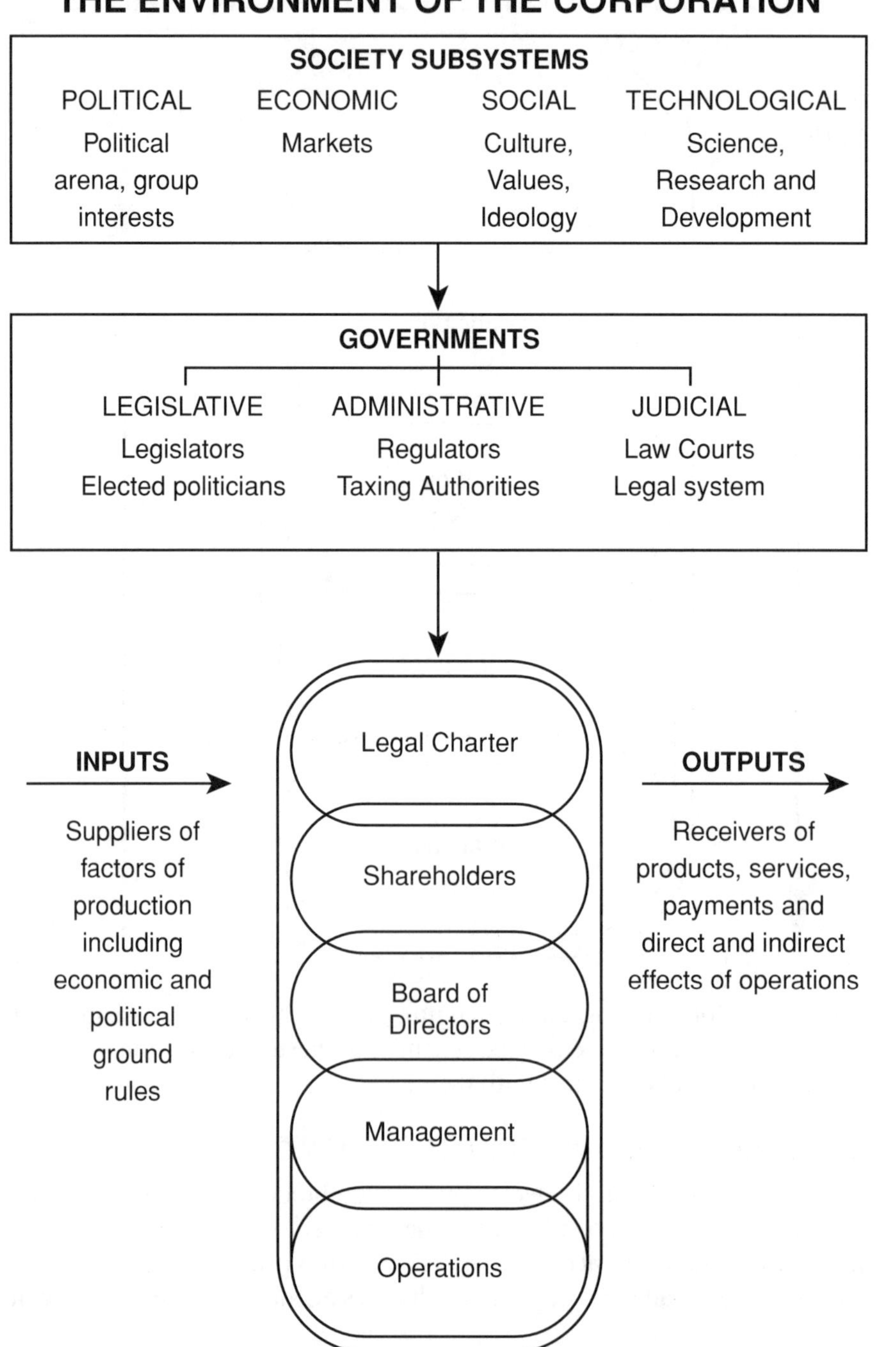
THE ENVIRONMENT OF THE CORPORATION
SOCIETY SUBSYSTEMS
POLITICAL
Political arena, group interests
ECONOMIC
Markets
SOCIAL
Culture, Values, Ideology
TECHNOLOGICAL
Science, Research and Development
GOVERNMENTS
LEGISLATIVE
Legislators
Elected politicians
ADMINISTRATIVE
Regulators
Taxing Authorities
JUDICIAL
Law Courts
Legal system
INPUTS
Suppliers of factors of production including economic and political ground rules
Legal Charter
Shareholders
Board of Directors
Management
Operations
OUTPUTS
Receivers of products, services, payments and direct and indirect effects of operations

the owners and the active managers, interpreting shareholders' needs and wishes to management and reporting on its stewardship to shareholders. It plays a pivotal role in keeping these elements of the system working towards a common purpose. If it fails to do this job well, it may be removed by shareholders through a democratic process at the annual meeting of shareholders. The board is held accountable by those who have given it power.

In *practice*, this model is seriously flawed. In widely-held companies shareholder input is seldom sought, and shareholder democracy is more often honoured in the breach. Annual meetings are generally perfunctory; nominating and voting processes are controlled by the board; some major shareholders hold disproportionate power. Communication between the board and shareholders is often sketchy, and the owners of the company are given very little basis on which to judge the effectiveness of their "representatives." The truth is that boards are too often self-perpetuating, more interested in retaining power than in responding to the wishes of shareholders.

LEGAL DUTIES OF THE BOARD AND DIRECTORS

The starting point of any job description of the board must be its legal base. Set in the broad context of corporate governance, the legal duty of the board is to "manage or supervise the management of the business and affairs of a corporation". The only qualifiers are that while so doing, directors are required to "act honestly and in good faith with a view to the best interests of the corporation" and to "exercise the care, diligence and skill that a reasonably prudent person would exercise in similar circumstances". One leading law firm described this duty in the following terms:

> Significant changes have occurred in corporate laws relating to directors. These have substantially increased the risk that the competence and perhaps the integrity of directors will be called into question in litigation, regulatory action or the media.
>
> The principal development is that the standard of care, diligence and skill to which directors are held has been substantially increased. It is only in the last fifteen to twenty years that there has been a legislated standard of care to which directors must adhere. Prior to that time the duties were defined by judges.
>
> While the courts enforced a high standard of honesty and

> loyalty to the corporation, they were lenient in their requirements for care, diligence and skill. The test was purely subjective: a director had only to behave reasonably having regard to his or her own knowledge and experience. The less informed he or she was, the less was expected. Furthermore, the courts did not expect or require a director to pay close attention to the affairs of the company. In fact, the courts decided that a director was not responsible for actions which were taken in his or her absence. This created a perverse incentive: the less diligent directors were about attending meetings the more insulated they were from liability.
>
> Legislation and regulation have changed this. The test is now more objective rather than subjective. And, sensibly, failure to participate — or lack of diligence — no longer will shield a director from liability.[2]

Since the 1980s, the legal liabilities and risks of directors have been steadily increasing. Directors are now accountable not only to the corporation and its shareholders, but also, under certain circumstances, indirectly at least, to employees, creditors, customers, suppliers, and governments. Directors are responsible not only for routine requirements such as fair dealing with shareholders, payments of wages, vacation, termination and severance pay, pension plan contributions, health insurance premiums, source deductions, and taxes, but also more complex matters related to competition and selected commercial practices, disclosure, breaches of securities legislation, insolvency, and environmental protection laws. The "due diligence" defence for directors in these matters requires that they individually and collectively take action to make sure they fully understand their responsibilities, duties, and legal liabilities, ensure that adequate warning systems and procedures are established and maintained to avoid problems, and that if and when problems arise they take personal, prompt, and effective action to ensure that management does what is necessary to remedy potential or actual problems. Most companies minimize the personal risk of directors' liabilities by buying directors' and officers' liability insurance, establishing corporation by-laws indemnifying directors from personal liability and, in some cases, setting up trust accounts for the payment of specific potential liabilities. However, in spite of the wide use of increasingly sophisticated risk management techniques, there is still widespread concern about the possibility of joint and several legal actions against directors, auditors, and controlling shareholders for potentially huge damages that are not covered by, or may be in excess of, liability insurance coverage.

In companies where losses are mounting and financial strength is being seriously eroded, the possibilities of insolvency, financial reorganization under the Corporate Creditors Arrangement Act (CCAA) or perhaps even bankruptcy and liquidation must be faced. When the possibility of insolvency, restructuring, or bankruptcy becomes a reality the legal rights of creditors must take priority in directors' obligations. Moreover, resignation may not be a good way out of a bad situation. In fact, resignation puts directors, boards and companies in the most unfortunate of catch-22 positions as described by one leading law firm:

> By resigning, directors generally cease to be responsible for obligations which accrue following the date of resignation. However, this is not always the case. [For example, liability for source deductions and taxes may continue for two years after ceasing to hold office.]
>
> Finally, a cautionary note must be sounded with respect to resignation. Not only does resignation mean that the director is giving up control and access to information of the corporation, but mass resignation by the directors may have a decidedly negative effect on how creditors view the corporation and its solvency, and might, thereby, increase the likelihood of claims being made against the directors.
>
> Further, there may be a question as to whether a director is neglecting his or her duties to the corporation by resigning in order to escape liability.[4]

Little wonder that spokesmen for directors of some failed companies facing potential ruin and personal bankruptcy have called for the replacement of corporate boards by advisory committees without legal liabilities.[5]

GOVERNANCE AS A POLITICAL SYSTEM

In order to understand how corporate governance works, it is also essential to understand the corporation as a complex political system, one that is ruled by individuals, groups and interests that attempt to control the appointment, decisions, and actions of those who manage its operations. The participants or actors are all joined together in a trading relationship in which they exchange tangible and intangible inputs for outputs; they give to, or withhold from, the system what it needs, and in turn receive, or do not receive, what they need from it. Shareholders pay for stock to get dividends and capital gains; managers give time, effort, knowledge, skills, reciprocal loyalty and trust in exchange for salaries, bonuses, pensions, security, perks, and loyalty, and trust; labour gives work and support for wages and conditions sometimes delineated in a union contract; suppliers exchange goods and services, loyalty and support for payment, and reciprocal loyalty and support; governments give legal charters and the protection of the law for tax revenue, employment, economic and political benefits; and so on. Participants are, at root, primarily motivated by self-interest and bound to all the others through a relationship marked by cooperation (to contribute to the success of the common enterprise) and/or conflict (to maximize the participant's self-interest and rewards, often at the expense of others). All are to a greater or lesser degree motivated by an ego-centred drive for power and control.

The corporate political process consists of multi-lateral bargaining interactions among the stakeholders involved. While the conditions that influence the purpose, propensity, methods, and intensity of bargaining are all important, we simply note in passing that some political scientists believe that a primary stimulant to bargaining is the awareness that compared to other individuals or groups, the bargainer is suffering from or fears relative deprivation or perceives the possibility of using power for self-interest. Bargaining vigor, strength, and aggressiveness — other important factors in corporate governance — generally depend on the bargainer's achievement drive, power and authority, coherence of demands, effectiveness, and ability to project demands in terms that are reasonably congruent with corporate goals and prevailing values.

How do these ideas apply directly to corporate governance? The board of directors is, in theory at least, the decision centre of a political bargaining arena composed of (1) shareholders (2) senior management, and (3) the other stakeholders of the firm (Exhibit 3.3). The central issues of corporate governance arise from the conflict among these three groups, all linked in complex, multilateral trading and political bargaining relationships that are ultimately refereed and arbitrated by the board. Some of the critically important, practical, and unavoidable issues are as follows: Who controls the firm, for what purpose, and in whose interest? In the fundamental

Exhibit 3.3

GOVERNANCE AND THE BOARD OF DIRECTORS
The Political Bargaining Arena of the Firm

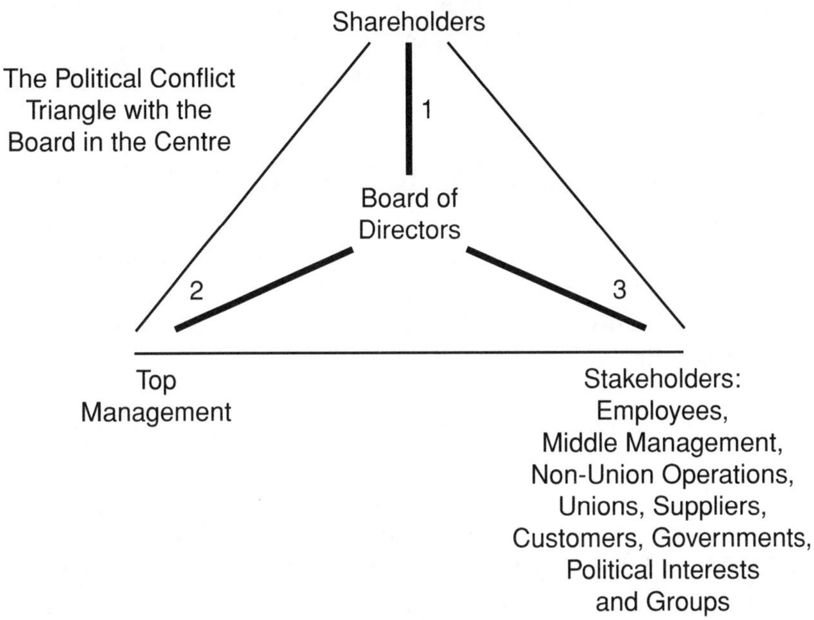

conflicts of interest among directors, shareholders, managers, and other stakeholders, who decides who gets what, why, how, when, and from whom? What is the job, authority, and responsibility of a director? Who hires, evaluates and, if necessary, fires the director? On what grounds? These basic issues are inescapable for anyone seriously involved in corporate governance.

Thus defined, corporate governance is anything but the mechanistic, abstract and esoteric topic implied by many legal theorists. What corporate governance is really about are issues of power and how it is used: who has the ultimate authority to rule the corporation? And how do the holders of power create, share, and sometimes destroy, shareholder wealth? As the Janzen case (Chapter 2) and many more like it warn, the reader should be under no illusions about the conflicts, high stakes, charged emotions, political machinations and legal battles often to be found in the goings-on of corporate governance. Corporate governance can bring out the best — integrity, wisdom, care, responsibility, affection, selflessness, and service — and the worst — greed, stupidity, irresponsibility, dishonesty, hatred and bad judgment — in human nature. It continuously confronts problems and issues about creating, and allocating corporate wealth, rewarding those who are successful and responsible, and disciplining those who are unjustly exploiting corporate power at the expense of others. It is almost impossible to exaggerate the importance of these issues, because they determine not only the rights and responsibilities of owners, managers, labour, and other stakeholders, but also the economic and social performance of firms, industries, and nations.

THE FIVE FUNDAMENTALS OF THE BOARD SYSTEM

Based on the current understanding and definition of the evolving duties of directors and the consensus of informed and reasonable practice, five fundamental precepts of the board system are now widely accepted. This current conventional wisdom regarding the board system can be summarized as follows:

1. **Shareholders are the source of the board's legitimacy and power**

The legal authority of the board derives ultimately from the property rights of shareholders, and the responsibility of the board is to act as agent for them. The board should keep shareholders and their advisors adequately informed so that as investors and owners they can monitor and evaluate performance and approve material changes. In reporting to shareholders the board is obligated to communicate to the fullest extent short of making them insiders or divulging vital competitive information.

2. **Boards are legally empowered and responsible to increase shareholder value**

Operating within the legal, economic, political, and social context of the firm, the board of directors has the authority and responsibility to control and guide the firm. The board's performance should be measured ultimately by the increase over time in shareholder value, the primary objective of the firm. Fair treatment of other stakeholders — employees, pensioners, customers, suppliers, creditors, governments, communities, and the public — is a necessary but not sufficient requirement.

3. **The chairman represents and answers to the board**

The chairman of the board is chosen by, manages, and is accountable to, the board. The job of managing the board is demanding, and requires independent leadership, commitment, focus, time, and talent on the part of the chairman.

4. **Boards delegate operations to management**

The board puts the best available CEO and top officers in charge and delegates to them the authority to manage the company. In its trusteeship and guidance roles the board is responsible for developing, implementing, and administering control and reward/punishment systems to monitor, evaluate, and improve company results, and to compensate, support and/or discipline and, if necessary, remove management on the basis of performance compared to goals and expectations and the requirement of high standards of integrity and ethics.

5. **Management is accountable to the board**

The CEO and his top management team report to the board. The role of management is to run the company and that of the board is to ensure that management performs as well as possible. While these two roles sometimes overlap and the boundary is often unclear, it is nevertheless fundamentally important that they be separated and not confused.

BOARD STRUCTURE AND PROCESS

The number of directors in any company is established in the bylaws, the detailed description of the legal constitution of the firm. The minimum legal requirement — if there is "public distribution and ownership by more than one person" — is generally for "not fewer than three directors at least two of whom are not officers or employees."[3] Some of the largest boards, big banks for example, have membership numbers in the twenties and thirties.

While minimum legal qualifications for directors consist of being 18 years of age, of "sound mind" and not bankrupt, most directors are in fact leaders from business, the professions, and public life: incumbent or former chairmen and CEOs, bankers, lawyers, auditors, politicians, and academics mostly from business, law, engineering, and science. And most are men.

Most current Canadian directors were "elected" through appointment by the controlling shareholder or the chairman/CEO. One survey of chairmen of large Canadian companies indicated that fewer than half (44 percent) had nominating committees and that even where a nominating committee existed, the CEO had considerable influence on the nomination process.[6] Over the last 20 years there has been a trend away from inside to outside directors, with the majority of directors in publicly owned companies now being outsiders or so-called independents.

To facilitate and organize the work of the board, most boards are organized into committees that undertake detailed reviews and supervision of various tasks and responsibilities. Committees of the typical board include the following: audit, executive, human resources and/or compensation, pension, nominating, and perhaps others such as finance, environment, corporate governance, public policy and/or government relations, conduct review (ethics, self-dealing), and special committees as required. In most companies the full board meets six to ten times and committees two to four times annually. However, depending on the nature of the business, its financial stability, the frequency of major decisions, and the need to address unusual problems or circumstances, meetings might be much more frequent.

Probably the most common aspect of all types of boards is that duly-constituted meetings follow parliamentary procedures, with proceedings recorded in minutes describing the legal record of the meeting, date, directors present and absent, other attendees, subjects addressed, positions taken by directors and resolutions and/or decisions proposed, seconded, approved, amended, tabled, or not approved. The fixed, common agenda — preliminaries formally convening the meeting and noting the chairman, secretary, and necessary quorum; approval of the minutes of the last meeting; business arising from the minutes; new business; and termination — follows a routine that can be viewed as either helpful or stultifying, depending on the chairman and the culture of the board. Nevertheless, the formal outline can readily accommodate regular or periodic reviews of operating results, profit and loss statements, balance sheets, and cash flow compared to plan and previous year; reviews and reports by management; periodic review of long-term strategic and short-term operating plans; reports from board committees; review and approval or change of recommended policies and decisions; compliance reviews related to health and safety, environmental, employment, and other regulatory requirements; pension plan funding and investment performance; outstanding litigation; and any other significant issues.

The typical board is managed by the chairman. He or she generally has a leading role in selecting and recruiting directors, often picking business friends or acquaintances who are known, and approved of, by most of the other directors. The chairman, with the assistance of the corporate secretary and senior staff, plans and organizes the meetings and agenda. Compensation for outside directors in larger companies runs around $15,000 to $20,000 as an annual retainer, a $1,000 per meeting fee and additional fees for chairing a committee, plus all expenses.[7] Management of the board almost always follows tradition and precedent. The culture is deeply ingrained from the past, proceedings are formal and behaviour is usually circumspect and ritualistic.

The survey of large Canadian company chairmen quoted earlier, provides interesting insights on a number of issues concerning directors and their roles;

- The average size of boards is between 12 and 13 members. On average, these boards lose one member per year. The highest level of turnover occurs on boards of privately-controlled companies.

- Three out of four corporations (74 percent) do not have a written job description for directors. This is especially true in widely-held public corporations, where only 5 percent report having specific job descriptions for directors.

- Nearly two-thirds of corporations do not have a standard procedure for briefing new directors as to their roles, duties, and responsibilities. Chairmen of widely-held corporations reported having briefing procedures in only 29 percent of the cases.

- The vast majority of corporations do not have a procedure in place whereby each board member's performance is regularly reviewed and appraised. Only 8 percent of privately-controlled companies, and 10 percent of widely-held firms report having performance appraisal systems.

- A little more than half (54 percent) of chairmen reported that their boards have a formal retirement age for directors; with the average age for retirement being 70. Some 81 percent of widely-held corporations have a mandatory retirement age, compared to only 49 percent of control-block companies.

- CEOs have some influence over the selection of board members in virtually all cases.

- The most important factors that chairmen use to evaluate a director's performance involve the director's judgment, regular attendance, preparation, and contributions at meetings. These and other factors are evaluated differently by chairmen of corporations with different ownership patterns.

- Very few companies (10 percent) have any formal mechanism in place to deal with an ineffective director. In effect, directors have a form of tenure, and it is very unusual and difficult to remove a director for nonperformance.

THE COST OF THE BOARD SYSTEM

The cost of a board of directors is regarded by management as more or less fixed, minor, and unavoidable. Little, if any, formal attention is paid to the matter. However, the boards of most large public companies are in fact very expensive. In addition to the obvious direct costs of fees and travel, living and entertainment expenses, there are a number of indirect costs which are seldom accounted for. These include management time, administrative and secretarial support, space costs, meals, directors' insurance, legal and professional services, perquisites, telephone and other communications. A typical medium to large public company board costs well over $1,000,000 per year when all these costs are considered.

The importance of assessing the effectiveness and benefits of such an expenditure becomes obvious. Such costs multiplied by the number of public companies suggest that the board system is an expensive institution to maintain. Whether it is effectively managed is the subject of the next chapter.

NOTES:

1. Chuck Midgette, ''Governance Rules Need Some Tweaking'', *The Financial Post*, May 4, 1996.
2. Tory Tory Des Lauriers & Binnington, *Directors' Responsibilities in Canada: What Works Best*, 1994, pp. 2, 3.
3. This wording is common in many corporation acts, including those of Canada and the provinces.
4. Private memorandum from Stikeman, Elliott, June 5, 1992.
5. Margot Gibb-Clarke, ''Court rules directors still liable after bankruptcy'', *Globe and Mail, Report on Business*, August 30, 1996 p. 139.
6. J.D. Kovacheff, *Managing the Board, A Survey of Chairmen of Canadian Corporations*, (National Centre for Management Research and Development, 1993).
7. These and other statistics about Canadian boards are reported regularly by the Conference Board of Canada and executive search firms like Korn Ferry and Spencer Stuart.

APPENDIX

THE DYNAMICS OF BOARDS IN TRANSITION: AN ANALYTICAL FRAMEWORK

The required understanding of the dynamics of the board system in transition must be based on an analytical framework that provides an overview of what to look for and how to put all the pieces together (see Exhibit 3.4). The key factors and their relationships are as follows:

1. The board system: the current function, structure and process of the board system as it exists and works in actual practice.

2. The environmental change forces impacting the board system: the related pressures for adjustment arising from the bargaining demands of the political, economic, social, and technological systems with which the board system has input-output relationships.

3. The problems and issues that result from the impact of environmental change forces (2) on the board system (1).

4. The ideal model of the board system: the normative conception of the board system that is the aimed-for long-term ideal, function, structure, and process guiding all planning for improvement.

5. Needed changes: the necessary adjustments in the current board system (1) to solve the problems (3) to make the board system conform more satisfactorily to the model (4).

6. Change action: the actual, practical action necessary to implement the needed changes (5).

From our experience and research, we believe these are the major factors and processes on which all thinking, planning, decisions, and action in regard to upgrading the board system are based, either explicitly or implicitly.

To illustrate how this dynamic works in practice, let us use this framework to explain briefly the regulatory mandating of the audit committee. As it worked in the 1950s, the board system (1) did not provide adequate control of financial auditing. Environmental problems (2) in the

Exhibit 3.4

CORPORATE BOARDS IN TRANSITION
Dynamics of the Evolution of the Board System

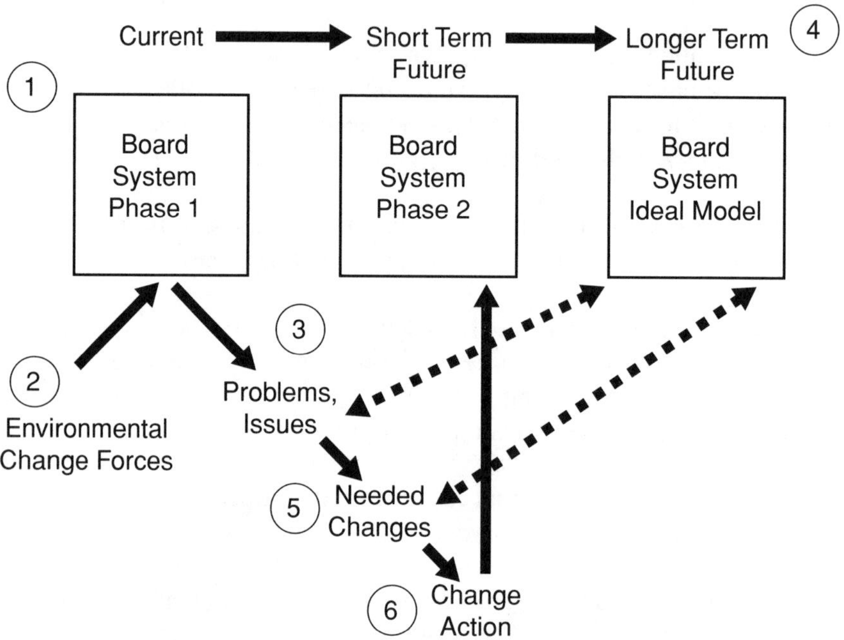

form of difficult business conditions impacted on many companies to cause severe financial problems. Several financial disasters (3) resulted, harming many shareholders and related stakeholders in the system—auditors, customers, creditors, employees, governments and so on. The ideal model desired by all (4) called for, among other things, satisfactory auditing and reporting. The pressure built for improvement and the proposed solution (5) was strong, mandatory, audit committees. The needed changes were planned and implemented (6) and the entire system adjusted to the new reality of the upgrading of function, structure and process in regard to financial management, auditing and reporting.

Chapter 4

HOW BOARDS WORK:

Appraising the Board System

"Our board of directors is like a bunch of ants running around having meetings on top of a big log carried by a turbulent current swiftly down a river. The ants think they are steering the log."
(Senior vice-president of one of the largest Fortune 500 companies)

The board system as described in the last chapter has been widely and harshly judged to have failed in controlling corporations so as to maximize shareholder value. Yet a paradox remains. Boards are still regarded by many as the all-powerful source of wise control and guidance of management, and, at the same time, belittled by others as pointless functionaries without real power or relevance to the strategic problems of business. Traditionalists of the ''legally-in-charge'' point of view hold that shareholders elect outstanding leaders (''potentates'')[1] to act on their behalf in appointing and supervising the best available managers, who are held accountable to increase shareholder value. Sceptics of the ''emperor-has-no-clothes'' point of view believe that directors are mostly ''pawns'' appointed by a controlling shareholder or a self-perpetuating management oligarchy to be ''window-dressing'' and ''rubber stamps.'' To what degree are either or both of these points of view valid?

To be credible, any proposal to reform and improve the board system must be based on a realistic and knowledgeable diagnosis of its strengths and weaknesses. Our purpose in this chapter is to present an evaluation of the board system and its performance, the realities of its structure and process that both enable and inhibit excellence in governance, what its great possibilities and severe limitations are, what the board system can and can't do, and what can and can't be changed. From this base, we shall proceed in the next chapters to consider the director's job and the function of the board in its critical role: overseeing strategic management.

STRENGTHS OF THE BOARD SYSTEM

In order to present a balanced evaluation of the board system it is important to begin with a brief overview of its major strengths. Any proposed remedies for its problems must be carefully analyzed and evaluated to ensure that they do not cause unintended side effects that harm or negate any of these factors:

The Board System Provides for a Needed Balance of Power Among Shareholders, Management and Other Stakeholders

As the board system has evolved (Chapter 2), it has been structured to provide a necessary compromise and balance among the interests of shareholders (capital gains and dividends); management (security, income, and advancement); and the protection of the company as a whole (including all its other stakeholders: employees, creditors, customers, suppliers, communities, and governments). Because contests for power and control cause confusion, conflict, and often ultimately failure, the board performs the function of a keel, providing the balance and stability that is necessary to keep the boat from tipping uncontrollably from side to side.

Boards Provide for Management Accountability

Since managers are human beings driven by self-interest, they need to be held accountable for their stewardship of assets and the use of their power to control the operation of the firm. History teaches that power without responsibility leads to abuse of authority and, in the longer term, the disintegration of the cooperation needed for the success and survival of any organization. If managers must be accountable, the only alternatives to the board system would be direct accountability to owners, an administrative impossibility, or to the government, an alternative that would be totally incompatible with free enterprise and democracy and a severe inhibitor to national wealth.

The Legal Base is in Place and Accepted as Standard Operating Procedure

Legally the board system is established, practised, generally respected and followed. It has stood the test of time and is relatively well litigated. The legal profession has been struggling for years to clarify many of the issues and conflicts involved and a comprehensive legal doctrine of the corporation has been developed. In spite of its faults and failures, it provides a strong, proven, workable base from which to govern and manage the firm. To understand how invaluable and indispensable this industrial foundation and infrastructure is, one only has to contrast business in most developed, western countries with that in China and the former U.S.S.R.

The Board System is Adaptable

Based on an abstract definition of board function and wide variations in practice, the board system is open-ended and flexible enough to be reformed and improved to fulfil an ideal role of direction with great effectiveness. Improvements can be made relatively rapidly and effectively in individual boards. Although general change in the system tends to be, and should be, more difficult and gradual, it can be done. Recent trends in legislation and regulation promise a major shift in the balance of power between the board and related parties.

The Board System is Open to Political Influence and Legislative and Regulatory Change

The legal foundation and rules of the board system are subject to the will of the public, expressed through the political bargaining arena, and can be changed as necessary through the political process. There is a workable balance between too little and too much flexibility or rigidity.

The Board System Can Work, Sometimes Very Well

Although there are many examples of the board system not working satisfactorily there are also many cases in which it has worked effectively, providing corporate governance that is first class in function, organization, process and result, not only for shareholders but for other stakeholders as well.

The Board System Attracts Many Good Directors

It is satisfying to be a competent director serving effectively on a good board. The enjoyable experience, associational richness, challenge, compensation, opportunity to learn and be informed and the possession of power and prestige available to only a few of the business elite, are highly rewarding for almost any individual. As a result the job has attracted, and will continue to attract, many able individuals.

Outlining these strengths helps to put criticism of the board system in perspective. The system is by no means fatally flawed or incapable of reform. In fact, the situation is just the opposite. In spite of many serious problems, the board system is not only conceptually strong, it is adaptable to reform, particularly the improvement of its management, which is our primary focus.

DIFFICULTIES AND PROBLEMS OF THE BOARD SYSTEM

Bearing in mind these strengths of the board system, let us review some of its major problems and difficulties.

The Job is Undefined

The duties of directors and boards, as described in the Business Corporation Acts of Canada, the U.S., the U.K., and many other countries whose rules are based on a similar legal doctrine, are not clear. The words describing their function — ''to manage or supervise the management of the business and affairs of a corporation'' — are nothing more than abstractions without any meaningful standards to guide or evaluate the carrying out of that function. The job requirements as defined in managerial practice vary widely depending on the ownership structure, the traditions and cultures of the board, the power and capabilities of directors, and the condition and strength of the corporation. To govern means to take responsibility for the most important issues and problems, to lead in taking decisions, and to do whatever is necessary to ensure corporate success in terms of long term profitability, growth, and survival. The lack of adequate definition of the director's job leads to uncertainty and confusion. Without specific performance standards, directors can avoid accountability and shareholders are uncertain as to legitimate expectations of performance. As long as the job is ambiguous and unclear, there will remain both managerial and legal problems in holding directors to their task and evaluating their performance, fundamental requirements for rational administration.

The Link Between Board Performance and Shareholder Value is Conjectural and Uncertain

Due to the complex chain of factors in the relationship of the board to operations, there is seldom, if ever, any observable direct or even indirect cause-effect relationship between the board and shareholder value (See Exhibit 4.1). The exception would be an unusual case of emergency decision and action by the board. Briefly stated, the board's most important

Exhibit 4.1

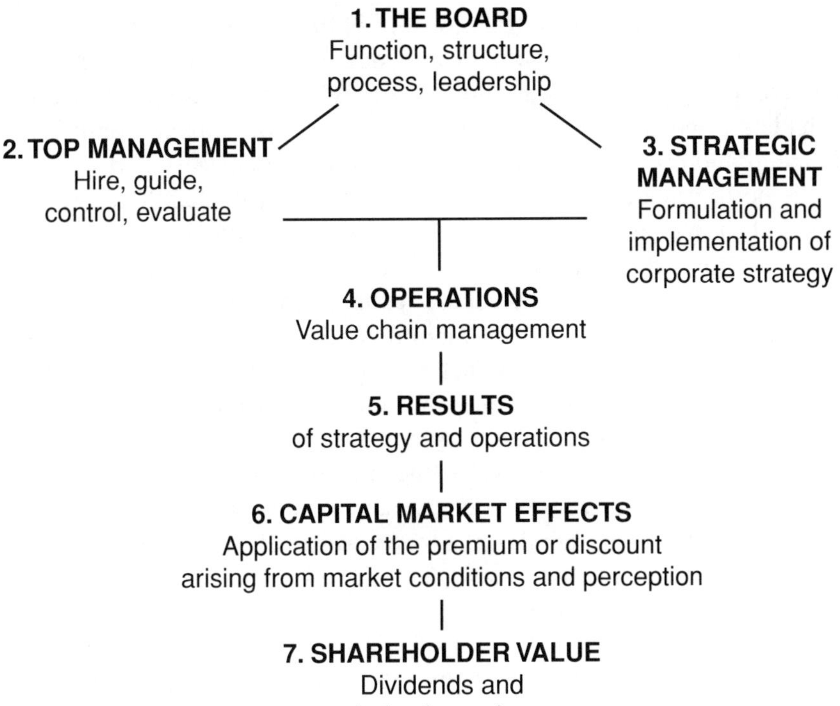

and direct relationship in the firm is with top management, through the CEO. In fact, many authorities contend that the board's prime function is to hire, monitor, support, evaluate, compensate, counsel and, if necessary, fire the CEO who, in turn, is held responsible for running the company. A concurrent relationship in the chain is between the CEO and his top officers and the strategic management structure and process of the firm. While directors have a direct input to, and feedback from, strategic management, their relationship with most of the activity involved is indirect, through the CEO and his top officers.

The next level of management and firm activities is the operational value chain — inbound logistics, operations, outbound logistics, marketing and sales and service — all of which must be well managed if the company is to show good results. These activities fall under the day-to-day supervision of middle and lower level managers and their relationship with the board, if any, is conjectural — so far removed as to be unreadable. At this level external factors, particularly market and competitive realities, trends and developments, have a major, sometimes decisive, impact on the degree of success attainable.

The next direct causal relationship is that of operations to financial results, operating cash flows in and out, noncash costs and revenues booked, and capital gains and losses through non-operating transactions. Calculated and adjusted, these sums, properly organized, comprise the financial and operating results that are reported internally and externally as the performance indicators used by management, shareholders, creditors, and analysts to evaluate management and guide decisions. Accounting for and reporting results is an art and not a science; these finite numbers give an aura of precision and accuracy that is not always justified.

Finally, depending on the chain reaction of the key factors outlined above and with the major impact of capital market realities — trends, hopes and fears about interest rates, inflation, public confidence, the supply and demand for a huge variety of securities, investments, and competitor actions — we arrive at intrinsic value (theoretical real value) and actual shareholder value (increases or decreases in the market price of the company's shares and dividends), the key end result in the chain of causal factors beginning with, but now so far removed from, the board of directors that any possible relationship is totally lost, in some cases perhaps even reversed. As one veteran director of a large company put it: ''Trying to make any changes here is like trying to pour water through a yard-thick layer of felt.''

Since the ultimate standard and measurement of board performance — the long run optimization of shareholder value — is no more than a conjectural and lagging performance indicator, evaluation of the effectiveness of any board must be based on the judgment of more observable intermediate performance indicators that can hopefully be assumed to determine the end results of corporate operations. Given these realities, the primary criteria, the key factors that a competent insider/diagnostician can observe and evaluate, for judging board performance are as follows:

1. Effectiveness of board function, organization, process and leadership (see Exhibit 4.2)

    - function: job definition, what the board does

Exhibit 4.2

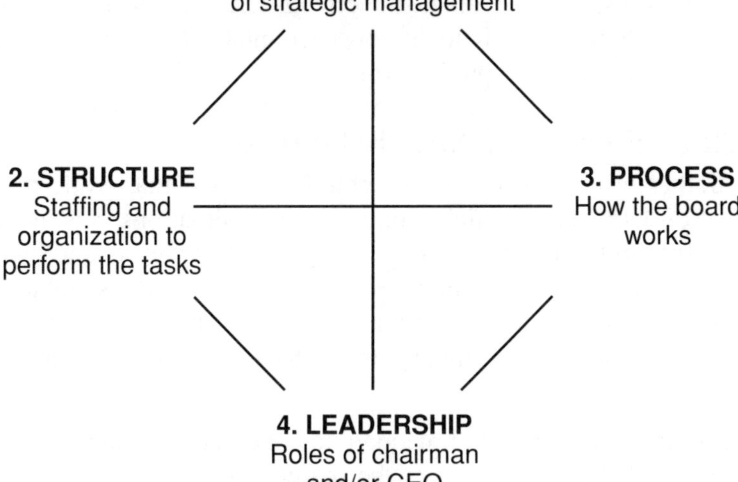

- organization: staffing and structure
- process: sequence of activities through which the board works
- leadership: roles of chairmen, lead directors and others who influence board proceedings

2. Quality of control and guidance of management
   - hiring, monitoring, evaluating, compensating and, if necessary, firing the CEO and officers
   - oversight, consultation, trusteeship
3. Quality of strategic management
   - strength and integration of corporate purpose, strategy, operations, results, organization and resources and their congruence with the environment

- effectiveness in formulating and implementing strategy to solve problems and capitalize on opportunities

These criteria for judging the effectiveness of boards are qualitative and subjective, beyond accurate and timely observation and evaluation by outsiders. This leads to the most important basic weakness of the board system: under ordinary circumstances it is extremely difficult, if not impossible, for outsiders to evaluate the effectiveness of a board. As a result, boards cannot logically be held directly accountable for shareholder value, the prime objective of the public firm.

Directors' Powers are Strictly Limited

Another basic problem of the board system is that while the legal power of directors is potentially total in certain situations, it is, nevertheless, strictly limited in practice by a complex set of checks and balances. Even the best directors, chairmen and managers who understand the art of using or manipulating the board power system can be handcuffed in attempts to upgrade strategic management. Key sources of power for individual directors are:

- the broad legal duties and mandate to supervise the management and affairs of the firm as agents of the shareholders;
- the power, personality, stature, knowledge, skills, and business and social network of directors;
- access to other directors and the chairman;
- the threat of dissent and consequent exposure and publicity that could negatively affect the public perception of the firm;
- the right to initiate questioning, dialogue and opposition in regard to any decision, policy or program.

Countering these strengths are a number of limitations that reduce, and sometimes nullify, the directors' powers, including:

- cultural, social, and political pressures to conform to the consensus of the board, and the process by which boards make decisions;
- formality and a traditional culture which often discourage questioning, dialogue, and dissent;
- time limitations of directors due to other commitments, jobs and responsibilities;

- reluctance to embarrass or confront the CEO/chairman, especially in front of management;
- need to avoid conflict because of the risks of confrontation and dissent, including potential loss of job, status, influence, income and perquisites;
- lack of information and/or certainty on complex, changing issues;
- management control of the information made available to directors;
- low director pay and busy schedules, discouraging time-consuming study and/or follow-up.

Given the pressures on one hand to participate actively and, on the other, to concur passively, it is understandable why so many directors are ineffective — they are simply unwilling or unable to size up difficult business situations, take a position on controversial issues, and in a tough-minded but cordial fashion, stand up for what is wise and responsible. As one director put it: "Most directors are like putty in the hands of management". Casey Stengel, the legendary baseball manager, is rumoured to have described his duties as a director of a California bank this way: "There ain't nuthin' to it. You go into the fancy meeting room and you just sit there and never open up your yap. As long as you don't say nuthin' they don't know whether you're smart or dumb." At least he was frank in admitting what really goes on in the minds of some directors! Living by Stengel's widely followed credo, six directors of one of Canada's largest banks are reported to have never once spoken up over a period of 11 years and 110 meetings.[2] (Did the bank's management know they would be gullible non-participants and appoint them for this reason or were they mysteriously struck dumb after joining the board?)

STANDARDS OF COMPETENCE AND PERFORMANCE ARE RISING

Notwithstanding the fact that directors' duties are seldom clearly defined and that their interventions seldom, if ever, have any traceable direct effects on operations, standards of competence and performance are gradually being upgraded as a result of increasing internal and external pressures. From within, increasingly active shareholders are demanding better performance in strategic management to improve shareholder value. From without, investment analysts are pressing for divestments and focus on core businesses. Political action groups and governments are combining to agitate for, and legislate, requirements for environmental protection, greater union powers, employment and pay equity, minority rights, and health and safety protection. The demands on directors' time and attention have grown exponentially, and performance requirements are similarly escalating.

DIRECTORS' LIABILITIES ARE INCREASING

Until the 1950s, directors' duties were relatively undemanding and liabilities, except for flagrant fraud, were inconsequential and unlikely to be imposed. The main requirements were honesty and loyalty to the company; misrepresentation and deals that benefitted directors personally at the expense of the company were prohibited. Duties were limited to the director's personal knowledge, involvement, and skill. In a legal defence for breach of director's duty, corporate lawyers were known at one time to advise "the less knowledgeable and diligent the better" — a director who didn't know about a problem could not be held responsible or judged guilty. One experienced, high-profile director reported that in those days he was occasionally advised by corporate lawyers not to attend certain board meetings because, if he did, he would be informed of matters or asked to ratify decisions that "it would be better that I not know about".

With the general upgrading of business practices and ethics, this era of directors' "duties" had generally ended by the 1950s. The standard of competence became the "care, diligence, and skill" that would be expected of a reasonable person in comparable circumstances. In legal actions related to controversy arising from board decisions, directors were protected by the "business judgment rule", the long-standing legal precept that, even in the case of a serious error in judgment, the courts would not second guess, challenge, or condemn a board's business judgments and decisions providing, of course, that fraud, illegality or bad faith could not be proven. In the 1980s, liabilities were widening and the business judgment rule was questioned and occasionally challenged. In effect, board decisions and actions or lack thereof were being opened to retroactive legal judgment.

By the 1990s, while directors' duties were still not generally specified, it was abundantly clear that much more demanding standards of "due diligence" were required as a defence against lack of disclosure, acts, or omissions that were oppressive to shareholders, unfairly disregarded shareholders or creditors, and transgressed environmental, employment, and health and safety laws. Several corporate debacles left big name directors "under the gun" and potentially ruined by corporate failures that, they argued, were beyond their control. Moreover, class actions based on contingency fees had become possible, removing a major legal barrier to those whose interests were harmed by what a board did or failed to do.

The bottom line in these developments is that today a good "due diligence" defence for a director in any legal action requires evidence that he or she could prove the following:

1. Adequate understanding of all important corporate matters — insight into the company and its environment, and knowledge of all significant actual and potential problems and opportunities, risks and concerns.

2. Effective control and direction of management — that the board was clearly in charge of management in terms of hiring, setting goals and standards, monitoring, evaluating, compensating and, if necessary, firing the CEO, and maintaining and supervising an effective information and control system and strategic management process.

3. Directors sought to be and were informed by management of all material problems, took personal, prompt, correct remedial action, and followed up to make certain that management actions were effective in rectifying any unsatisfactory situation.

In summary, the director's duties have expanded greatly, with stringent liabilities for acts of commission or omission that are harmful to shareholders and other stakeholders subject to an increasingly onerous "due diligence" defence. As one leading lawyer put it, "Attempts to codify the duties, responsibilities and liabilities by directors and officers and to judge them through hindsight may well be the beginning of the end of an era when it was fun to be a director."[3]

CONFLICTS BETWEEN THEORY AND PRACTICE

One of the most important practical problems of the board system is that it depends for its proper functioning on the understanding and reconciliation of many conflicts between theory and practice. To govern effectively, directors must strike a balance between precepts that say they should on one hand observe one principle, but on the other hand must also obey a conflicting principle. Some of these paradoxical conflicts are as follows:

1. **Paradox:** Many if not most of the public shareholders who legally own widely-held companies have been limited-term investors inter-

ested in return on their investment and not in proprietorship and management responsibilities. As the dean of business historians, Harvard Business School professor Alfred Chandler, observes: "the public shareholder ... played no appreciable role in creating modern industrial enterprises or in the building of the industries in which they operated."[4]
Problem: The proposition that ordinary public shareholders should be actively involved in corporate governance will always be somewhat artificial and contrived. The practical reality as Chandler has pointed out, is that management is necessarily in charge of the widely-held firm and directors are under some degree of management control.

2. **Paradox:** Directors are legally responsible for supervising the management of the firm, but full-time management has the day-to-day presence and thus controls the planning and operations, the information system, and organization.
   Problem: How can directors be responsible without really being in control? How should the unavoidable problems arising from the generic tensions and conflicts between the directors and management be handled?

3. **Paradox:** Legally the source of power and legitimacy comes from all the shareholders, but in reality power usually rests in a major shareholder and/or management.
   Problem: How can directors be responsible when they do not have the ultimate power to decide and act? How should directors function when their purpose, to optimize value for all shareholders, conflicts with the self-interest of major shareholders and/or management?

3. **Paradox:** To act as responsible agents for shareholders, directors should aggressively push management to optimize shareholder value, which often conflicts with management self-interest — job security, compensation, perks, risk-aversion, and tension reduction.
   Problem: How should directors balance supporting management and risk demanding too little, and criticizing management and demanding too much?

4. **Paradox:** The board should delegate operations to management and not interfere, but also be in control, know what the problems are and make sure that management is doing its job well.
   Problem: How do directors simultaneously avoid or balance negligence and being too passive on the one hand, and "micro-managing" and being too aggressive on the other?

5. **Paradox:** Directors, in the end-result, should be congenial team players who support cabinet solidarity and, at the same time, should be mentally tough, self-reliant, responsible individuals who will "take a position" and dissent from board group-think as necessary.
   Problem: How does a director balance collegiality with individual independence of thought and responsibility? What are the tensions involved, and do the almost-overwhelming pressures for conformity coopt individual warnings and dissent?

6. **Paradox:** Boards must make decisions but, in the words of one veteran director, "a board meeting is a lousy place to discuss a problem."
   Problem: How can directors have the kind of discussion and dialogue necessary to understand, and, if necessary, debate issues and agree on decisions when the format of board meetings often prevents this? Management has often already decided the issue, time to consider and discuss is limited, proceedings are formal, the agenda is full, the necessary information and analysis are not available and the culture rules against this approach.

7. **Paradox:** In an annual meeting, the niceties of shareholder democracy are all observed — directors are elected, major decisions approved, and reports given — all decided and prearranged by management. Spontaneous nominations, suggestions, and questions from the floor are generally discouraged, thwarted, or ignored.
   Problem: How can shareholders have any power, voice or influence when incumbent management and their chosen board control all the instruments of shareholder democracy?

8. **Paradox:** In most boards, the CEO — who is responsible for running the company — is also the chairman, and as such responsible for leading the board in monitoring, evaluating, paying, and, if necessary, replacing the CEO.
   Problem: In companies where the jobs of CEO and chairman are combined, the CEO tends to control the operation and deliberations of the board and management has more power than the board.

9. **Paradox:** To do the director's job conscientiously an out-of-town director generally needs to spend considerable time to prepare, a good part of a day to travel, and a day at each meeting. The director who is an officer of another company or has his or her own company contributes as much as $7,000 to $8,000 worth of time per meeting to the corporation. Compensation in return would probably be $2,000 to $3,000 before taxes.

Problem: There is a tremendous gap between what directors are expected to contribute and how much they are paid. This probably means there is an increasing reality gap between what boards are expected to do and what they actually do.

These paradoxes — and many more could be cited — illustrate the complexity of judgment and balance of conflicting principles that must be accommodated and applied for the board system to function. To make such judgments and compromises even more difficult, the proper synthesis of many conflicting rules of governance varies widely by company and situation. Take, for example, board control and delegation. In dealing with a takeover bid, a board must take control in a manner that would be totally inappropriate for changing the product/market strategy of a division or raising a large amount of capital for future expansion.

Almost all business "principles" are relative and situational, relevant and true in some circumstances, but not in others. It is therefore impossible to frame a statement of board system rules that would be universally valid. Unless it is under the rule of highly competent directors with the experience, knowledge, skills, and attitudes necessary to make it work under many different circumstances, the board system is highly vulnerable to misuse and consequent ineffectiveness. This requirement of ever-changing, wise application of different competencies and judgments under different circumstances is both a great strength and a great weakness of the board system.

DIRECTOR INDEPENDENCE IS A MYTH

It is now a given with regard to the board system that a majority of directors be independent of management and/or the controlling shareholders. While the term "independent" may have legal meaning, practically speaking it is an oxymoron when applied to directors.

Since the quality of directors and their judgment is critically important, institutional shareholders, legislatures, and courts have put much emphasis on the independence of directors. This emphasis took on importance in the 1950s and 1960s when the differentiation was between "inside" and "outside" directors (employed or not employed by the company), inside directors being severely downgraded because they were obviously in no position to make contributions independent of the management party line. If by independent one means self-sufficient or self-governing, not subject to the influence and power of others, such a director is a myth, neither existing nor possible. The complex process of proposal and election as a director means that the new director owes his or her proposal, induction, and membership in an exclusive club to those who suggested, investigated, nominated, and elected him or her.

Even more obvious, as soon as the new director has cashed the first cheque and accepted the first perk, favour, or word of approval, he or she has been initiated into the group and is subject to all the rewards and punishments that arise from a not-too-subtle constellation of relationships. As several important institutional shareholders have pointed out "to have fairly independent directors who represent shareholders, change is necessary"[5] with respect to the entire nominating and election process and the monitoring and evaluation of each director's track record. The fact of the matter is that all directors represent and are related to someone and something. Independence is a state of mind, not a relationship. The truly independent director is one who may from time to time have conflicts of interest, but who recognizes them, declares them, can put them aside, and can address the issue at hand with rationality and a high level of objectivity.

DIRECTORS, CHAIRMEN, AND BOARDS VARY WIDELY IN COMPETENCE

The most critical problem of the board system is that the management competence of directors, chairmen, and boards varies widely from unsatisfactory to excellent. Our research indicates that for every excellent director, chairman, and board that is doing outstanding work in leading a company to success there is an unsatisfactory counterpart, incompetent and irresponsible, along for the ride at the top of a company that has failed or is drifting in that direction. The widely-reported failures of governance at many leading companies are probably just the "tip of the iceberg," a few of the many cases that prove the point.

That this is so should not be surprising because, as we have pointed out, the board system has many weaknesses and the job is not clear. The legal duties are to direct management, but there is no direct causal relationship between the board and company results or shareholder value. There are no agreed competency qualifications for directors or chairmen. There is no formal training or accreditation. The management of boards almost always follows outdated tradition and precedent. The culture is deeply ingrained from the past, behaviour is circumspect and ritualistic. The typical board is managed by the chairman, who usually recruits directors who are business or personal friends approved by most other directors. In practice, boards are seldom accountable to anyone except themselves and there is little, if any, systematic evaluation of performance. Given these fundamental anomalies and often insuperable faults in the function, structure, process, and leadership of boards, it is perhaps surprising that the board system performs as well as it generally does.

One way of thinking about and assessing and diagnosing the problems of the board system with a view to practical reform is to understand that directors, chairmen and boards can be broadly graded in categories ranging from clearly unsatisfactory, to poor, average, good, and excellent. Some criteria for ranking boards as a whole are outlined in Exhibit 4.3. Analogous criteria for ranking individual directors and chairmen are outlined in Chapters 9 and 11.

In the absence of any evidence to the contrary, this suggests the existence of the normal, bell-shaped curve of distribution of competence in boards as a whole. While there may be significant variations in the competence of individuals within any board, or indeed in the competence of individual board chairmen, in the end it is the performance of the board as a whole, that is as a system or team, that is important to the shareholder. The overall effectiveness of a board working as a team is not necessarily the sum of its parts. Every director does not have to have demonstrated competence on every issue; indeed some who are completely at sea on many items coming to the board may provide extreme competence on one or a few other issues that are infrequently discussed, but which are critical to the company's strategic direction. By the same token, a board comprising highly competent, experienced directors can often survive mediocre leadership from a chairman. The important measure in governance is the output of the board as a team working together, not the brilliance (or lack thereof) of its individual members.

The existence of the normal bell curve in regard to board effectiveness suggests a distribution roughly along these lines:

	Unsatisfactory	**Poor**	**Average**	**Good**	**Excellent**
Percent	10	20	40	20	10

Obviously, for individual directors and chairmen, there are wide variations from this general distribution of overall board effectiveness. In some boards, previously rated as highly prestigious only because no outsiders really knew what was going on behind the closed doors, most or all members have proven to be unsatisfactory as they presided over disastrous mistakes, declines, and failures. Some boards with potentially strong individual directors have been frustrated and blocked from successful performance by mediocre or authoritarian chairmen, or unwise, dictatorial controlling shareholders. In other boards, because of the context, circum-

Exhibit 4.3

BOARDS CLASSIFIED BY EFFECTIVENESS

Rating	1 Unsatisfactory	2 Poor	3 Average	4 Good	5 Excellent
Company Relative Performance	Lowest, actual or potential failure, insolvency	Below average, serious under performer, erosion of shareholder wealth	Mediocre, average	Above average	Highest, leader in profitability, growth, strength, and prospects
Management Strength	Totally inadequate	Weak	Mixed	Competent	Outstanding
Strategic Management	Potentially disastrous	Incompetent	Questionable	Solid	Very strong
Board Management	Extremely negative	Weak	Problems	Improvement planned and underway	Enlightened, very strong
Shareholder Relations	Terrible	Bad	Passable	Satisfactory	Strong
Contribution in Consulting and Trusteeship	Ineffective, irresponsible, negative	Inadequate	Mediocre	Reasonably good	Outstanding, highly effective
Overall	Major mistakes and disastrous losses	Serious weakness and ineffectiveness	Status quo maintained	Good solid performance	Exceptional success

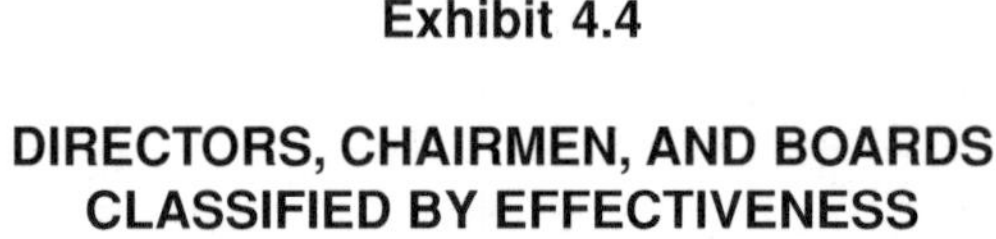

Exhibit 4.4

DIRECTORS, CHAIRMEN, AND BOARDS CLASSIFIED BY EFFECTIVENESS

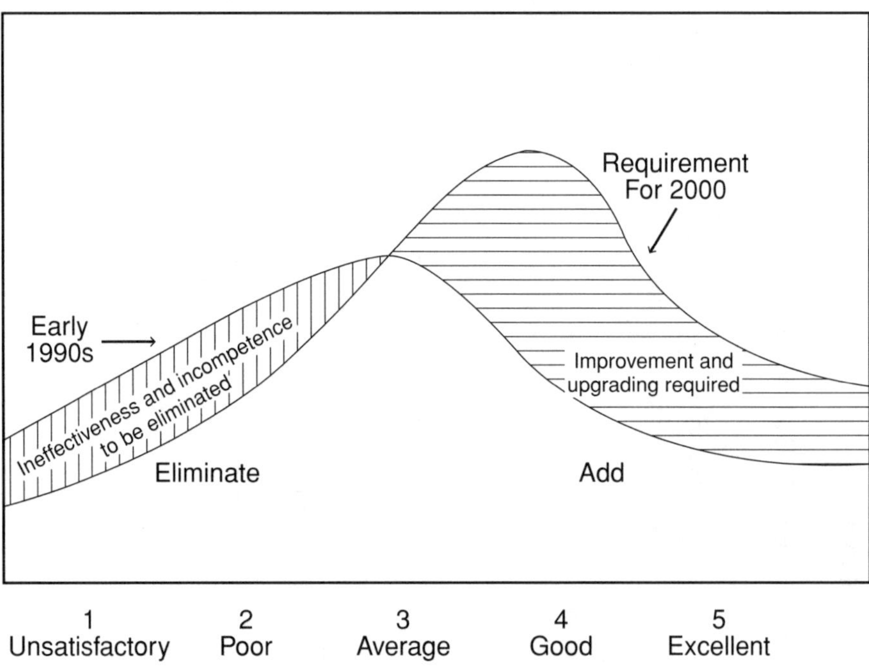

stances, and interpersonal dynamics involved, some potentially outstanding directors turn in mediocre performances, and some otherwise average directors turn in outstanding performances. Nevertheless, we believe that a distribution on the scale shown above is reasonably descriptive of the current general quality levels of Canadian boards, taken as a group.

While there is anecdotal evidence of some performance improvement, especially over the past decade, the greatest single challenge confronting the board system is to markedly upgrade the quality level of boards by concentrating on upgrading the roughly 30 percent that currently rank in the poor and unsatisfactory category. In other words, the bell-shaped curve of the mid-1990s needs to be pushed hard to the right (see Exhibit 4.4) if the board system is to be successful in overcoming the problems of the next few decades. In this development of more effective boards, improvement in the management of the board is the answer and the challenge that we are addressing in this study.

Notes

1. This dichotomy is described and analyzed in Jay Lorsch with Elizabeth MacIver, *Pawns or Potentates: The Reality of America's Corporate Boards*, (Boston, Mass: Harvard Business School Press, 1989).

2. Rod McQueen, ''Under the Gun,'' report in *The Financial Post*, May 4, 1996. p. 6.

3. Henry J. Knowles, Q.C. of Wooley, Dale and Dingwall in an address to The Risk and Insurance Management Society Inc., Calgary, Alberta, October 15, 1986.

4. Interview with professor Alfred D. Chandler, Jr. as reported in the *Harvard Business School Bulletin*, (April 1990), p. 48.

5. See, for example, Robert A.G. Monks and Nell Minow, *Power and Accountability* (New York: Harper Collins, 1991), especially Chapter 3.

Chapter 5

THE CANADIAN PROBLEM: Major Shareholders Control Most Boards

The fundamental *Canadian* issue of corporate governance is that the nation's business is dominated by companies in which a major shareholder, sometimes with a relatively small equity ownership, can control the board of directors to the detriment of minority shareholders who are effectively powerless to resist. Such shareholder control blocks exist in a number of forms: in subsidiaries of other companies, whether foreign or Canadian; in companies with a majority shareholder, or in companies where minority shareholders hold controlling votes either through a shareholders' agreement or through multiple-voting shares. There *are* examples of U.S.-style widely-held companies in Canada, and they are important in key industries such as banking, but proportionately they play a much smaller role in Canadian industry.

What this means in governance terms is that many, perhaps most, Canadian directors and the shareholders they represent are often along for the ride, with limited or no real power to govern the companies for which they are legally responsible.

To illustrate the governance issues that arise in this context, consider the following cases.

CROWNTEK CANADA

Crowntek Canada, with several divisions operating in a wide variety of businesses, was the 60 percent-owned Canadian subsidiary of a large U.S. parent company. The Canadian company had gone public on the Toronto Stock Exchange in 1974, largely in response to the Trudeau government's push for Canadian ownership. A competent board had been appointed, including six Canadian outside directors, its CEO and CFO, and three top parent company officers.

The Canadian company was one of 27 geographically-decentralized, national units, all heavily dependent on the U.S. parent for top management, strategy, planning, technology, product development, production know-how, treasury management, auditing, and special services. From the first days of Crowntek Canada's public ownership, the directors were confronted with a seemingly-endless succession of fundamental conflicts of interest with the parent company. The board, in a serious but discreet manner, fought a constantly-losing rearguard action against the parent company's dictates on such issues as product mandates and export market assignments; plant investments, start-ups, machinery and equipment specifications and procurement; capital budgeting; working capital and cash flow management; transfer pricing; charges for management services and technical know-how; tax calculations and strategy; management promotions and transfers in and out of the subsidiary (which was viewed by the parent as a prime training ground for management); and marketing and sales management.

The most visible of these issues related directly to the publicly-reported financial statements of the Canadian company, where transfer prices and parent company charges became the focus of bitter accusations by shareholders at the company's well-attended annual meetings. The Canadian company's president, always an American, often found himself in the embarrassing position of being forced to defend parent company policies and decisions that had been privately protested to the parent by Canadian directors as unfair and unwise.

During the 1970s and 1980s, the parent company chairman/CEO had been highly supportive of the Canadian subsidiary, viewing it as a vital investment in the company's future in this country. But, with the increase in international competition in the 1990s, the passage of NAFTA, and the retirement of the long-serving CEO, the Canadian directors could clearly sense the irresistible pressure to approve major decisions that would benefit the parent at the expense of the public shareholders of the Canadian company.

For some of the Canadian directors, who admittedly bore only minimal responsibility, the negatives of the job — time, futility, frustration, criticism by shareholders, and the growing realization that they were being used as ceremonial figures in a meaningless legal ritual — were starting to outweigh the positive rewards of pay, perquisites, prestige, and the association with other quality board members. Privately, two of the Canadian directors discussed resigning.

* * * * *

JONES CORPORATION

The April Nominating Committee meeting of the Jones Corporation board was lengthy and heated. David Smith, the committee chairman and a long-serving independent director, had planned the agenda carefully. It was an important meeting, because no fewer than three of the 14 board members had announced their intention to retire at the annual shareholders' meeting, scheduled for September. All three had reached or passed the board's newly-installed retirement age of 70, and their retirement was a significant element in a long-term governance plan which Smith and the committee had prepared and presented to the board a year earlier. The plan had been unanimously and enthusiastically approved by the board as a whole, including the three retiring members.

Smith's intention was to have a thorough discussion of the qualifications sought, and to solicit names of prospective candidates from the other three members of the nominating committee, two of whom were independent directors. The third, Max Woodford, 35, son of the founder, voted the family's controlling interest through their majority holdings of the company's multiple-voting "A" shares, which carried 100 votes per share; the widely-held "B" shares had one vote per share. The "A" shares in total represented only about 30 percent of the total equity of the company, so that the Woodford family commanded a majority of the votes while owning only about 15 percent of the total equity. Max Woodford's father was one of the three retiring directors.

To David Smith's dismay, when the committee discussion turned to considering replacements for the three retiring directors, Max Woodford interrupted him and, without any consideration of desirable qualifications, put forward three names of individuals that he had met and befriended through the Young Presidents Organization. In the discussion that followed, Max let it slip that in fact he had already asked the three individuals to serve, and that they had all agreed to do so. He made it clear that he felt that nomination to the board was his prerogative as controlling shareholder, and that any further discussion was pointless.

* * * * *

EDSON (CANADA) LIMITED

Richard Bradley was the nonexecutive chairman of Edson (Canada) Limited, the Canadian subsidiary of a large U.S. manufacturer of small appliances. Sixty-five percent of the shares in Edson Canada were owned by the parent and 35 percent were widely traded on the Toronto Stock Exchange. The Canadian company had been purchased in 1980 by Edson, Inc., but in 1995 the parent company had sold 35 percent of its shares in a secondary offering in Canada in order to raise cash for a U.S. acquisition. Edson Canada operated with a good deal of autonomy from the parent, possessing its own board of directors and product development, marketing, and finance functions in addition to two large factories in Ontario and Quebec. Financial performance had been excellent in a highly-competitive industry, characterized by frequent new product introductions and substantial advertising and promotional expenditures.

One morning in early December, Richard Bradley received a telephone call from Mario Castelli, president and CEO of the parent and a member of the Canadian board. Castelli outlined a major cash squeeze facing the parent company; performance in the U.S. had not been good, prices and margins were depressed, and the company's principal bankers wanted Edson to pay down some of their unsecured debt. Castelli told Bradley that the parent company wanted the Canadian subsidiary to declare a special dividend at year-end, which was less than a month away. The company had never paid dividends, but the parent needed a large infusion of cash and was "putting the arm" on the Canadian company to help.

The large amount required would necessitate the Canadian company taking on substantial additional debt. The Canadian balance sheet was strong, but to pay the dividend would severely hamper the company in several ways — particularly in product development and marketing — and would also result in the unwanted risk of having to shoulder a large increase in interest expense at a time when sales were slowing down. Although the Canadian minority shareholders would share in the dividend, it was clear that this would be a material set back for Edson Canada.

* * * * *

THE COUNTRYWIDE NEWS COMPANY

The Countrywide News Company was run in a highly-authoritarian manner by a tough and aggressive entrepreneur who bought, sold, and manipulated his way to a minority control position in a growing newspaper chain. Well known and highly influential in political circles, he had attracted an outstanding group of friends and business leaders to his board.

With many problems in the company and the industry, it was inevitable that the board frequently faced controversial issues. In one meeting, during which a particularly thorny issue had been raised, the discussion began to turn to the apparent disagreement of some of the top managers and directors with several controversial changes that had been largely dictated by the chairman/CEO, who was the controlling shareholder. After about ten minutes of generally-negative comments and some sharp questioning, the chairman suddenly lost his temper. His face reddening and the veins in his neck bulging, he angrily smashed his fist on the table and shouted: "Dammit, you guys don't think I can run this — outfit, do you?" What had been an animated discussion ended instantly, and a heavy, foreboding silence engulfed the room. After a long, tense pause in which no one dared speak or look at anyone else, the senior outside director finally broke the silence: "What's the next item on the agenda?" he asked calmly. The meeting proceeded.

After the meeting was terminated, the chairman wandered over to a group of three outside directors who were discussing the blowup. Unapologetically, he said to no one in particular, "Sorry I had to get a little rough back there, but I had to let you guys know who's the boss around here."

* * * * *

CONTRAST WITH THE UNITED STATES

These cases illustrate a number of the problems and issues that arise in Canadian companies controlled by a major shareholder, in some cases foreign corporations and in others by large, powerful Canadian-based owners. These issues are familiar to any director who has served on the boards of such companies. They are, in a very real sense, "The Canadian Problem," because such companies comprise the majority of Canadian corporations.

This is in sharp contrast to the United States, where the overwhelming majority — roughly 70 percent — of large corporations (see Exhibit 5.1) are widely-held, without any identifiable major shareholder. Why the difference, and does it matter?

Exhibit 5.1

THE 500 LARGEST CANADIAN AND U.S. COMPANIES, CLASSIFIED BY OWNERSHIP AND CONTROL

Type of Company	Canada	United States
Privately-owned	20%	3%
Control Block	50%	18%
Widely-held	15%	70%
Public Utility	10%	9%
Government-owned/controlled	5%	—
Total	100%	100%

Note: These are estimates based primarily on examination of *Financial Post* (FP500, 1996) and *Fortune 500* (April 29, 1996) listings. We recognize the limitations of this sort of analysis. There is an order of magnitude problem in looking at the "top 500" companies in Canada and the U.S. Sales figures are not necessarily the best indicators of size or power. Despite these limitations, the data do demonstrate significant differences in the two countries.

The strikingly-different pattern of ownership has clearly emerged out of the equally diverse business histories, cultures, and sizes of the two countries.[1] Canada has had a much longer colonial tradition than the U.S., and as a thinly-populated, resource-rich country it has relied heavily (and still relies) on outside capital for the development of those resources. Private wealth has been concentrated in a relatively few individuals and families. Capital markets, by comparison with its southern neighbour, remain relatively thin and undeveloped, and many major developments — particularly in transportation and communication — have required substantial government involvement. Indeed, the hybrid corporate forms of public utility (government-granted monopoly) and Crown corporation (government ownership) remain important players in Canadian business, and the problems and issues of corporate governance where there is government ownership or control, with concomitant ultimate political control and accountability, become complex indeed.[2]

Perhaps for many of the same reasons, Canadian capital markets in the post-World War II era saw the development of public companies with dual-class share structures, that is, nonvoting, subordinated, or restricted-voting shares. A dual-class share structure has common equity that has been divided into two classes of shares with different voting rights. Such shares allow control to be disproportionate to the amount of equity invested, reducing or eliminating the power of the vote, the foundation on which corporate democracy is based. Such shares were originally introduced primarily as a way for family-controlled Canadian companies to retain control while seeking external equity capital. Today, over 200 companies listed on the Toronto Stock Exchange have such shares. A similar situation does not exist in the United States, where the concept of "one-share, one-vote" has generally prevailed.[3]

PATTERNS OF OWNERSHIP

Whatever the reason, the pattern of corporate ownership in the two countries is dramatically different. In order to categorize ownership patterns in the two countries we have broken ownership into the five groups: privately-owned; control block companies; widely-held; public utility; and government-owned or controlled (the so-called "Crown corporation"). We define the five types of ownership as follows.

Privately-Owned Corporations

These are companies with no public ownership. Usually owned by the founder and perhaps members of his or her family, they are usually, but not always, small and medium-sized firms operating in the most market-oriented sectors of the economy. Characteristics often observed include owner-manager domination; authoritarian, top-down organization; entrepreneurial, nepotistic culture; rapid growth; vulnerability to changing business conditions; and often heavily reliant on bank credit. Many of these companies, especially in their early stages, have only a token board of directors to satisfy legal requirements. As they grow, the contacts of the owner widen, the business becomes more complex, and the founder often increases his board to include additional trusted friends, associates and advisers.

Control Block Corporations

These are firms in which there is a clearly-defined owner (or owners working together under a shareholders' agreement), but where there are also other shareholders. This pattern often emerges from the founder's wish or need for outside capital, requiring the sale of equity to others. Where the shareholder owns 51 percent or more of the common shares, he or she is clearly in control, can elect or depose any director without much difficulty, and is essentially free to run the company subject only to legal requirements protecting minority shareholders.

Companies can also be controlled by a major shareholder having less — often much less — than 50 percent of the equity. However control must usually be exercised judiciously, as other shareholders can, and sometimes do, combine to oppose or thwart his decisions.

Widely-Held Companies

This is the stereotypical Fortune 500 company, with ownership widely dispersed and not organized. No one owner, or group of owners, controls enough votes to overrule management, and management is, in effect, self-perpetuating. In Canada, the major chartered banks provide a good example, due to provisions in the Bank Act limiting ownership.

In many companies previously widely held, there has been a market trend towards a shift of ownership from individual shareholders to large institutional investors, principally mutual funds and pension funds. While many of these institutions have in the past chosen not to exercise their shareholder rights, there is growing concern among them about the quality of corporate governance in Canada.

Public Utilities

These are companies like Bell Canada or Union Gas that have a protected monopoly in industries with a high degree of government regulation. Strategic decisions on rates, geographical coverage, product policy, capital investment, and diversification are controlled explicitly or implicitly by a political process directed by government.

Crown Corporations

Companies where the controlling shareholder, whether 100 percent or majority, is government. In such companies, objectives, strategy, policy and operations are not driven by profitability so much as by political and social considerations. They are controlled indirectly by government through legislation, control of the board, and funding and oversight. Direct intervention by political leadership, though rare, is not unknown. Such companies are expected to act as an arm of government policy.

Given these different forms of ownership, what can we say about the patterns that exist in the United States and Canada?

It is axiomatic that to understand the job of the corporate director, one must first understand the nature of the ownership of the corporation; the director is there, after all, to represent the shareholders, i.e. the owners. The role and responsibility of the director of a 100 percent privately-held corporation is markedly different from that of a director of a widely-held corporation. Similarly, the director of a company that is controlled by a large shareholder but which also has minority shareholders, has a different role from that of the director of either the private company, or the widely-held corporation.

In attempting to judge the effectiveness of individual directors and of boards as a whole, one must first understand their roles and functions. This provides a beginning understanding of the context in which they function and a base yardstick against which their performance can be judged. It follows that it is meaningless to generalize about the "role" of directors in all companies: one must look first at the pattern of shareholding in order to develop a reference point for the "job description" for any director.

Parenthetically, the failure of researchers to differentiate the different patterns of control, and thus director functions and responsibilities, has led to a great deal of confusion and controversy, with inconclusive results. This is perhaps understandable, since much of the research on directors and boards has been done in the United States, where the predominant control pattern of medium and large-sized corporations has been widespread ownership. Generalizations based on U.S. experience are manifestly often not appropriate for Canada, and may seriously mislead the public, the media, the legal profession, and government policy advisers interested in governance.

In Exhibit 5.2, we attempt to break down certain characteristics of corporate boards by pattern of ownership. In other words, we seek to probe further into the nature of the directorship function in companies that have different ownership. We examine specifically how ownership affects the locus of power and authority; the role of directors; the criteria for selecting directors; the limitations on directors' functions; information requirements and availability; and standards for judging performance.

OWNERSHIP STRUCTURE AND THE DIRECTOR'S JOB

Against the backdrop of very different ownership structures in Canada and the U.S., we return to the premise that ownership structure is a major determinant of what a director's role should be. In other words, a director's "job description" should be determined by the control pattern of the organization.

Specifically, Exhibit 5.2 shows that where share ownership is diffuse, control tends to shift to management. The job of the outside director in such companies is quite different from that in companies where there is a control block. The issue facing directors in widely-held corporations is how to prevent management from usurping the board's functions through its control over the agenda and the information flowing to directors. Directors must strive for true independence on behalf of all shareholders. If they fail, management will tend to run the company to suit its own interest and maintain self-perpetuating control over succession.

In contrast, the director in wholly-owned, private corporations is there as a friend, confidante, and adviser to the owner. In many such cases, outsiders should normally be named as members of an advisory committee and not as directors, with the fiduciary responsibilities that directorship implies. Typically chosen because of friendship, personal loyalty and business experience, the director in a private company often has no personal financial stake in the company. His or her role is as a skilled adviser, provider of another viewpoint, and backstop/supporter/door-opener with banks, customers and others. As the shareholder interest is obviously represented directly by the owner, the outside director is expected to provide the widest possible range of advice. The responsibility for taking or leaving the advice is the owner's.

Similarly, the director of a Crown corporation will almost certainly be "politically correct" as a prerequisite. However directorship skills are required. Decisions taken will ideally be business decisions, tempered with strong sensitivity and concern for the public interest. Not an easy task, and not always successfully accomplished.

Exhibit 5.2

CORPORATE GOVERNANCE BY TYPE OF FIRM

Key Factors	100% Privately Owned	Control Block: Majority	Control Block: Minority	Widely Held	Public Utility	Crown Corporation
Key characteristics	Firms owned by individuals with no public ownership.	Owners retain or buy over 50% or more of shares and sell or leave a minority interest to the public.	Owners sell more than 50% of the shares but retain a block that gives effective control.	Shares distributed widely with no control block. Typical U.S. *Fortune 500* company.	Public ownership of monopoly with a high degree of government regulation.	Government ownership, instrument of government public policy.
Role of shareholder(s)	Owners have total power to manage without restrictions except for business and legal constraints.	Control block owner all-powerful except for legal restrictions and moral responsibility for fairness to minority shareholders.	Minority control block must retain the support of enough shareholders to keep majority of votes.	Fragmented and powerless except under unusual circumstances. Institutional activism increasing.	Powerless except for protection of regulators.	Government owners in total control.

Exhibit 5.2 (*cont'd*)

NATURE OF OWNERSHIP AND CONTROL

Key Factors	100% Privately Owned	Control Block		Widely Held	Public Utility	Crown Corporation
		Majority	Minority			
Locus of power and authority	Owners have total control.	Majority shareholder has total control except for legal restrictions protecting minority shareholders.	Largest minority shareholder controls if supported by coalition equalling a majority. "Shareholders agreement" often dictates control.	Management has effective control except under very unusual circumstances.	Strategic decisions controlled by government regulations.	Government controls through civil service under direction from the prime minister and political advisors.
Primary role of directors	Friends and advisors. No formal power, work through influence and counsel.	Friends and advisors to majority owner and representatives of minority shareholders.	Advisors to effective control owner, representatives of all shareholders.	Legally trustees for shareholders and overseers of management. In reality to ratify management initiatives.	Public relations, rubber stamps, and window-dressing to give public acceptability.	Public relations, rubber stamps and political window-dressing, position is usually a reward for political services rendered.
Selection criteria for directors	Personal relationship, friendship and advice.	Personal relationship, friendship, advice, management know-how.	Personal relationship, public acceptability as a representative of minority shareholders.	Relationship with chairman or nominating committee: reputation, power, leadership, experience and record.	Experience, public image, political acceptability.	Services rendered to the government political party, often "political hacks".

Exhibit 5.2 (*cont'd*)

NATURE OF OWNERSHIP AND CONTROL

Key Factors	**100% Privately Owned**	**Control Block** **Majority**	**Minority**	**Widely Held**	**Public Utility**	**Crown Corporation**
Limitations on directors' functions	No power or influence except through personal relationship with owner.	Little power except to influence controlling shareholder and management and defend minority shareholders.	Power and influence depends on shareholder agreement and balance of power.	Chairman/CEO control of information and agenda. Unwritten "club" rules.	Government regulations control geographical coverage, products, prices, profits and operations.	Act of Parliament and political oversight defines operations. No deviation from law allowed. Support of government political party mandatory.
Information availability required	At judgment of owner.	Only on key issues, especially affecting minority.	On entire operation.	Comprehensive coverage of all important aspects of the company.	Financial and operating data.	Routine matters for legal ratification.
Standards for judging performance	Loyalty, support to owner, help and advice.	Relationship with controlling shareholder, manner, cordiality.	Cooperation with controlling shareholder, protection of minority shareholders.	Value added as overseer of management, contribution to increasing shareholder value.	Appearance, legitimacy as window-dressing.	Value as figurehead, service to government political party.

CANADA: CONTROL BLOCK COUNTRY

Most directors in Canada function in a situation where there is a definite control block, but where there are also minority shareholders. Whenever other people's money is invested the director has a fiduciary responsibility. Where the controlling shareholder has clear representation on the board, either directly or through associates, the job of the independent director centres on constantly reminding the board of its fiduciary duty, especially to minority shareholders, while being realistic towards the wishes of the controlling shareholder and/or his representatives. The independent director must endeavour to see not only that justice is done, but that it is seen to be done, to all shareholders.

Controlled companies can usefully be divided into two categories: (1) controlled subsidiaries, where the major shareholder is another corporation, and (2) control block companies, where the company is autonomous, but is controlled by a single shareholder, shareholders' agreement, or other such arrangement. The outside director's role in the two cases is largely similar, but the types of issues confronted may be significantly different. In the controlled subsidiary, the management requirements and strategy of the parent will frequently conflict with the interest of the minority shareholders. In the controlled autonomous company, issues tend to centre on differences in the financial requirements of the major shareholder and the minority.

The Controlled Subsidiary Case

As the introductory cases clearly demonstrate, the job of the independent director in a controlled company is often ambiguous and difficult. The director owes his job ultimately to the controlling shareholder, and he can be removed if the shareholder decides he should go. Yet the independent director has a fiduciary responsibility to the minority, and his loyalty must be to the best interest of the company — not the same thing as the interest of the major shareholder. Furthermore, in the case of the foreign-controlled subsidiary contemplating a plant closing, the director may have to present the case for a particular community, for the Canadian employees, or for the national interest as a whole. Movements of capital, people, and products among controlled subsidiaries pose many issues of equity to minority shareholders, and difficult decisions for directors.

The Autonomous Control Block Case

Analogous issues also face the independent director of autonomous Canadian companies with a controlling shareholder. The majority shareholder may wish to pursue a course of action — declaring a special dividend, or transferring a key top manager — that the independent director believes is not in the interest of minority shareholders. Sorting out the director's responsibility to "all the shareholders", or to represent "the company's best interest" is frequently very difficult — particularly when it means disagreeing with the major shareholder who may be sitting across the boardroom table.

NEEDED: MADE-IN-CANADA CORPORATE GOVERNANCE

The differences in the issues faced by independent directors in the U.S. and Canada are sufficiently great as to call for very different standards in judging the performance of corporate boards and individual directors in the two countries. It also suggests that corporation laws and regulations governing the behaviour and responsibilities of independent directors in Canada should not necessarily mirror those of the U.S., but should be designed to reflect more accurately the nature of the Canadian business environment. Corporate law and regulation directed at the governance problems of large, widely-held corporations is not appropriate in an economy dominated by control-block companies, as Canada clearly is today.

By the same token, the task of managing boards of directors in Canada will generally be quite different from that in the U.S. The job description for independent directors of controlled companies, the Canadian norm, will be quite different from that for directors of widely-held companies. Major differences will be found in the criteria for selecting directors, the amount and type of information provided to them, the standards for judging their performance, and the level and type of their compensation.

Canadian writing on the subject of governance and, not surprisingly, Canadian corporation laws, auditing standards, and regulations all tend to reflect U.S. developments. There seems to be an implicit assumption that the two systems, U.S. and Canadian, are essentially the same. Yet, as we have seen, there are substantial differences. And these differences mean that the job of most independent directors in Canada is substantially different from that of their counterparts in the United States. We need corporation laws and regulations that reflect the reality of Canadian corporate governance, not some pale, belated shadow of the U.S. We need more and better made-in-Canada corporate governance research, and we need shareholders, boards and directors that understand the differences and govern themselves accordingly.

NOTES

1. The classic history of business in Canada is Michael Bliss, *Northern Enterprise: Five Centuries of Canadian Business* (Toronto: McClelland and Stewart, 1987). This masterful work is an indispensable reference for anyone seeking to understand the economic evolution of Canada. Interestingly, its index contains no reference to boards, directors or governance — perhaps a reflection of the times when it was written.

2. A number of books have been written on this uniquely Canadian corporate form. See particularly *Corporate Governance: Improving the Effectiveness of Crown Corporations*, Conference Proceedings, October, 1994, Department of Finance and Treasury Board of Canada. Also, *Directors of Crown Corporations: An Introductory Guide to Their Roles and Responsibilities*, 1993, prepared by the Crown Corporations Directorate of the Department of Finance and Treasury Board Secretariat, in collaboration with The Conference Board of Canada and the Canadian Centre for Management Development.

3. The most comprehensive work on restricted voting shares has been done by Professors Brian Smith and Ben Amoako-Adu of Wilfrid Laurier University. Several publications outlining their research have been published by the National Centre for Management Research and Development at the University of Western Ontario.

Chapter 6

THE DIRECTOR'S DILEMMA: Two Conflicting Codes of Behaviour

Huge legal battles pitting directors against allegedly-wronged shareholders are now common in the arena of corporate governance. In these legal actions, with potentially devastating effects on personal reputations and wealth on the line, victory or defeat will turn on how judges and/or juries define the duties of directors and boards and whether impassioned arguments by plaintiffs' and defendants' high-priced lawyers prove they were or were not satisfactorily carried out. Consider, for example, the Fraser Trust Company case.

THE FRASER TRUST COMPANY: A GOVERNANCE DISASTER

In 1992, control of the Fraser Trust Company was taken over by Vanco, a diversified financial holding company based in a large Western city. Buying 28 percent of Fraser, Vanco became its major shareholder, and quickly and decisively took control. Within a year or two, Vanco had implemented a complete transition in the purpose, strategy, top management, and board of directors of Fraser, thereby transforming a relatively conservative, slow-growing, and long-successful financial institution into a more aggressive, growth and profit-oriented, risk-taking subsidiary with complex governance, financial, and management relationships with other companies within the Vanco organization. As the Vanco philosophy, management, and operating methods took over, it was reported that Fraser became completely enmeshed in Vanco, and was increasingly under the direction and control of Vanco's hard-driving chairman/CEO and major shareholder, the key strategist and mastermind of the Vanco group. He and his inner circle strongly influenced subsidiaries such as Vanco through holding companies, all under his control and all committed to implementing Vanco's centrally-planned strategy, management methods and values.

For over 50 years, Fraser had been known as a "widows and orphans" stock, widely held in trusts and retirement plans. Fraser's prestigious board, now dominated by several key members of Vanco's brain trust, numbered 25 members, of whom 16 were "outsiders" and nine were from the Vanco group. The board included ten lawyers, several of whom were widely known and for whom Fraser was a major client, three accountants from related companies, seven active or retired CEOs, and five well-known personalities from public life. One informed observer described the board as "one of the most prestigious groups of business and community leaders ever to serve as window dressing and rubber stamps going through the motions of corporate governance".

The board's operating process and concerns centred on considering and approving lengthy and detailed material mandated by different levels of government, and on matters of potential self-dealing and conflict of interest common to many financial institutions. Questions of strategy and value creation for the company's many shareholders were left primarily to Vanco and were seldom, if ever, discussed by the Fraser board. The board had executive, audit, human resources, investment and conduct review (ethics and self-dealing) committees. Reporting to Fraser were three domestic and two foreign-regulated financial companies, with their own overlapping boards and similar committee structures. The Fraser board met 12 times per year, each meeting day being filled with committee and subsidiary company board meetings. Preparation and meeting requirements were onerous. Directors were paid modestly, well below the opportunity cost of their time.

Shortly after taking control, and not satisfied with Fraser's growth and profitability, the Vanco top level control group installed in Fraser a new CEO who was under heavy pressure to push aggressively for increased growth and profit. Under his tough leadership, Fraser expanded rapidly into loans to Californian and Mexican real estate developers, invading new markets by lending to relatively weak local companies (at relatively high interest rates) at a time when the real estate market cycle was booming. For a year or two this strategy appeared to work well, with growth and profits hitting new highs. Then, with mounting management ambitions, rising share prices and unfailingly optimistic management pronouncements and forecasts, disaster hit. Plunging real estate values, rising bad loans, management weaknesses, and information system and control problems all seemed to multiply. Within six months the rosy picture attested to in annual and quarterly reports and widely reported management statements turned into red ink. To make matters worse, it was alleged that as Fraser's financial problems were worsening — a situation suspected to be feared by the inner circle but not reported publicly — the company had paid dividends, redeemed securities and terminated Vanco support commitments, all to the benefit of Vanco.

Within a year Fraser failed completely. The company was put into bankruptcy and parts auctioned off at fire-sale prices. Shareholders, many of whom had recently paid up to $20 a share for the stock, had lost everything. Enraged and bitter, they were given little explanation and their complaints were dismissed out of hand. The public stance of the Fraser board was that the directors had done all they could but "had been deceived by management." Some thoroughly disillusioned directors privately complained that they had little knowledge of what was going on and even less power to change anything. "It's now easy to see," as one put it, "that we should have been an advisory committee only with no legal liability."

As the smoke cleared, and shareholders realized how badly they had been burned, a group of militant shareholders launched a class action alleging oppression against the directors of Fraser and Vanco and their auditing firm for an amount of over two billion dollars, of which apparently less than one-quarter was covered by directors' and officers' liability insurance. The lawyers leading the shareholders' cause began to amass documentary and oral evidence tracing all the details of the collapse of Fraser, including minutes of all board meetings in the period under review. Working with consultants the lawyers then drew up a list of the crucial questions upon which the legal case and the financial fate of the directors involved would rest:

1. What specifically are the currently-accepted duties and responsibilities of the board of directors in discharging their duties to govern and supervise the management of the corporation?
2. Did the board of directors exercise and carry out their required duties and responsibilities?
3. Did the directors keep themselves prudently and adequately informed of the business and affairs of the corporation prior to its failure and demise?
4. Did the board exercise proper standards of foresight, wisdom, and prudence in fulfilling their duties and responsibilities to the corporation?
5. Did the board of directors adequately maintain their independence from Vanco in performing their duties and responsibilities to the shareholders and the corporation?
6. Did the directors exercise adequate independent control over management or were the directors under the control of the management of Fraser and the officers and directors of other subsidiaries of Vanco?

The major legal battles that resulted from this, and similar cases, were regarded by many to be an indicator of the future of claims for retribution pursued by plaintiffs through class actions. The crux of the issue was: *what specifically is the job of the director?*

* * * * *

A CHOICE FOR DIRECTORS

Enlightened and responsible directors today increasingly face a profound and perplexing identity crisis. As a result of unsatisfactory company performance, tough competition, difficult business conditions and increasing stakeholder demands, the director's responsibilities, job, and code of behaviour are all changing. The disappointing performance of many North American companies demands that the abstract legal mandate that ''directors shall manage or supervise the management of the business and affairs of a corporation'' be defined and applied more specifically and effectively. As a result many directors are increasingly being forced to choose between their old, traditional role — cooperative ''rubber-stamps'' and ''window dressing'' — and an emerging, new role, of professional, active, enterprising, and, if necessary boat-rocking, contributors conscientiously overseeing management and responsibly adding significant value to corporate governance.

For the many directors now experiencing this challenge the issue is clear: are they primarily fronts for entrenched managers or a controlling shareholder, or are they effective contributors in control of a responsible and effective governance process that ensures long-term corporate success? The fundamental issue in this conflict is whether the power to govern is ultimately controlled by managers primarily for their own interests or by independent directors for shareholders and a wider constituency. As one recent book has put it, the question is whether directors will be ''pawns or potentates''.[1]

To illustrate the problems involved, consider these examples of typical situations that all too frequently confront most directors:

- In Company A, a director is concerned about four years of disappointing performance. Key results — profits, return on equity, cash flow, and shareholders' value — are mediocre and slipping. Management is not coping satisfactorily. No turnaround is in sight or planned. The rest of the board seems to be not overly concerned.

- In Company B, management is proposing an acquisition. Much work has been done without board consultation and the deal has progressed to the point of a presentation requesting approval. One director presses his concerns about several problems. The chairman is obviously annoyed by his questioning. The meeting has gone well past its usual time and most other directors, while unenthusiastic, seem ready to vote for approval so that the meeting can be terminated.

- In Company C, a director is concerned that his relationship with the chairman/CEO is cooling. The director has been concerned about many problems. The company's results have been indifferent. Strategic planning is fuzzy and lacks adequate competitive analysis. Head office overhead expenses seem too high. The chairman appears to be building a bureaucratic staff that is not respected by operating division heads. The chairman's personal expenses seem to be out of control and he has subtly but adamantly blocked a closer audit of the logbook of the corporate aircraft. The frequency of friendly interaction between the director and the chairman has declined. Each suspects that the other has not been supportive behind his back.
- In Company D, the audit committee, composed of older, intimate friends of the chairman/CEO, presents for approval a balance sheet recording an unrealistically high valuation of certain assets. Under the pressure of bad results, the valuation figure has been finessed past a reluctant external auditing firm. One director is concerned that the market value of the assets is materially less than the stated book value.

Many directors trade such stories, and there is much evidence that they are not uncommon experiences. Interesting actions are proposed and argued along with rationalizations of what the director did in the circumstances. The common denominator of these situations is that they boil down to two very different courses of action. One is based on the "old" code of behaviour: Be a good guy. Cool it. Don't push. Avoid a hassle. Don't cause confrontation. The other is based on the "new", professional code: You're duty-bound not to overlook such problems. Take responsibility. Rational analysis. Integrity. Ethics. No cover-ups. Don't back down. Other directors are just as concerned as you but are waiting for someone else to take leadership in confronting the issue.

In our experience, action in such situations is very much guided by the implicit and unwritten precepts that should govern a director's conduct. Among the many directors with whom we have discussed and experienced such practical problems, there are clearly these two conflicting views of what is proper: the "old" and the "new".

The unavoidable difficulty and stress in choosing between or, even tougher, judiciously and diplomatically combining these two role sets involves profoundly difficult issues for directors. The conflicts affect personal integrity, legal liabilities, ethics, professional responsibility, friendships and loyalties, prestige and egotism, wealth and income, even justice and revenge. When a director is torn between loyalties to these two codes of behaviour, he must resolve and manage this conflict in regard to his definition of self and role, purpose, behaviour, relationships, and commitments. With such difficult and unavoidable choices, it is obvious to us that the psychological and professional stress on directors is mounting. In fact, many are questioning whether the rewards of the job still outweigh its costs; some are living with a personal compromise based not on resigning but on reducing commitment to the job.

These two conflicting ideas of the rules of conduct are competing for the allegiance of directors' minds and actions. Their choices will have widespread effects and profound implications for corporate governance; they will determine not only decisions in individual firms, but in the long run, collective performance in industries, national economies, and throughout the capitalist system. Our purpose in this chapter is to explain the old and the new codes of proper director conduct, the rules for success in the past and how they are changing for the future (Exhibit 6.1). Until now, these codes have been largely unwritten.

THE OLD CODE

This is the traditional code of behaviour that has been followed for decades by senior directors in many relatively successful and stable companies. Well known to insiders, it has been passed by observation and experience from one generation of directors to the next without ever being written down. We learned this code ourselves many years ago through experience and observation of outstanding veteran directors who were our role models in many companies. We believe it to be a fair description of the way directors were *supposed* to behave, except in rare emergencies such as the firing or death of the CEO, or mergers and acquisitions when active decision-making duties were forced on directors. The "10 commandments" of this traditional code and culture, once widely accepted as standard practice and still observed by many directors and boards, are as follows:

1. Total Loyalty to the Chairman

The chairman of the board, who is usually the CEO as well, is the boss. Since the most basic business maxim is that you must get along with

Exhibit 6.1

SUMMARY OF THE OLD STYLE AND NEW STYLE CODES OF BEHAVIOUR

	OLD STYLE	NEW STYLE
Function		
Board	Legal direction, formal, ritualistic and routine	Trustee and management review and counsel; open, collegial dialogue
Roles		
Chairmen	Structure and use board for personal support, formal, legal functions	Structure, use board for general long term benefit of company
Directors	Passive, support the chairman and management	Active, work to make a difference for the good of the company
Directors' reasons for joining board	Prestige, recognition, rewards	Opportunity to contribute, make a difference, meet challenges, build relationships
Relationships		
Directors to Chairmen	Unquestioned personal loyalty to chairman	Main loyalty to company, support chairman when right, encourage to change when wrong
Directors to Directors	Minimal, formal	Network, stay in touch, mutual support
Directors to Management	Only through channels, minimal, superficial, no contact outside meetings	Open, frank, as necessary for information and understanding, legitimate to stay in touch
Meetings	Stiff, formal, controlled, short	More relaxed, less formal, more open time for questions, discussion
Perks	Individual private arrangements with chairman	Reasonable policies applied to all
Climate	Guarded, uptight, legalistic, minimal dialogue	Open, relaxed, collegial, time for discussion

the boss, chairmen can demand and get at least the appearance of unquestioned loyalty. Even if serious mistakes and problems are obvious and the mood is tense and foreboding, don't openly oppose the chairman. This is the first and most important old rule of conduct for any director.

An underlying reality influencing nearly all board relationships is that either the chairman chose the directors or they chose him. If he chose them, they are obligated to him for the opportunity to join an exclusive club with prestigious fellow-members, pay, and perks. Moreover, he can eliminate and blacklist them if they cause him problems. If they chose him, self-interest compels them to support him wholeheartedly in order to boost his chances of success and thus prove they made a wise choice.

Some chairmen act as though they are almost honour-bound to eliminate any criticism or serious questioning. As a matter of power and honour, they will not countenance any real or implied challenge or opposition, even if it takes an occasional expression of anger, perhaps even a temper tantrum, to make the point. Roger Smith, former chairman of GM, made this pattern of behaviour abundantly clear in his vexatious and extravagant campaign to eliminate Ross Perot[2] from his board.

Old-style directors understand this rule and usually back the chairman, or at least don't visibly oppose him, even when he is wrong and they know it. Any negative implication, no matter how subtle, about the conclusions, recommendations, or competence of a chairman makes a director stand out as someone who is potentially dangerous and doesn't know the rules. If he continues, he will soon get a reputation as such and be subtly eliminated from the club.

For most directors, it is in their own best interest to clearly manifest this total loyalty. Different types of directors are subject to different pressures to conform to this rule. For *inside* board members, the chairman is their boss; anyone who ever reached the board level in a corporation understands what this relationship means in terms of career and politics. Most *outside* directors are CEOs; many follow an implicit reciprocal code: "do unto other CEOs what you would have done to you". Overlapping boards, complex networks of relationships, and other factors often mandate that CEOs respect another chairman's turf. In problem situations the fear of "there but for the grace of God go I" compels many CEOs to support each other. Understandably, CEOs tend to be sympathetic because they understand the pressures of the role as perhaps no one else can.

Lawyer-directors who have the company as a client have an obvious conflict of interest. Most never bite the hand that feeds them. In addition, some lack business experience and judgment.

Investment bankers not infrequently become directors, in part to find or protect business. This hope would obviously be jeopardized by any implied criticism of the chairman. While there are undoubtedly many able and independent *retired executives* serving as directors, some appear to be looking for a sinecure, fees, and perks and have little to contribute. As one in a contentious situation put it recently, ''I'm right outside the company information loop and don't have any contacts in the industry so I couldn't take a position on this problem''.

In companies with a control block, directors who are hangers-on, relatives and personal retainers of the chairman or major shareholder often lack training, ability, experience, and judgment and are in a dependent position that precludes them from any objective opinion on doubtful issues.

2. Support Management at All Times

Since the old-style director remains detached from the operations and internal problems of the business, this requirement is self-evident. The implications of this part of the credo are many. When the company's problems or unsatisfactory results are explained away in the most positive light, accept whatever excuses and rationalizations are offered without being too difficult.

If, in response to a question, you are told ''management discussed this problem before the meeting'', back down gracefully and say no more. If an important item comes as a surprise added to the agenda under new business, don't raise any potentially contentious questions.

To understand the spirit of this requirement you must realize that management is on the job full-time and you are not; they know the business and you don't; they are inside the information loop and you are not. Today's public shareholders are seen primarily as investment managers who are often along for a short-term ride. This means that the only practical way the widely-owned modern corporation can work is for the board to accept that management is in control and go along except under very unusual circumstances.

3. Be Compatible

This rule means that you should always try to get along well and never let differences surface. Because there is so much ego and politics involved in board relationships, the personal and professional are unavoidably mixed and it is difficult to differ with fellow directors on an issue and expect them to remain friendly. For some old-style directors, this requirement is perhaps best summarized in two simple syllogisms that help avoid any interpersonal difficulties:

i. Board members are your friends and colleagues. You don't criticize a friend. Therefore, you don't criticize the opinions and conclusions of other board members.

ii. You don't criticize anyone's views unless they are wrong. You don't criticize the views of other board members. Therefore, other board members are never wrong.

Any experienced director knows that a board is a political minefield. When you look at the permutations and combinations of networks and relationships and the interpersonal trading and stakes involved, you realize that you should be very guarded and say as little as possible. In fact, some old-style directors have survived very difficult circumstances and appeared to be very wise by seldom opening their mouths.

4. Be Legally Correct

The board is basically a legal entity and its fundamental issues are legal. As stakeholder surveillance tightens, legal issues increase and liabilities mount, raising the fear of legal actions and personal penalties, this is a top priority.

Most business mistakes and bad judgments, no matter how serious, can be covered up, ignored, or excused, but legal errors are critical because they are open to examination and challenge, and may involve personal liability for directors. This means that lawyers should go over everything that could have any legal significance. Minutes should be short and carefully crafted by a shrewd and cautious lawyer who can anticipate any possible problem. Personal notes about sensitive matters should be destroyed so they can never become evidence in a legal action. If in doubt on any issue, create a paper trail, pay large sums for insurance, get legal opinions and comfort letters, document everything, and go to sufficient lengths to make sure that no one can ever pin responsibility for mistakes or negligence on the board.

5. Participate Correctly and Constructively

Vocal participation and support are counted on by the chairman and management — up to a point. This means that all directors are expected to contribute, but strictly within limits. Don't upset the chairman or your colleagues by raising more than your fair quota of questions. Since most board meetings run three hours more or less with only 20 to 30 minutes of discretionary time available, your fair share of air time is generally a few minutes at the most.

Don't waste time. There are many items on the agenda to be covered in a short period, and this does not allow time for follow-up questions or dialogue. There is a great deal of ceremony and fixed routine to any board meeting, and this should not be threatened or thrown off track. Remember the meeting is on a tight schedule because at the end there is usually an elaborate lunch or transportation arrangements that cannot be kept waiting.

Never ask really tough questions or press a point with visible indication of real misgivings. The required ritual calls for you to be properly cool and aloof even if deeply concerned that something is wrong.

Bear in mind that if you are less than enthusiastic or not always supportive of management's initiatives you are probably wrong because (a) you don't know all the facts in the situation, or if you do, (b) you are off-base because you are showing a negative attitude.

6. Don't Take the Job Too Seriously

Part of fitting into any board is to not overreact or get into things too deeply. If you get to know too much about the company and the industries in which it participates, you will get into a depth and range of concerns that will cause problems both for you and the rest of the board. To crusade aggressively for change or improvement may be upsetting to management and other directors.

Don't spend too much time preparing for meetings or studying problems because this will get you interested in things about which you should not be concerned. Remember that if you spend a lot of time on company matters, as suggested by two leading authorities on board affairs,[3] most other busy outside directors can't do this. If you get to know too much you'll embarrass and threaten them. Make sure that you can never be accused of "micro-managing."

If you are a new director you are safe from any meaningful participation for at least a few meetings. You will be pointedly seated at the far end of the table and other directors will neither expect nor want to hear too much from you. Older, senior directors especially will expect you to know your place.

Avoid the many mistakes that you might make by getting too interested and involved. If you take the job too seriously, you'll need more information and will want to develop a network of contacts in the company and its industries. Such improper behaviour is monumentally resented.

In summary, read the material that is sent to you. Be generally aware of what is going on. But don't be too concerned or probe too hard for weaknesses.

7. Go Through the Right Channels

In any board situation there are a number of organizational subtleties and proprieties that should always be observed. First, and perhaps most obvious, directors should communicate only through the chairman. Don't network in the board, company or industry. Never go "behind the chairman's back" and contact other directors outside the meetings. In order to be blameless in your support of the chairman, keep contacts with management and sometimes certain other directors to an absolute minimum, and when they cannot be avoided, talk about sports, social events, or items in the morning paper; do not discuss the company, its problems, or people. Particularly, avoid subordinate managers who could get you and themselves into serious trouble by discussing what is really going on.

8. Be Discreet

Discretion at all times. This means primarily watch what you say and to whom you say it. Support the necessary tradition that calls for cabinet secrecy and confidentiality, solidarity and unanimity. Any company organization is a complex, political system in which, for some top people, questions related to power, influence and hidden agendas are of more concern than the real work needed to make the company succeed. If you take a position on any issue, this may be threatening to someone whose ambition or vulnerability[4] motivate him to misrepresent your position and pass messages along that are meant to undermine your position with other members of the board, particularly the chairman. When in doubt, remember that total discretion is to say as little as possible.

9. Take Your Perks and Keep Quiet

You don't have to read *Barbarians at the Gate*[5] to know that chairmen like to accumulate markers in their political banks by "doing things" for those on whose support they rely. This part of a chairman's job is a very personal, complex, and private exchange relationship with separate individuals and groups on the board. The stock-in-trade in this exchange is favours carefully chosen to have particular value to the individuals involved: tickets for a big game in the company box, golf at Augusta, $400 tickets for a sold-out show, special fees, corporate aircraft detours to West Palm Beach or the desert on Friday and back on Monday, the World Series, the Superbowl, the Stanley Cup, big fights, the Kentucky Derby, salmon-fishing, grouse shooting, Wimbledon, Ascot, and a hundred more.

If the chairman does something nice for you that is obviously costly, don't ask if you should pay personally. Don't embarrass him. Don't tell anybody else. These are simply minor expenses lost in the shuffle, little things one does for another. How you will be expected to repay him will become obvious when the time comes.

10. Don't Rock the Boat

In order to enter into the proper spirit of an old-time board of directors, this is a general requirement applied to all of the director's behaviour. The board is a long-standing legal requirement; in the minds of some older chairmen/CEOs, a necessary evil. This being the case one should make the best of the situation in a pleasant and civilized manner. Directors are friends and peers, members of an exclusive club. In this setting no one should ever be embarrassed, threatened, or criticized.

Remember that your share ownership, if any, is usually minimal. After a few years on the board, you are more an employee than an investor or a representative of shareholders. Govern yourself accordingly. Stay out of trouble.

For decades, on many boards, careful observance of this unwritten code of conduct has enabled a director to be successful by the standards of other members of the elite group that endorsed and preserved them. Following these rules brought invitations to serve on many boards; breaking them could bring quick notoriety and shunning.

THE NEW CODE

Since the old code of behaviour became so widespread and deeply ingrained over so many decades, key questions must be addressed: Why is it not working? What are the change forces that are causing the old precepts to evolve to the new?

The most obvious cause of change in directors' behaviour is that the results now being produced by the old boy boards are in many respects unsatisfactory. Individually, the performance of many, perhaps most, companies in the *Financial Post* 300 has been disappointing. Some widely-reported, spectacular failures have served to focus public attention on board incompetence and negligence. Many big-name directors have been publicly disgraced, suffered major financial penalties and a few have gone to jail. Collectively, in industry after industry, many large North American companies have been unable to hold their own in international competition.[6]

When companies are in trouble, shareholder value is being eroded, and the whole economy is suffering, attention inevitably turns to the boards of directors which are ultimately responsible. Responding to pressures from management, boards in some companies have badly abused shareholders. Unjustifiably high compensation, golden parachutes, greenmail payments, poison pills, and other devices that sacrifice the interests of the other stakeholders to those of management are properly judged as scandalous by many investment managers and the public. Legal issues related to mergers, acquisitions, takeovers, and management LBOs have raised the attention levels of dissident shareholders, some of whom have initiated court actions in defense of their rights. The increasing threat of law suits, damages, financial penalties and losses, and public disgrace is of major concern to directors.

The concentration of ownership in control blocks in many companies has caused a public sensitivity as to the power structure and decision-making processes that can lead to self-dealing and abuse of minority shareholders. In general, stakeholders' surveillance of the corporation is becoming more sensitive, widespread, and penetrating. As more boards are influenced by outside directors, the power to govern is shifting away from management to the wider constituencies of the corporation for whom these directors are agents. With the increasing shortage of well-qualified directors, it is more difficult for chairmen to find candidates who will knuckle under to the old code of behaviour which is now widely judged to be incompetent, unprofessional and, in some cases, unethical and illegal.

As the rewards for outside directors have not kept pace with higher levels of risk, expectation and legal requirements, directors have become less willing to accept the responsibility and workload involved. The sources of attraction to the job become less important than the sources of resistance to accepting it.[7] These and many other pressures are resulting in a new concept of the job of a director with a more professional code of behaviour. The new style emphasizes the following precepts:

1. Manage the Business and Affairs of the Corporation

Directors everywhere are becoming more sensitive to the fact that their legal mandate, authority and obligation is to "manage or supervise the management ... of a corporation" with the requirements that they "act honestly and in good faith with a view to the best interests of the corporation", and "exercise the care, diligence and skill that a reasonably prudent person would exercise in comparable circumstances."[8]

This job is usually defined as overseeing strategic management, selecting the CEO and approving the top management, monitoring and assessing performance, taking corrective action as necessary, taking over in serious emergencies, and reporting to shareholders. While directors oversee the direction of the corporation, and delegate day-to-day operations to its officers, they are duty-bound to become more active in guiding management to the extent necessary to carry out their responsibilities.

Since unsatisfactory results, serious problems, emergencies, and changes in control are being experienced more frequently in more companies, the old myth that the board is not management and does not manage — if ever true — is rapidly being eroded in theory and discarded in practice. A timeless and widely accepted definition of management is "getting things done through people". This being so, the board has always been responsible for management and leadership and the real issue to be addressed is defining what management roles directors should play, not debating their responsibility for doing their job.

Many companies are run by chairmen/CEOs whose knowledge, skills, attitudes, experience, track record and ability to solve current problems leave a lot to be desired. And, in many unsatisfactory situations, the old board remedy of replacing management may be a simplistic, slow and inappropriate response to the problem. The duty of a director to bring clear and obvious added-value to the situation requires that new code directors be able and willing to exert their best efforts to contribute what is necessary and appropriate for improvement. If directors don't step in and assist as necessary in times of crisis and serious trouble, who will?

Competent directors are increasingly conscious that they can delegate authority but never responsibility. The inevitable result is that more and more directors both proactively pursue and passively are drawn into the job of "management". That this is a major change leading to uncharted waters, no one would deny. However, this trend can probably not be reversed and the confusion and problems involved cannot be avoided. Obviously, cooption of the board through "upward delegation" must always be avoided. Directors will have to find a new balance between unavoidable participation in and necessary detachment from management.

2. Function as a Trustee and Consultant

The new code holds the director to high standards of professional behaviour, performance, competence, honesty, faithfulness and loyalty as a trustee for the constituencies whose continued support is critical to survival of the corporation. Although shareholders are at the top of the list, employees, pensioners, customers, suppliers, local communities, and the public must also be considered. As trustee, the director is responsible for the effectiveness and efficiency of the company in achieving its required performance.

As a consultant and guide to top management, the director has a broad responsibility to size up the company, diagnose its problems, review and assess, and if necessary, change what management proposes to do, and direct the process of getting it done. Effectiveness in this job demands penetrating insight and analysis, ability to rank problems in order of priority, forecasting ability to understand the most likely future scenarios, an action agenda and understanding of the network through which plans are implemented. Any director who is unwilling or unable to carry out these two demanding roles — trustee and consultant — is unfit for the job.

3. Take the Job Seriously and Do It Well

In one respect the director's job can be described as campaigning for what is right and against what is wrong in managing the firm. Since the director must be unfailingly courteous, diplomatic and professional, his or her influence must be based on knowledge, experience, wisdom and rational argument. To work in this manner a director must be very sensitive to what is going on and prepared to take a position based on informed analysis and wise judgment, and avoid or minimize personalities, emotion and power plays.

This requires extensive preparation and many hours of review and analysis. In fact, several authorities on the job of a director argue that to function adequately directors must spend a great deal more time than is currently the practice. The new-style director errs on the side of doing too much rather than too little. He goes beyond accepting minimum legal requirements to proaction. He is not just along for the ride, relying on his peers and management to do all the tough jobs.

4. Do What is Right

As an agent whose duty is to act for the shareholders, the conscientious director is bound to pursue excellence in professional conduct and ethical principles with as little compromise as possible. On major issues particularly, he must take a prudent, tough-minded position and not back down without good reason.

Even the best managers who otherwise turn in an outstanding performance in decision-making and implementation are wrong occasionally. In such cases the director's job is to be a check and balance, and this requires resistance to what does not make sense. Common targets include bad decisions, ineffective execution, unsatisfactory human resource management, over-emphasis of the short term at the expense of the long term, abuses of power through excessive management compensation, unnecessary head office spending and overhead expenses, unchecked hubris, and the pursuit of self-interest to the detriment of the best interests of the firm.

Frequently, doing what is right requires the fortitude to oppose the majority and risk being unpopular, at least temporarily. In some cases, when doing what is right means challenging the chairman, insisting on the recognition of an opposing point of view or inconvenient facts, perhaps even resigning, real courage is required. Sometimes doing what is right unavoidably leads to trouble, for which one usually pays a price. In such cases, it is well to remember the wise words of a veteran director who advised one of us: ''It is better to be in trouble for doing what is right than not be in trouble for doing what is wrong''. Or, we would add, for getting into really big trouble when others find out what went wrong.

5. Support Those Who are Worthy

The new director operates on the assumption that support is given and earned primarily on the basis of performance and rationality, as contrasted with tradition and political considerations. CEOs and other top managers vary widely in styles, ability, and competence. There is bad in the best and good in the worst. Therefore directors are unwise to be credulous and trusting and to give uncritical support to anyone. To bring checks and balances to the system, the effective director should always be somewhat skeptical and critical. Even when a company is successful, the new-style director is concerned that changing conditions require adaptation. As a result, questioning the status quo must never stop. If success is more a journey than a destination, continuous improvement is always necessary and in this pursuit a director should never be satisfied.

Pervasive problems in top management that warrant continuous monitoring and opposition include lack of adequate attention to developing strategic and operating problems, bureaucracy, bad judgment, excessive self-interest, and ego trips. The director's duty is to be on guard and bring discipline to bear as necessary.

6. Use the Board Routines and Infrastructure

The operation of any board is based on communications, information, meetings, committees, routines and relationships. The new code of behaviour calls for the director to use this complex system skillfully in pursuing success for the company. Some of the most obvious ways of ''working the system'' are discussed below.

Many problems that are too dangerous to be confronted head-on with a chairman can be deflected to committees. Committees such as executive, audit, compensation and human resources, nominating, governance, public affairs, and environmental concerns, supplemented as necessary by special committees, can be used effectively by directors to influence decisions related to many sensitive issues.

The use of proper procedure in regard to minutes provides many possibilities. Directors can insist that questions or statements be recorded in minutes and that follow-up reports be given by management. This enables an astute director to get issues on the record and to work items into the unavoidable section of any properly-run meeting in which business arising from the minutes should be addressed. Directors may ask for special presentations and reviews and/or informal sessions that serve notice of concern and allow management to prepare properly to deal with debatable issues. Many directors use effectively the art of building a one-on-one relationship with the chairman and communicating concerns at a time and in a manner that heads off or cools problems.

There are many simple and straightforward techniques to encourage discussion of points of view that a chairman may be anxious to pass over. For example, a director exposed the weaknesses of one proposal by asking whether the management team that had worked on it was unanimous in its recommendations. After some hesitation and embarrassment it was admitted that they were not, and important problems and counter arguments were outlined by a senior manager who would not otherwise have been able to raise problems and state his opinion. When outside professionals such as auditors, lawyers or consultants on environmental, health and safety and other regulatory problems report to the board, ask the question: "If you were a director is there anything you have encountered in all your extensive work for this corporation which would cause you concern?"

Experienced directors use a variety of legitimate techniques and tactics to press points and keep management on the hook.

7. Get the Information You Need

Managers frequently give directors information that is inadequate, incomplete, disorganized, late, or in reports that are so long that key facts are lost in masses of detail. The new code calls for directors to ask for and insist on receiving the information necessary to describe the evidence, analysis, and conclusions upon which major decisions are being based. In a properly-run board, directors insist on due process, with no surprises. If necessary, on major decisions they will insist on longer or special sessions and in-depth presentations by the managers involved so that they will be able to assess and explore the evidence and reasoning on which they are basing conclusions and decisions.

8. Build Good Relationships in the Board and its Organization Network

Any board is part of a complex organizational and political network. This includes the chairman, managers, friends and contacts, all of whom are subdivided into different coalitions on different issues. The new behaviour code calls for directors to stay in touch with these groups. In this manner, directors can understand how others perceive and react to the problems and strategic agenda of the company. This enables one to test the comfort levels of colleagues on the board and to have the backing of different coalitions in regard to different problems and initiatives. Directors need each other's help, support and power to avoid the divide-and-conquer routines that are often practiced by management. This applies particularly to the coordination of committees restricted in their concerns so that sensitive matters can fall between terms of reference and are left unexamined by directors.

Every individual in the board network will vary in regard to self-interest, relationships, experience, judgment, analytical ability, support for management, private agenda items and so on. The new code of behaviour takes all this as being legitimate input into the process and relationships related to governance. Instead of backing off, the enlightened director builds on this structure and uses it in his pursuit of what needs to be done to make the company more successful.

9. Work on Getting the Culture Right

Many traditional boards are legalistic, stuffy, formal, and ritualistic. The new behaviour code calls for informality, dialogue, openness, humility, and positive attitudes. In older boards, where it is not legitimate to behave according to the new code, it is necessary for directors to insist that meetings and relationships be loosened up and dialogue, exchange, even at times debate, be encouraged. In many cases the old "board-speak" style frequently uses language that is indirect, abstract, subtle, and condescending. It needs to be replaced by communication that is more direct, frank, open, specific, substantive, analytical and judgmental.

10. If Necessary, Rock the Boat

The new behaviour code assumes that a director cannot make an adequate contribution to the proceedings of a board without occasionally rocking the boat. All companies make mistakes, many serious ones. Some mistakes are excusable but many are not. All mistakes are costly, and some carry potentially-devastating personal liability for directors. Repeated leadership mistakes lead inevitably to decline. This means that in any board all initiatives and plans need to be reviewed, challenged, constructively criticized and occasionally disrupted, perhaps even killed. Even in the best-managed companies, decisions need to be fine-tuned and improved. In every director's experiences there are meetings that he or she would like to be able to erase and do over again in order to take a different position, sound the alarm, or oppose something that was approved with disastrous results. There is no escaping the reality that behind every major mistake stands a board that is responsible and perhaps should have known better. The new code requires that directors be responsible for ensuring that there is a healthy tension between them and management for unsettling the tranquil drift that is found in too many companies.

Making the New Code Work

Most directors will manifest a mixture of old- and new-style behaviours, sometimes changing with circumstances. Experienced directors all know colleagues who, on casual observation, appear to follow the new style but, when under the gun, revert to the old, or vice versa.

Old-style directors need to be stroked by attention to their egos, status, and prestige. The new want straight talk, substantive content, and performance. Mistaking one for the other can lead to serious mistakes. For example, one outstanding young CEO described being recruited for the board of a major company in these words: "The chairman was giving me all this baloney about how great they were and how great they thought I was. I had only one question for him: What difference will I be able to make on your board? From his puzzled look I knew what the answer was. I turned him down."

Often the clues that identify a director's style are slight. Board members often do not listen well enough to understand the real meaning behind what others say. A director's apparently simple comment or question may have a meaning and intended impact much different than those perceived by a chairman who is a poor listener.

Similar to all other organizations and persons, boards and directors are constrained by structure, processes, rules and assumptions that are the results of history, tradition and past problems. We believe that even under the new and changed circumstances of the '90s, many boards and directors often live by the old code of conduct.

All board members need to face up to the obvious problems inherent in both codes. The old is unsatisfactory and out of date. Whatever its justification in the past, it has proven ineffective in getting the job done today. It has contributed to a worrisome decline in many formerly strong, leading companies.

To live by the new code is a tremendous challenge. The first problem is that it requires a degree of wisdom, knowledge and judgment that not all directors have. It takes great strength and courage. In addition, it takes time and hard work.

Judgment and experience are required to draw the fine line between the contrasting extremes and appropriate behaviour. A number of questions must be faced. How does a director find the right balance between negligence and meddling? In making demands of management, how does one find the balance between requiring too little and too much? Or between being quietly supportive and curiously and constructively critical in attitude? How does one decide between spending too little time and too much? How does one find the right balance between individuality and team play? How can a better balance be struck between the risks and rewards for being a new-style director? To make the problem even more difficult the balance will change according to companies, circumstances, personalities, professional ability and relationships.

THE CHAIRMAN: KEY TO CHANGE

In considering and comparing the old and new styles it is important to stress that either style is *learned behaviour*, and that it typically is learned at the first few meetings attended by a new director. The pattern is set by the chairman and to a lesser extent by the other directors and attending management. Chairmen tell you very quickly, mainly by body language and the way they handle questions, whether active participation is welcome or not. Other directors tell you a lot by the way in which they do (or do not) participate. Even the seating at most boards tends to put the new boy in his place. Management's response to questions (whether forthcoming or defensively abrupt) also signals what the acceptable style is.

A board's culture and style is determined mainly by the chairman. He controls the process by his power over a number of critical levers — who is on the board, its psychological climate, attitudes and values, formal and informal interactions, the structure of its committees, how it is paid, the timing of meetings, what gets on the agenda, the management of the information flow to directors, and the subtleties indicating approval and disapproval of individuals, initiatives, and positions. All of these, and more, determine how a board acts. A board chairman who wants old-style behaviour can certainly get it; by the same token, a chairman who wants an active, challenging, committed board can get that too. It is certainly possible, but very difficult, for a board seeking a more active role to push it on a reluctant chairman; more often, the frustrated director goes along or drops out.

Examples abound of many old-style boards with old-style chairman. They *hate* questions. Their agendas are programmed to the minute, and they become tense, fidgety, and abrupt if the board strays from them. Such boards are usually composed of mainly nice guys, retired CEOs, lawyers, and investment bankers who don't say or do anything to upset the *status quo*. A typical board meeting might last precisely three hours, of which three-quarters is presentations by management or regular, on-going agenda items. Lunch is served sharp at noon in the adjacent dining room, and one could be in the middle of selling the company, but discussion would have to terminate then and there for lunch. In one such case it has taken subsequent chairmen and an almost complete board turnover to change the *modus operandi,* and there is still much progress to be made.

A variation on the autocratic chairman style is the use of the executive committee. Here, the information and key issues are hoarded for discussion and decisions by a small group of like-minded directors, with the rest being relegated to a decidedly secondary role. This can be equally destructive, especially for the directors who are left outside the inner group.

By contrast, there are also examples of new-style chairmen, who pick strong people for their boards and let them know that digging deeply into issues is not only permitted but actively encouraged. They make it clear to directors that the board's issues are professional, not personal, and that they expect loyalty to be primarily to the company rather than to themselves. They are open and nondefensive in the way they expose issues and problems. They encourage free-ranging discussion. They work for consensus, and know when to back off. Meetings leave plenty of time for discussion; boiler-plate resolutions and staged presentations get short shrift. Special meetings are scheduled when necessary to deal with key issues. Directors are kept informed between meetings. Networking and social activities are encouraged.

If the leadership in developing the board culture must come from the chairman, a big issue for the chairman is what he wants and expects from a board. He or she has to think this through very carefully. Then the question becomes: if a chairman wants a ''new-style'' board but has, for whatever reason, inherited an ''old-style'' system, how does that chairman achieve the transition?

NOTES

1. Jay W. Lorsch, with Elizabeth MacIver, *Pawns or Potentates* (Boston: Harvard Business School Press, 1989).

2. See Doron P. Levin, *Irreconcilable Differences* (New York: Plume, 1990).

3. See Arch Patton and John C. Baker, ''Why Won't Directors Rock the Boat?'' *Harvard Business Review* (November-December 1987), p. 11.

4. See Abraham Zaleznik, *The Managerial Mystique* (New York: Harper & Row, 1989), especially chapters 10 and 11 on Organizational Politics and the Corruption of Power.

5. Bryan Burrough and John Helyar, *Barbarians at the Gate* (New York: Harper & Row, 1990).

6. Significantly, these problems are basic to the performance of capitalism. It is paradoxical that just at the time of the greatest victory for capitalist ideology, corporate governance — its very foundation — is being weighed and found wanting. In many North American companies individually and collectively, the governance process hasn't been able to accomplish what must be done to maintain an internationally competitive position in sales, market shares, profits, return on investment, benefits for direct and indirect stakeholders, and, ultimately, the standard of living.

7. William A. Sahlman, ''Why Sane People Shouldn't Serve on Public Boards,'' *Harvard Business Review* (May-June 1990), p. 28.

8. Peter A. Atkins and Eric L. Cochran, *Directors' Duties in Corporate Takeovers, Mergers and Acquisitions: Historical Roots and Current Perspectives*, unpublished internal paper for the firm of Skadden, Arps, Slate, Meager & Flom.

Chapter 7

OVERSEEING STRATEGIC MANAGEMENT: The Director's Job One

"Board involvement in formulating and implementing corporate strategy has always been a sensitive issue. Although it is standard procedure for managers to brief directors on the evolving strategy and structure at the annual meeting dedicated to that purpose, it has always been understood that the 'ownership' of the current strategy remains firmly in the hands of the chief executive and his or her management team."
(Gordon Donaldson[1])

"Our board is just a bunch of old 'has-beens' playing politics, but we keep them so far from customers, factories or anything that's really important that they can't do any real harm."
(Division manager in a Fortune 500 company)

Widespread differences in practice, confusion and strongly-held views about the proper role of the board in regard to corporate strategy mean that the nature and extent of directors' involvement in the management of strategy varies widely from company to company. Consider for example, two cases, one where the board played a decisive role in the strategy ultimately adopted, the other where the board was shut out of the strategic process by management.

Company A was a moderately large, widely-held international company in the upstream oil and gas business. Due to an acquisition in Latin America, it had great success in replacing its reserves, and had brought considerable production on stream just as oil prices had started to rise, after several depressed years. The company had prospered, and, with its substantial cash flow, accumulated large cash balances exceeding $500 million. At the company's annual two-day strategic planning retreat, management put forward a plan which involved a number of major capital investments in different parts of the world. Discussion with the board revealed that several directors were concerned that the company's shares were undervalued on the market, and that the company represented a highly-vulnerable take-over target. At the end of a sometimes-heated discussion, the decision was taken to cut out a number of the capital investment proposals that featured more marginal prospective returns in favour of a revamped investor-relations program, a revised dividend policy that included a special dividend, and a plan to buy back some of the company's stock — all designed to enhance the market value of the company's shares and fend off prospective raiders hoping to acquire the company on the cheap.

* * * * *

Company B was a large, widely-held industrial equipment manufacturing company, firmly under the control of a long-serving, domineering, financially-oriented chairman/CEO and his management group. The board included several retired CEOs who offered little resistance to being relegated to a generally passive and supportive role. The annual strategic review took place at one of the eight regular board meetings. The planning process was handled completely by the management, under the direction of the CEO, and a bulky strategic plan was presented to the board for approval. Addressing the company's three major challenges — high manufacturing costs, deteriorating quality relative to German and Japanese competitors, and a firmly-entrenched, militant union — the strategy called for huge investments in plant relocations and automation as the key to a turnaround. Discussion and questioning at the board was perfunctory, and when an outside board member raised serious questions about the company's vulnerability to financial, manufacturing, and workforce problems, he was put down brusquely by the chairman. "Leave it to us", he was told. "We know what we're doing. This plan is the best answer to our problems."

Over the ensuing three years, the required investment in automated machinery and computer-controlled manufacturing systems ballooned over budgets, manufacturing problems worsened, market share continued to drop, and strikes and union violence erupted. As a result, several significant institutional investors, alarmed at major losses, combined to force the board to fire the chairman/CEO, shake up management, and reverse the strategy in an attempt to get the company back on track.

* * * * *

STRATEGIC MANAGEMENT DEFINED

Facing many difficult business challenges and the insistent demands of investor activists for re-engineering and restructuring to improve shareholder value, one of the most important issues for both boards and management is corporate strategy: What is the strategy? Does it promise steady gains in shareholder value? How is it crafted, implemented, audited, and strengthened? Does it provide a strong foundation for all other aspects of management? These central issues lead unavoidably to the question of the role and responsibility of the board in overseeing corporate strategy.

Control of the strategic agenda is at the heart of the governance issue. Failure to understand the appropriate roles of the CEO-management team and the board of directors in the development and implementation of strategy leads inevitably to confusion, conflict and, in many cases, disastrous results.

The complex realities of corporate governance, the board system, and the director's job, as described in the previous chapters, make it critical to understand that the board's vital function: **"to manage or supervise the management of the business and affairs of a corporation" in practice means to supervise the strategic management of the firm.** The purpose of this chapter is to describe what this means, and how it should be done. It is absolutely fundamental to any understanding or discussion of board responsibilities, the directors' job, and all that follows — the definitive benchmark of effective professional governance.

THE STRATEGIC MANAGEMENT SYSTEM[2]

To begin, it is necessary to define terms.

Strategy is the distinguishing pattern of the most important characteristics of the design of the firm: the deployment of its resources, including research and development in its current and hoped-for future businesses, product/market scope and focus, and geographical coverage; and the operations, marketing, finance, and organizational policies that govern how it pursues its purposes and competes.

Management is leadership in planning, budgeting, organizing, directing, and controlling. Combining these two concepts:

Strategic management is a systematic process for planning and implementing the decisions and action necessary to ensure success in terms of increasing not only shareholder value, but also profitability, growth and competitive strength. Its goal is to ensure the strength of, and congruence among, the seven key factors in any business: *purpose* (vision, mission, objectives and goals), *strategy, organization* (tasks, personnel, structure, systems, and culture), *operations*, *results,* and *resources* of the business as it is integrated in the context of its *environment,* and

Strategic agenda management involves sizing up a company's situation; isolating the few critically-important issues that will determine success or failure; concentrating attention, power, and resources on these key issues; and guiding the managers involved through an issue-management cycle to a successful conclusion, not only for each individual issue but also for a series of collective sequential issues. In other words, this involves leading management in deciding the things that a company must do to get from where it is, to where it needs to be.

Strategic management therefore includes and links the following tasks:

1. Sizing up the company's situation, based on a detailed appraisal of the strengths, weaknesses, and interrelationships of the key factors in the business;

2. Identifying and analyzing the most strategic issues, the problems and opportunities that will determine the firm's success or failure, i.e., setting the strategic agenda; and

3. Approving goals, and monitoring the organization, especially top management, as it works through the cycle of management activities necessary to deal successfully with each major issue confronting the firm. Especially important is the allocation of capital, which should be viewed as investments in strategies, and the follow-up on the results of the capital so invested;

4. Giving leadership and support to "the fighting in the trenches" with "a passion to implement strategy and otherwise move the business forward".[3]

Strategic management in this form was developed in the 1960s, has been widely adopted and has long been taken for granted as standard operating procedure for the proper way to run a business. It is also true that there have been many problems in the way the model has been implemented. Often it has been too formal and ritualistic; strategic planning and operations can become disconnected; the system can lack and often inhibits creativity; personal vision and entrepreneurial thrust and drive are frequently blocked or discredited. *Nevertheless, strategic management remains the basic system for running a business*—the only alternatives are administration by expediency, over-reliance on "bubble-up" from the bottom ranks, individual charisma, controversial fads, trendy but unproven methods, gimmicks, and idiosyncratic methods that don't pass the tests of time and the real world.

The job of strategic management has always included all of the so-called "new" duties of the board of directors, such as:

- adoption of and participation in a strategic planning process, including organization planning and development;
- ensuring the adequacy and integrity of internal control and management information systems;
- identification and analysis of the principal strengths, weaknesses, opportunities, threats and risks of the company, and planning and implementing appropriate organizational systems and programs to manage them.

This system, strategic management, is the structure and process that directors and boards must understand, act within, and oversee effectively if they are to fulfill their role within the prevailing scheme of corporate governance. It is the essence of the board's job.

THE PRACTICE OF STRATEGIC MANAGEMENT

Prevailing practice is that in controlled corporations the major shareholder calls the strategic shots, and in widely-held corporations, as Donaldson says, "ownership of the current strategy remains firmly in the hands of the chief executive and his or her management team".

Conventional wisdom reinforces this position. The initiative for the strategic planning process originates with management or a controlling shareholder. Because they have limited time and lack intimate knowledge of the business, directors seldom have much to say other than to approve the ultimate strategy; their principal role is to see that there is a strategic management process in place, to monitor results against the agreed-upon goals, and to reward or punish management depending on the achievement of those goals. The reasoning is quite compelling.

Most of the management texts agree. Michael Porter, the guru of competitive strategy, almost completely dismisses the board's role in determining strategy (see Chapter 1). Courses in business policy or strategic management, where strategy is the central theme and which typically assume widely-held ownership, have little, if anything, to say about boards and their participation in the strategic process: strategy determination is seen as a management responsibility. One searches in vain for references to strategy in most of the writings on governance and boards.[4] "Ownership" of strategy rests with management. . . . "and for good reason", says Donaldson.[5]

> In order to be effective, every organization requires not only a clear and unambiguous strategic mission but also the confidence that its top management has the authority and ability to carry it out. By nature, the typical board of directors is poorly designed and ill equipped to provide hands-on product and market leadership. The majority of its members usually lack the industry-specific experience, the company-specific knowledge, and, most important, the time necessary to turn broad strategic vision into operational reality.. Board members give their undivided attention at most once a month for six or eight hours at a time. They can hardly be expected to have the detailed command of the issues and the requisite independent judgment necessary to make compelling proposals to counter those of management.[6]

All of which is true.

THE CASE FOR BOARD INVOLVEMENT

Yet, paradoxically, under law the board is ultimately responsible not only for the execution of strategy, but for the success or failure of the strategy itself. The law is unambiguous and unequivocal—the directors are responsible, not management. The board cannot excuse itself for poor performance by saying. "It was management's strategy, not ours. Blame management, not us. We were just there to see that the strategy was carried out."

In a series of articles written in the *Harvard Business Review* in the early 1980s, Kenneth R. Andrews argued persuasively that directors needed to become more involved in the process of strategy formulation.[7] His position was roundly criticized by a number of CEOs, who saw it as a threat to their power. Andrews' suggestion was contentious at the time, but viewed from today's perspective, he was surely right. Clearly, for the board to do its job the directors must be actively (not passively) involved in overseeing the process of both determining and executing strategy. It is fallacious to suggest that, because management usually has responsibility for initiating the strategic process, it therefore has "ownership" of the current strategy. There are required roles to play for both the board and management, but the roles are different and should ideally be based on the unique strengths that each party brings to the process. The nature of those roles, and the balance between them, will be specific to each company.

Major variables that influence the extent of board involvement in strategic management include:

1. The board-management-shareholder relationship: the strategic involvement of the board depends on who is in control, and how those in control work with other stakeholders and participants.

2. The chairman/CEO split: if the CEO is also the chairman, or if the chairman's job is seen as relatively weak, the CEO is in a position to control the board and its involvement in strategic management.

3. The competence and ability of the board: if the directors are relatively weak and/or lack the time and commitment, they will be unable to contribute significantly to strategic management.

4. The company and board "culture": if a company culture of board noninvolvement is deeply ingrained, it may be hard for those outside the in-group to break in and get leverage on the strategic management process.

5. Company strength and success: if management is doing a good job and results prove it, there is less immediate reason or pressure for the board to become more deeply involved.

6. The size and nature of the company: it is easier for a board to understand, track, and be involved in a relatively small, focused company operating in markets near to home.

7. The degree of technical sophistication involved: it is difficult, if not impossible, for a board to be highly involved and proactive in strategic management if that board is unable to understand the science and technology involved in product development, operations, or marketing.

In many cases, directors do not have either the time, technical expertise, or industry knowledge to make much contribution to the early stages of strategic planning. But an effective board does possess other qualities and skills that are vital to the development of an effective strategy, and which are not usually qualities and skills possessed by full-time management. Not the least of these are general management experience, objectivity, political savvy, financial know-how, international skills, and judgment of human beings. An effective board brings important added-value to the process of determining overall strategy, as well as to monitoring the strategic management process itself. An effective board must be an active participant in strategy determination, and the board and management must be unified in pursuing the chosen strategic direction for the company.

What Does the Board Bring to Strategy?

It is true that the board's role in strategy determination is limited, sometimes severely so, due to lack of time, technical expertise, or knowledge of the industry. It is the board's job to see there is a competent CEO and management to provide such input. What a good board brings to the discussion is independence and objectivity; experience in similar situations in other industries; the ability to challenge "sacred cows"; breadth of judgment; a longer-term perspective, unhampered by career considerations or company politics; specialized knowledge in areas such as politics, science, technology, law, or the operation of financial markets which a career manager would be unlikely to possess; and, ideally, an understanding of stakeholders and their points of view—reinforced in most cases by being themselves shareholders of the company.

In the introductory Company A case, the directors had a broad business perspective, were sensitive to the problem of undervalued shares, knew the vulnerability that was entailed, and pushed a strategic direction that gave greater priority to activities on the management agenda designed to enhance share value rather than the broader long-term growth strategy favoured by management. This meant a revised capital budget, and included revamping the company's long-established dividend policy and initiating a buy-back of company shares, neither of which had been suggested by management.

In Company B, the directors were shut out of the process, and discouraged from even attempting to raise strategic issues. Management saw its strategy as being driven by worsening competition, manufacturing and cost problems, and union power and demands. They attempted to correct the situation by betting on huge investments in automation. It is unlikely that the board, had it been truly involved, would have concurred with this strategy—but it was never given the opportunity to weigh the issues and raise questions that might have averted disaster.

> Management and the board have unique and distinct perspectives on strategy. Managers are charged with turning strategic vision into operational reality. Of necessity, they must focus on one strategic path at a time and pursue it relentlessly to maximize its potential for corporate profitability. . .The board's mandate in strategic oversight is distinctly different. Its responsibility is to represent the perspective of investors and question the strategic path itself. . . Management may think it's dealing with disloyal boards at times, but from directors' perspective, they are the ''loyal opposition''. Although the two perspectives converge when board and managers are *developing* strategy, management's role in *executing* the strategy precludes it from also objectively evaluating the strategic path once it is in place.[8]

Ultimately, the board (which usually includes the CEO) must control the company's strategic direction if it is to carry out its oversight responsibility. Much of the work of strategic management can and should be delegated. Where there is a track record of strong, aggressive and strategically-oriented management, the board's role may simply be to help avoid any mistakes, questioning and in some cases delaying or heading off initiatives that may not have been adequately considered. But responsibility for the outcome cannot be avoided. Companies that ignore directors' potential for contribution to the strategic planning process do so at considerable peril. What is required is recognition by both board and management that responsibility for strategic planning is a shared responsibility, that each party has a contribution to make, and that it is critically important to understand the extent and nature of those contributions.

BOARD ENGAGEMENT IN STRATEGIC MANAGEMENT

Regardless of any differences in their job definitions, abilities, or motivations, every board and director is unavoidably compelled to be continuously involved in the structure and process of strategic management. The deep personal engagement of all directors is not only implicit in their responsibility for due diligence in all their board responsibilities, but also explicit in the following circumstances:

1. Critical discontinuities, such as:
   - major changes in top management; the replacement due to death, retirement, or separation of the CEO and other key managers,
   - change, or major threat of change, in ownership or control,
   - threatening developments in competition, markets, technology, or economic conditions, and
   - appearance of major opportunities, such as possible acquisitions, expansion, or divestments.
2. Periodic major reviews, including:
   - redefinition or reconfirmation of purpose — vision, mission, goals and objectives,
   - approval of a strategic plan,
   - approval of annual operating and capital budgets,
   - approval of specific major capital appropriation requests, and
   - annual performance and compensation reviews of the CEO and senior management.
3. Routine interaction with management:
   - monthly and quarterly reviews of operating results,
   - periodic progress reports and updates on special projects or initiatives,
   - informal discussions with individual directors and managers,
   - plant tours and special off-site meetings,
   - requests for issues and opportunities to be put on board agendas, and
   - review of board meeting minutes and follow-up inquiries on topics discussed.
4. External interactions and research:
   - reaction to investment analysts' reports which question or criticize company performance and results,
   - monitoring of media reports concerning the company and its political, economic, social, and technological environments, and

- outside business and social contacts that often yield useful, sometimes critically-important, information.

It is clear from this list that a committed director is more or less continuously "on duty". As a director of several companies put it: "Consciously or unconsciously I am working for all the companies on whose boards I sit most of my waking hours (and many of my nonwaking hours as well!)". A key issue in judging the competence of any director is whether he or she views these often-discontinuous and seemingly-unrelated tasks as random chaos, or is able to integrate and coordinate the various pieces into an instructive picture in which all the details come together in the framework of strategic management. Committed directors are in a continuous learning mode, studying, reading, observing the events around them, relating them to the strategic issues facing their companies, and communicating with the chairman, CEO, and/or other directors. Without this ability and insight, directors are living on their intellectual capital and becoming obsolete, abdicating their responsibilities, and putting their companies at risk.

In a formal sense, the board typically is regularly involved in strategic management at four points:

1. approval of a strategic plan;

2. approval of annual operating and capital budgets;

3. approval of specific major capital appropriation requests; and

4. annual performance review and compensation of the CEO and senior management.

The board's first and most important involvement comes with the approval of a strategic plan. Unfortunately, too often this plan is developed by management in isolation, and the first the board sees of the plan comes at the end of this process, where it is presented for approval. By then, the plan has often involved untold man-hours of staff work and management time, and the board's role is reduced to tinkering with details—far too late in the process for meaningful input. The case of Company B, referred to earlier, represents a classic of this kind.

To deal with this problem, some companies are introducing board input at the beginning, not the end, of the strategic planning process. As a first step in strategy formulation, the board meets in special session on its own, without the pressure of a normal board agenda. As illustrated in Exhibit 7.1, the annual strategic planning cycle begins with the CEO and key management personnel leading in conducting a multi-year review of past performance, and a wide-ranging *tour d'horizon* or review of the firm's environment, identifying issues and options followed by board discussion. Minutes are kept and conclusions summarized, providing a starting point for the detailed preparation of the strategic plan by corporate staff and management. Their completed work is then presented to the board at the normal approval stage, and the approved plan is used as a guide for management in developing tactical programs, budgets and long range financial plans.

Implementing these decisions represents a progression from the very broad (the strategic plan) to the very specific (individual operating budgets, capital appropriation requests (CARs), and the annual performance review and compensation decisions). Strategic plans are generally reviewed annually but changed infrequently—say every few years. Approval of operating and capital budgets for the corporation and for major divisions, is typically done once a year. Spending against those budgets for specific major capital items is done by CAR, and a number of CARs may come before any board meeting in an irregular pattern depending on the capital intensity of the business, the spending limits of the CEO, and competitive factors. Logically, most CARs should arise from the implementation of the strategic plan; in fact, the link between the two is frequently lost in a barrage of technical and financial detail, and CARs often end up being evaluated on an isolated, case-by-case basis.

The board's final step in the strategic management process comes at the end of each year, with the annual performance review and determination of compensation for the CEO and senior managers. Most boards today have a compensation committee that evaluates performance, sets performance standards for the next year, and recommends salaries, bonuses, long-term incentive payments, and benefits based on performance to the board for its approval.

THE STRATEGIC AUDIT

How should the board organize itself so as to carry out its strategic management responsibilities most effectively?

We agree with several commentators, most recently Donaldson, who have called for the board itself, or of a board committee, to take responsibility for the task of a strategic audit, (as opposed to overall strategic planning) in much the same way that existing audit committees evaluate

Exhibit 7.1

A COMPANY'S STRATEGIC PLANNING CYCLE

- Each year the management of the company undertakes a strategic planning process in order to set the overall strategic direction and clearly define long term operating, marketing and financial objectives.
- This year the company adopted a new process, with each operating unit preparing its own strategic business plan.

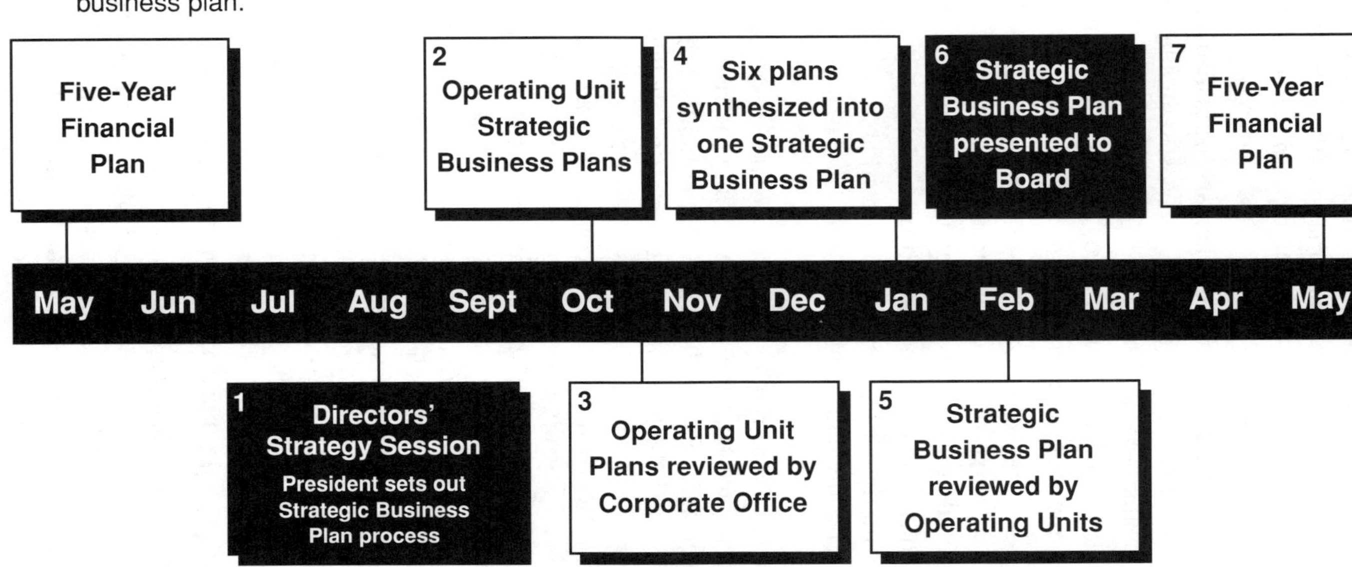

the financial statements indicating the health of their companies. While the ideal would be for the full board to handle this responsibility, the realities of time and workload may well lead to delegating responsibility for the audit aspect of strategy to a committee of the board.

> . . . there is no existing mechanism in most governance processes for formal strategic oversight. A sustainable, effective process means assigning specific responsibility and leadership to particular members of the board, in much the same way that other committee assignments are made. . . The committee should select the criteria for review of strategic performance, oversee the design of the database, and establish a review process. It should ensure the integrity and continuity of the ongoing data collection and reporting efforts, identify issues for discussion with the CEO, keep the full board abreast of the evidence, and schedule both regular and special meetings.[9]

One of the principal objectives of designing the system in this manner is "to reduce both the appearance and the reality of confrontation over disputed turf. The robust egos that normally inhabit the boardroom are highly sensitive to actions that appear to challenge their authority. . .a regular, formal review process dedicated to the discussion of strategic performance with the CEO reduces the likelihood of an adversarial atmosphere. Equally important to a calm and thoughtful exchange of views are meetings in which the only people present are the outside board members and the chief executive."[10]

The principal advantage of the strategic audit committee structure comes when there is a large and relatively unwieldy board. With a smaller, involved board the issues of strategy are of such fundamental importance to the job of every director that all directors should participate, in the interest of avoiding the creation of a "two-tier" board where some directors are involved in the mainstream of activity and others are left outside.

MANAGING THE STRATEGIC AGENDA[11]

If strategy is a shared responsibility, then the board shares its responsibility for strategic management with the CEO who is almost always a director as well. Because he wears both hats, the CEO is the key to making the system work. What distinguishes the best CEOs is superior ability to manage the company's strategic agenda.

Strategic agenda management is the essence of the CEO's job, and is vital to any company's success. It is the all-important link between planning and action, visionary leadership and front-line operations, purpose and results, strategy and tactics, between general and functional management, and between the board of directors, where overall responsibility for the company's performance rests, and the lower levels of management, where operational action is implemented.

Consider the case of John Webster, CEO of an international company recently taken over by a major shareholder. When he took the job, he faced a difficult situation. For some people it would have been sufficient to maintain operations, turn off, and let the strategic agenda be dictated by the major shareholder. However, here we see how a strong CEO with good support can overcome trying challenges and frustrating problems.

From the beginning of his tenure, John Webster had a strong, clear strategic agenda that he effectively communicated up and down the organization. In his first meeting with the board, his organized approach and systematic style became evident. His method was to delegate routine operating matters and spend his time on special tasks that he thought to be major problems, opportunities, or challenges. Over a period of several years, his agenda contained from four to nine key issues at any one time.

John's agenda was based on detailed, first-hand understanding of the business. Well experienced in the industry and deeply involved in the company's operations, he had wide contacts with whom he stayed in touch. Although there was a comprehensive formal strategic plan approved by the board, it had little effect on his agenda, which influenced the strategic plan rather than vice-versa.

His agenda often changed substantially and quickly as he responded to new developments, over many of which he had no control. His agenda was flexible; there was constant and urgent probing, experimentation, movement, and closure. But his agenda priorities were always clear. Key managers were never in doubt as to how agenda items were ranked in importance, attention, resource allocation and relation to other initiatives. The agenda was shared, discussed, and debated openly.

The company's reward/punishment system was clearly integrated into this process. Managers who really performed to clear items from John's agenda were well known to benefit through gains in status, salary, promotions, stock options, and bonuses. Managers who responded negatively to John's agenda were known to pay the price for their lack of positive contribution. Not surprisingly, a professional, performance-oriented, hard-working, and reward-conscious culture developed.

John Webster's management of the company's strategic agenda was most obvious in board meetings when he reported on operations and results. The board agenda was organized around the key strategic issues. His remarks, always related to the strategic agenda, highlighted the progress of current items and the phasing in and out of new and old items respectively. His style was to have other managers report on agenda items under their authority; it was clear from their remarks that the agenda was used as a central organizing framework throughout the management ranks.

Every company is unique, and what is effective in one company may not work in another. Webster's obvious strength in strategic management made the board's job relatively easy. Not all CEOs are blessed with a similar grasp of the job. In another company the board went through a difficult time in searching for, and deciding upon, a CEO. In the end, they chose an individual who had outstanding skills in virtually every respect, but who lacked a strong instinct for strategy. In deciding to hire him, the board recognized and committed itself to compensate for this shortfall by becoming more actively involved in the strategy process. As a relatively small board led by an experienced non-executive chairman, they set aside time in several meetings each year for lengthy discussions with the CEO about the longer-term direction of the business, and the consequent strategy with regard to investments, acquisitions, shareholder relations, and the like. The board also monitored the strategic agenda closely, performing many of the activities that strategy-minded CEO like Webster might have done in his company. Results were outstanding — the CEO provided extremely strong operational leadership of the company, and the board's active involvement in the strategic management process ensured that these efforts were being channeled in the right directions.

CONCLUSION

In governance, all that can be said for certain is that the board is ultimately responsible for strategic management, and its engagement in the process is both inevitable and unavoidable, regardless of motivation, ability, understanding of the job, culture, or leadership. Overseeing strategic management is truly the board's Job One.

Many, if not most, boards fail the test of providing added value to the strategic management process, and thereby fail in their most important function. What is needed to upgrade performance and prevent debacles?

1. A better understanding of strategic management, and the board's relationship with management in carrying it out;

2. An almost-obsessive concern on the part of all directors to see the process improved, attitudes changed, and a determination to "get on with the job";

3. Insistence on operating the company according to a strategic agenda, with continuous tracking by the CEO and the directors themselves;

4. A better focus of the entire board on strategic issues, and, if appropriate, creation of a strategic audit committee;

5. Improved ability to monitor and use information to question, make suggestions and guide management in managing the strategic agenda;

6. Integrating management job descriptions, hiring, evaluation, compensation, and all other aspects of management with the concept of strategic management.

All boards and directors are, by the very nature of their authority and responsibility, inextricably involved in overseeing strategic management. The issue is not whether they *are*, but how they *should be* involved, with clear standards of performance so that they can properly fulfill their expanding and increasingly-important due diligence requirements as directors of a public corporation.

NOTES

1. "A New Tool for Boards: The Strategic Audit," *Harvard Business Review*, (July - August, 1995).

2. This point was emphasized in review comments on this chapter by Purdy Crawford, Chairman, Imasco Limited.

3. This section is based on Donald H. Thain, "Strategic Management, The State of the Art," *The Business Quarterly* (Autumn 1990), p. 95.

4. A good example is the extensive interview with C.K. Prahalad, one of the recent gurus of Strategic Management, in *Strategy and Business* (3rd Quarter, 1996), p. 88 Prahalad dismisses the strategic role of "external governance" — shareholders, boards and CEOs — in one sentence.

5. Donaldson.

6. Ibid.

7. Cited in Donaldson.

8. Donaldson, p. 103.

9. Ibid.

10. Ibid.

11. This section is based on Donald H. Thain, ''Managing the Strategic Agenda: The CEO's Job'', *The Business Quarterly* (Spring, 1993).

Chapter 8
WHY BOARDS FAIL

Why have boards failed? This critical question, now a defining issue in corporate governance, remains largely unaddressed. In the absence of any agreement on the answer, it is impossible to tackle logically the ultimate issue: What should be done to make boards more effective? Without agreement on diagnosis, how can a correct prescription be made for improvement?

Our purpose in this chapter is to provide an explanation for the failure of corporate boards as a basis for advancing the needed turnaround in corporate governance. Clearly, in spite of the general criticism of boards and the obvious failure in individual cases, not all boards fail. Some, to our first-hand knowledge, work extremely well in fulfilling their governance responsibilities to shareholders, stakeholders, and the public at large. Such cases, of course, seldom get reported. It is only the spectacular failure, the aberration, that draws public attention. The existence of well-functioning boards proves that the system can work as intended — there is nothing so fundamentally wrong with the system that it cannot be corrected. The challenge is to understand why some boards fail and others succeed and to apply the lessons learned to all boards.

Useful insights and valid conclusions about why boards fail must be based on a clear understanding of how boards work and what goes wrong when they get off the tracks. To illustrate, let us consider a case that describes some of the basic problems common to most board failures.

THE INTERNATCO COMPANY

Internatco was a large, Canadian-based international manufacturing firm that derived half its sales from the automotive industry and the rest split among machine tools, electronics, and aerospace. It had been run for over 20 years by Tom Benson, chairman and CEO, and before that for 30 years by his father, the founder. Tom Benson's firm hold on the company did not come from stock ownership; the company had gone public in the 1930s and the family had sold all but a small percentage of the shares. Rather it came from talent, hard work and sheer will-power — the father's determination to establish a great enterprise and to turn it over to his son, and the son's consuming ambition to succeed his father and to eclipse his father's accomplishments. Tom Benson was widely known, a proud, hard-driving and occasionally brilliant risk-taker, trained for the job from an early age by his father with whom he had a sometimes tumultuous love-hate relationship. Now aged 68, he had not slowed down, nor had he brought along a successor.

Internatco's prestigious 19-member board of directors included two of Tom Benson's brothers who, other than voting in support of the chairman, seldom participated in meetings. Also on the board were three members of management and a former president, four prominent and politically-connected lawyers for whom the company was a major client, three entrepreneurial CEOs who were suppliers and long-time friends of the chairman, a retired member of the federal cabinet, a prominent socialite, an investment banker, and a retired banker who had been instrumental in financing much of the company's growth. The outside members of the board averaged 67 years of age.

The board met six times a year. Meetings tended to be short and formal. The chairman often joked about completing the company's well-attended annual meeting in less than 30 minutes, barely time to run through the necessary legal formalities. The content of board meetings was generally limited to a review of operations and the approval of the legal documentation of deals and initiatives, carefully crafted by management and company lawyers under the close supervision of the chairman. Beyond financial statements and oral operating reports, little information was given to directors. Required homework and meeting preparation was minimal. Board meetings ran smoothly, with little dialogue beyond a few superficial questions and perfunctory comments usually emanating from the most outspoken of the three CEOs. Comments were invariably directed to the chairman, who usually responded himself, with authoritative, terse answers, occasionally asking a member of management to comment. Meetings were called for 10 o'clock, and generally concluded around noon for drinks and a four- or five-course gourmet lunch featuring two or three outstanding wines and concluding with cigars. A warm camaraderie was shared. Describing his role, one director said, "I was invited on this board by Tom's father, and I'm really here as an honoured guest to be a good spectator and cheerleader."

The board had two committees: a three-man audit committee, chaired by the senior lawyer-director, that met briefly once a year to approve the year-end financial statements, and a long-standing five-man executive committee, constituted to act for the board in an emergency, but which never met. Nevertheless, committee members received $3,000 a year for their services.

As a result of a four-year decline that management blamed primarily on foreign competition, changes in technology and markets, and unsuccessful foreign ventures, particularly in Europe, the company faced a crisis when two banks threatened to call large loans, which could have precipitated insolvency. To stave off impending disaster, the chief financial officer, directed by the chairman, proposed to satisfy the banks by selling a major division of the business to a competitor.

This proposal caused serious disagreement in the board over the alternatives for divestment, valuation of the assets proposed for sale, and the implications for strategic planning — all requiring expensive special services, evaluations and reports from auditors, lawyers, investment bankers and consultants. Over a two-week period, three emergency board meetings were convened in unsuccessful attempts to sort out what had become a complicated and intractable set of issues. Back in his luxurious office after a contentious, frustrating late-evening meeting, Tom Benson confessed to a director who was a friend and supporter: "What a terrible situation! Here I am nearing the end of my career surrounded by incompetents, traitors, and financial pickpockets and with no way out of this mess except to sell a good business that we should never let go. My poor old man must be turning over in his grave."

Media comments on the company's subsequent collapse speculated on whether it was caused by bad management or unfortunate circumstances, and why the board had been unable to anticipate and prevent the crisis.

* * * * *

COMPANY FAILURES ARE BOARD FAILURES

There are many reasons why companies fail. For every spectacular terminal failure as in Internatco, there are dozens of cases where companies have been brought to their knees by major mistakes — mistakes of strategy, execution, judgment, or risk-taking, organizational paralysis and leadership failure.[1] In every case, the buck stops with the board. Directors are elected to represent the shareholders; failure to represent the shareholders' best interest is a failure of the board. Avoiding major mistakes, either of commission or omission, is precisely why directors are there. They cannot avoid this responsibility.

It is, of course, very difficult for a director to interpret and act in timely fashion on the signs and symptoms of incipient decline and impending trouble. If what he or she perceives to be distant early warning signals of trouble are unclear, perhaps even controversial, there is the risk of being written off as a "Chicken Little" who is overplaying what may turn out to be false alarms that the sky is falling. If, on the other hand, a director waits for the solid confirmation of hard evidence and trouble, the problems will be at the door and any possibility of taking preventive or evasive action will have come and gone. With such difficult problems and judgments involved, the challenge of leadership in foreseeing and taking preemptive action to avoid trouble is one of the most important measures of the wisdom and ability of any director.

Company failures are board failures. Why have boards failed? The case of Internatco and countless others we have experienced and/or observed in our careers as directors have led us to conclude that there are at least six major reasons why boards fail: failures of leadership, failures of power and legitimacy, failures of job definition, failures of competence, failures of culture, and failures of board management (Exhibit 8.1). All are related. We propose to look at each in turn, building our analysis from our own experience as directors, and illustrating the issues by reference to the case of Internatco.

1. Failures of Leadership

Quality of board leadership is undoubtedly the most critical of the key factors determining board success or failure, so much so that the problem of, and solution to, board underperformance can be traced almost always to a failure of leadership.

As first among equals and the key link between the directors, shareholders and management, the chairman impacts heavily on the functioning of the board. As the primary planner and manager of the board's work, and leader of discussion at board and shareholder meetings, the chairman sets the tone, style, and pace. In attitude, manner, commitment, wisdom, judgment, social skills, integrity, and work capacity, he or she inevitably provides a model for all other directors.

While all directors are equally responsible for the duties of the board, their contributions are magnified or diminished depending on the chairman. *It is no understatement to say that the leadership ability and performance of the chairman is the most significant determinant of the success or failure of any board.* This was certainly the situation in Internatco: the company's and the board's ultimate failure can be traced to the focus of power in this one person.

Exhibit 8.1

**THE SIX LINKS
IN THE BOARD VALUE CHAIN**

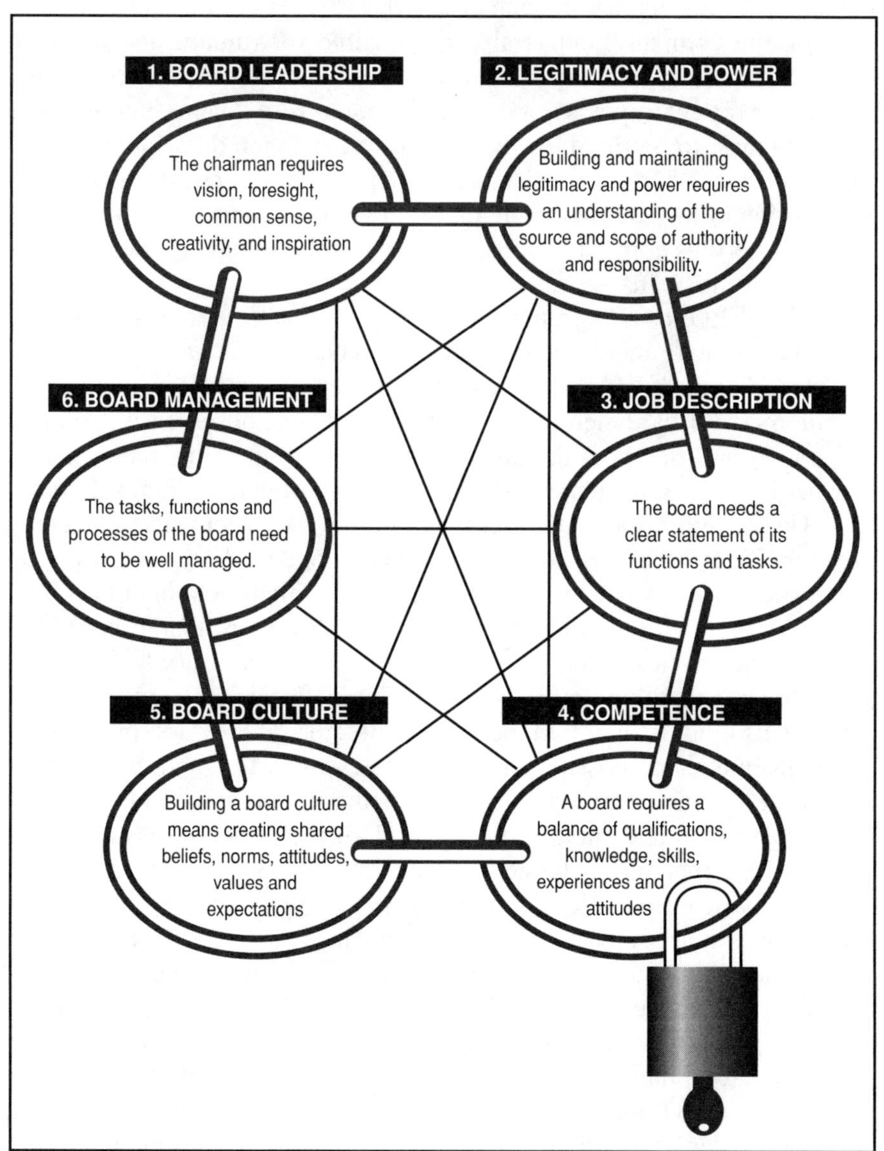

Many if not most of the problems of ineffective boards can be minimized or turned around if the board is led effectively. This means that the board, to be effective, requires leadership, and the leadership can ordinarily come only from the chairman. But who is the chairman? In most North American boards, the chairman and chief executive officer are the same person. That means that in such cases, the CEO is not only in charge of running the company, but is also responsible for running the board to which he or she is, in theory at least, accountable. It also means, inevitably, that the job of chairman is not only part-time, it is secondary in priority to the CEO task, to be fitted in whenever it can. The job descriptions of the two positions, where they exist, are sufficiently different that under pressure the job of the chairman will almost always get short shrift. Moreover, there is a serious conflict of roles which severely inhibits the sound management of the board.

Most CEOs have risen through the ranks of management, and identify their success with their management role. The result is an attitude, often unstated, that the board is a burden on management, and its influence is to be minimized. Board members are seen as part-time observers and outsiders, knowing little about the business but second-guessing management, another layer of bureaucracy getting in the way of getting things done.

These conflicts and attitudes are built into the system, and when they are embodied in the one position, it is small wonder that the performance of the board suffers. The most prevalent and debilitating fault of the CEO/chairman is an attitude that the board is nothing more than a necessary evil: "I have to have a board, so I'll do the least necessary to fulfill my obligations — anything more is an unwelcome intrusion on my time and turf." This kind of chairman then keeps directors in the dark, provides as little information as possible, avoids threatening issues, and runs tightly-regimented, formal meetings. A good meeting for this chairman is one that is short, routine, and stickhandles around all the important issues of the business. Internatco is a classic example.

The basic problem for many chairmen is compounded by the fact that they are less than competent at their job, and lack the knowledge, attitudes, skills, and experience to run a good board. The job is seldom defined, qualifications are seldom thought through. Chairmen who have come up the management ladder have usually been appointed because they were good operators, had strong functional expertise, the support of a strong mentor, and good political skills, or they represented a powerful faction, function, or department in the organization — scarcely sufficient requirements for the job of chairman.

2. Failures of Power and Legitimacy

The authority, responsibility, and influence of individual boards vary widely depending on the power they assume, and the legitimacy of the source of that power. This power determines whether a board has any reasonable hope of performing what it is legally required to do — to "manage or supervise the management" of the corporation.

If the board has the support and confidence of the firm's constituents, especially the shareholders, and if the constituents actively fulfill their rights and obligations as owners, the board can function as legally mandated. If not, its power tends to be taken over either by a major shareholder or by management, and its role is reduced to rubber-stamping decisions made by the real power holders in the organization.

In Internatco, the board was clearly captive to the chairman who, by virtue of his inherited role and dynamic leadership, the passivity of other shareholders and — as CEO — his domination of management, controlled all the levers of power. The board had no legitimacy other than that bestowed by the chairman, and hence no real power to carry out its legal responsibilities.

The chairman, in keeping the board on a short leash, did himself a great disservice in the end. By concentrating power in his own hands, he created a board of "spectators and cheerleaders" who were content to go along for the ride, never questioning or challenging the strategic decisions that ultimately caused the company's downfall. Ordinary shareholders lacked any voice, in part due to their own failure to exert their ownership rights. The institutions set up to give them a voice — the annual meeting, the proxy process, the nomination of directors — were merely charades whereby the board went through the motions of consulting the owners, but was never challenged or held to account. The larger minority shareholders — institutions such as pension funds, mutual funds, money managers, and insurance companies — abdicated their ownership responsibilities and left the field to the major patriarchal figure, who also headed management. The board was "elected" by the dominant CEO and chairman thus breaking the essential accountability link with the ordinary shareholders. The result was autocracy, not shareholder democracy; power without accountability, a disaster waiting to happen.

3. Failures of Job Definition

In any occupational situation where someone is failing in a task, a logical first step for analysis is to review the job description — what is the task? Applied to directors and boards, this indicates a fundamental problem. As explained in Chapter 4 the legal definition of the board's job is an abstraction lacking substantive meaning. Boards do not, cannot, run businesses in any active sense: they delegate this task to management. The best they can do is set or approve purpose and strategy, appoint officers, monitor their performance, and hold them to account for results. Yet, in many cases directors are not accountable and are appointed by the very managers who are supposed to report to them.

For whatever reason, meaningful job descriptions — standard practice at all other levels of the organization — are almost nonexistent at the board level. Formal or systematic job training for directors is similarly absent. Small wonder that fundamental issues frequently arise: is the purpose of the board to maximize value for shareholders, or is it to serve non-owner stakeholders, to maintain jobs, provide security, and preserve the environment? Should the function of the board be viewed narrowly — to hire, counsel, compensate, and if necessary, fire the CEO, or broadly — to review, change, approve and monitor corporate goals and strategy, to review management performance, interact with shareholders, and take over active management in an emergency?

The ambiguity and breadth of the legal definition of a director's responsibilities leads to a wide variance in how the director's job is defined in practice; misunderstanding and miscommunication on the part of regulators, shareholders, directors, and management; and widespread confusion in discussions of governance issues. Most corporate boards lack any detailed, realistic, practical job description for directors, or operate with only the briefest and most superficial statement of directors' terms of reference; the same is true of chairmen. Lacking specific guidelines or standards of expected performance, board members are forced to rely on signals picked up from the chairman or their peers. Moreover, such job descriptions as do exist are constantly changing, reflecting changing societal expectations of corporations in such areas as environmental, health and safety concerns, increased company and board liability, and growing awareness of the board's crucial role in the process of strategic management.

Lack of agreement and precision on what boards are supposed to do makes it virtually impossible to measure whether any given board is effective or not. In addition, the uncertain cause/effect relationships between what a board does, company performance, and shareholder value, while important, are so indirect and affected by so many other variables, that they cannot be accurately determined. If one of the board's principal functions is to prevent management from making strategic mistakes, how can this be measured and assessed? For example, how is avoidance of error reflected in financial performance?

The lack of objective measures of board effectiveness leads to a situation where directors individually, and boards collectively, are to all intents and purposes unaccountable, and can absolve themselves from blame for almost any mistake as long as they have acted within the law. The "business judgment" defence absolves directors from responsibility for most of the critical issues that come before the board, with the result that it is almost impossible to pin down responsibility and accountability.

4. Failures of Competence

There are no meaningful qualifications for directors or chairmen of corporations. The legal qualifications — that a director be at least 18 years old, legally sane, and not bankrupt — set so low a hurdle that virtually anyone can be appointed a director, and mean that many directors are incompetent to perform any job even remotely similar to that of controlling and guiding a corporation to achieve maximum shareholder value. Couple this with inadequate understanding on all sides concerning the job to be done, and it is not surprising that the criteria and selection processes for new directors are poorly designed and often inappropriate. The result is a wide variation in the competence and ability of board members, ranging from totally unsatisfactory — so lacking in necessary knowledge, skills, attitudes, wisdom, experience, and integrity that they are a completely negative influence — to outstanding, master professionals who are consistent contributors and pillars of strength, no matter what the problems or circumstances. Wide variations in the competence and effectiveness of directors (and chairmen) lead in turn to substantial differences in the capability and potential of boards.

In Internatco, the selection process was entirely controlled by the all-powerful and self-willed CEO/chairman. Tom Benson and, before him, his father, assembled a group of highly compatible, supportive cheerleaders with little if any careful thought as to the needs of the company or indeed, himself. Over the years, the board had become a cohesive but unquestioning social club. This group was clearly incapable of anticipating or grappling with strategic issues or acting on them effectively. When the financial crunch came, it was too late, and they were seen as "incompetents" and "traitors" by the chairman who had appointed them to be unquestioning supporters.

Events of recent years have dramatically raised the bar for directors. Minimum requirements for serving on a corporate board today are considerably higher than they were even a decade ago. Knowledge of derivatives and other complex, new financial instruments was not an entry requirement for most directors serving today. The rapid growth of sophisticated information systems of the last ten years has bypassed many directors. Marketing strategies have been revolutionized by the growing availability of data bases and the targeting of high potential buyers. Environmental and social issues have transformed strategic thinking in many industries. New organizational theories and practices have changed the nature of work, and the relationship of corporations to their employees. Today, the prospective director needs knowledge, skills and attitudes similiar to the equivalent of a good, recent MBA degree (plus an abundance of good, old-fashioned common sense and experience) just to understand what is going on in the boardroom.

In many industries, boards are being left behind because of changes in the technology of the business. In fields such as computers, communications, entertainment, the media, and pharmaceuticals, future success will depend largely on the choice of technologies. Many directors are not up to the task. As one CEO explained it:

> This company faces make-or-break decisions in which the fundamental issues are technological. Unfortunately, the outside members of our board are not scientists, and they lack the knowledge to understand the technological change we are going through. I have *tried* hard, — special briefings, study sessions with experts, consultants' reports, you name it — but there is nothing I can do to bring them up to speed. It's just too difficult for them to understand.

Knowledge is power. In such circumstances, the board has little choice but to leave the most important strategic decisions in the hands of management, thereby abdicating its most fundamental responsibility.

5. Failures of Board Culture

Every board has a culture — the shared attitudes, values, experiences, norms and personal relationships that have built up over time and that govern what directors can and cannot say and do, and what subjects are taboo, "the undiscussibility of subjects that are undiscussible." Boards operate on the basis of unspoken and unwritten rules; there is an established pecking order, not obvious to the casual observer, that takes time to understand. In many boards, the culture has been so deeply embedded that most directors are not even aware of the possibility of doing things differently. This culture can be tremendously resistant to change. For the new director or chairman who wants to initiate significant change, inertia and resistance to change can be a major challenge.

Board cultures vary widely from what we have termed the "old code" — passive, accepting, deferring to the chair, and supporting management no matter what — to the "new code", where participation is the norm, constructive dissent is encouraged, and where meetings are active. Culture largely determines whether the board will approach its tasks with a take-charge attitude, or simply go along for the ride, following the path of least resistance. Internatco is a particularly vivid example of an "old-style" culture with deep roots, and little, if any, prospects of change. Boards, particularly those ruled by the old culture, tend to follow and react to management, thereby failing in their leadership and guidance responsibilities. As a result, directors do not perceive problems until they are informed by management, usually long after it is possible to avoid serious consequences.

6. Failures of Board Management

The failure of many boards is due to bad management of the board itself. In such boards, the performance of administrative tasks is so inadequate that the board is severely constrained in doing its job.

The size of a board, for example, can have a major impact on how effectively the individual director can work. Despite recent trends towards reducing board size, the boards of many public companies today are too large to be effective problem-solving groups. Most research on problem-solving group performance puts the optimum group size at eight members, give or take one or two. The boards of some financial institutions are as large as 30 members or more; a more normal pattern in industry would be boards of 12 to 18. Oversized boards result in several problems — individual directors' participation time is severely reduced and/or even eliminated; much board work has to be delegated to committees, reducing the involvement of directors in many issues; evaluation of director performance becomes difficult if not impossible; motivation suffers; the system is less open to criticism and possible change; and it becomes easier for management to control the board by divide-and-rule tactics.

When a board is too large, its flexibility is drastically reduced. Meetings cannot be held on short notice or in response to crises without key members being absent. Agendas must be adhered to. Discussions must be limited. Time availability drives the board and its work. Formality and ritual become the norms.

The critical test of board administration is in how well the board information function is managed. Three common problems prevent boards from doing their jobs.

First, most information provided to directors focuses on past financial results: sales, costs, profits, assets and liabilities. All are indicators of problems, opportunities, and decisions from the past, usually so long ago that little can be done about them except to react with defensive tactics. The real purpose and spirit of strategic management is to create the future of the business by anticipating and taking action on problems and opportunities, and guiding management to achieve a competitive edge in confronting them. To function effectively, boards need information on leading indicators: customer satisfaction; developing trends in markets; technological forecasts; new product development; competitors' objectives, future scenarios, strategies and actions; employee attitudes; and the like. When this kind of future-oriented information is not made available to boards, their guidance function is largely nullified.

Second, except for routine matters, management controls the agenda and all information made available to the board. When the information necessary to consider a course of action is selectively screened and censored, the monitoring, consulting, and control functions of the board are severely hampered.

Third, there is a fine line between providing too much information to the board and too little. There is an art to managing the information needs of the board, and this should be one of the major elements in the chairman's job description. In many companies, the information package is sent out too late, is too thick, takes too long to read, is difficult to understand, leaves problems buried in the numbers, and is not focused on relevant action options. Many directors, busy with other matters, lack the time, ability, or commitment to wade through it all and make their own analysis of company-supplied information. This effectively leaves power in the hands of those who do. By the same token, too little information, or information provided too late, can be equally damaging.

Recent years have seen a rapid expansion in the responsibilities of boards and board members, and a corresponding growth in the workload expected of directors in carrying out their duties. How that workload is managed is an important variable affecting the effectiveness of any director. Poorly-organized meetings and information flow can have a negative effect on how well a director performs; good board management releases the time of directors to focus on significant matters central to carrying out their responsibilities and improves the productivity of the board as a whole.

The basic tasks on which the effectiveness of board operations depend include:

1. sizing up the company and monitoring its problems, opportunities, and strategic agenda;

2. planning the board's work, as determined by the company's situation and strategic agenda;

3. calling, arranging, and conducting board and committee meetings as necessary to get the board's work done;

4. organizing the board to divide and coordinate the work, and staffing the board and committees to enable that process;

5. planning, preparing, and distributing the information needed by directors to perform their duties properly;

6. designing and implementing an optimal compensation system for senior management;

7. developing and following a process to evaluate and upgrade the effectiveness of directors individually and the board collectively;

8. developing and implementing a process for defining the board's succession needs and the means for meeting them; and

9. acting and communicating in emergencies and special situations that arise between regularly-scheduled meetings.

In an effective board, all these tasks are well done. There is a good sizeup of the overall situation facing the company, and a sense of its strategic direction. The work, problems, and opportunities are well understood, and planning is comprehensive and sensible considering the company's unique circumstances. Time is well planned and directors are not overloaded; there is a clear focus on key issues.

Effective administration of the board will not make up for failings in other key variables. But poor management of the board not only hampers its effectiveness, it can create frustration among its members and lead to underperformance or resignations from turned-off directors.

KEY SUCCESS FACTORS FOR AN EFFECTIVE BOARD

In this analysis of the main reasons for board failure, we have begun to put forward the beginnings of a model for board success, the other side of the coin. The corresponding six key success factors in building an effective board are:

1. outstanding leadership;
2. unquestioned legitimacy and effective power;
3. enlightened definition of function, role, and responsibilities;
4. outstanding competence;
5. a supportive, functional culture; and
6. efficient management of function, structure, and process.

These six key factors are clearly interrelated; each builds on and supports the others, reinforcing each other and multiplying their cumulative effect for good or bad. They are the levers which must be controlled by those seeking to improve the quality of any board, and they must be operated in conjunction with each other. Focusing effort on any one element will not produce the effect desired, although, if one of these factors is "first among equals", in our experience it is leadership.

In unsatisfactory boards, problems arise in all six areas (Exhibit 8.2) — leadership is jealously guarded to ensure that the CEO's or major shareholder's will is supreme; power has generally been pre-empted by management or a major shareholder; the job of the director is to support management or the major shareholder as the case may be; competence declines because it is not legitimate to exercise the leadership capability of directors; the old "don't rock the boat" culture prevails; and management of the board is manipulated to maintain management domination and keep directors away from vital issues. Any one of these problems would be bad enough; in combination they are almost impossible to overcome without drastic change in leadership and attitudes.

The long list of recent corporate debacles raises the issue of why these mistakes are made, often by the highly prestigious boards of leading

Exhibit 8.2

SIGNS AND SYMPTOMS OF PROBLEMS IN BOARD EFFECTIVENESS

1. **BOARD LEADERSHIP**
   - Lack of leadership in focusing on central issues
   - Chairman lacking the knowledge, attitudes, and skills required for effective leadership
   - Board functions that are overlooked, downgraded, or blocked by chairman
   - Important topics and problems avoided because of sensitivity and resistance of chairman
   - Board preempted by CEO who is chairman

2. **LEGITIMACY AND POWER**
   - Ordinary shareholders without power and voice
   - Unaccountable minority control blocks
   - Management takeover and preemption of boards
   - The jobs of CEO and chairman combined

3. **JOB DEFINITION**
   - Job definition unclear and disconnected from company's strategic agenda
   - Lack of evaluation of board performance and director effectiveness

4. **COMPETENCE**
   - Lack of meaningful qualifications for directors and chairman
   - Too many inside or related directors
   - Lack of needed expertise and knowledge
   - Lack of ordinary shareholder point of view

5. **BOARD CULTURE**
   - Board held in grip of a negative, dysfunctional culture
   - Board passive and reactive
   - Failure of directors to dissent
   - Inability to change approach or unwillingness to upgrade board operations

6. **BOARD MANAGEMENT**
   - Board not coming to grips with critical problems
   - Poor administration of board tasks
   - Disappointing and frustrating meetings
   - Poor organization of board committees
   - Lack of needed, well-organized information
   - Board too large to function effectively
   - Unsatisfactory compensation system
   - Lack of board succession plan
   - Ineffectiveness in emergencies or special situations

companies. And why, long after problems are obvious, does it take so long to start the necessary corrective action? Our analysis suggests that such problems arise from either major shareholder or management control of board concerns and processes, leading to incompetent chairmen and directors who don't understand their job, bad decision-making procedures, lack of relevant information, and hubris and complacency resulting in a deeply-rooted and dysfunctional culture.

Such results are not an inevitable outcome of the system. There are many boards that are models of effective governance — that do the job that they are intended to do. Unlike the failures, which attract widespread public attention, they function quietly and efficiently, serving their shareholder-constituents in the pursuit of long-term shareholder value. Most thoughtful and experienced directors know what has to be done to turn around the malaise of corporate governance — improving the quality of leadership, making boards truly legitimate by winning the confidence of shareholders, adopting explicit director and chairman job definitions, upgrading director competence, improving management of board processes, and working towards a new board culture of effective, challenging teamwork. These are the means by which boards can be made to function as they should. The balance of this book will be devoted to discussing each in more detail.

NOTES

This chapter is based on our earlier article, ''Why Boards Fail'', *The Business Quarterly* (Spring, 1995).

1. For more detail see Benson P. Shapiro, Adrian J. Slywotzky and Richard S. Tedlow, ''Why Bad Things Happen to Good Companies,'' *Strategy & Business*, Booz Allen & Hamilton, Second Quarter, 1996, p. 16.

Chapter 9

BOARD LEADERSHIP:
The Job of the Chairman

Leadership is the key success factor in the board system. In improving board effectiveness the problem and the solution begin with the chairman. Our purpose in this chapter, the first of seven examining key success and failure factors in the board system, is to describe and comment on the chairman's job — the role, its challenges and problems, and our recommendations — and return at the end to the question of whether the two jobs of chairman and CEO should be combined or separated. We begin with a case describing how in many companies the chairman takes on the job.

THE MEGA CORPORATION

At the annual meeting of the Mega Corporation, John Cunningham was presented to the shareholders as the new chairman and CEO. Cunningham had risen through various operating jobs to become president and chief operating officer, where he compiled an impressive record. When the long-time chairman and CEO approached retirement age, a committee of the board evaluated possible successors, both from within and outside the company, and recommended Cunningham. The board accepted the recommendation prior to the annual shareholders' meeting, where the appointment was routinely announced.

In subsequent months, Cunningham was immersed in a constant round of meetings as he attempted to take over and put his own stamp on the company's strategic agenda and direction. Many of these meetings required extensive travel to the company's principal plants and subsidiaries around the world. He chaired his first board meetings and attended several committee meetings, becoming more at ease with the directors, some of whom he had known only in passing.

Cunningham's priorities were primarily with major competitive problems, strategic planning and organization. Working with the board was well down on his list of items needing attention, especially as the board had just put him into the job. Gradually, as he became more comfortable with his role as chairman, he ran the board meetings more tightly, controlling the agenda and pushing critical items through to decision. The meetings and discussion were sometimes useful, he thought, but the time and effort necessary to organize and prepare for them were generally not well spent, and represented something of an intrusion into his very demanding job of running the company. To free himself for the several critical tasks on his agenda, he delegated most of the planning and preparation for board meetings to the company secretary, an experienced lawyer. In most cases, he could hardly wait until the meetings were over so he could get back to the more important task of addressing the pressing problems facing the company.

* * * * *

John Cunningham's experience is reasonably typical of most new chairmen/CEOs, and his evolving relationship with the board is not too far from the reality of most North American businesses. In it lie the seeds of a central problem.

The problem centres on the evolving relationship of the chairman and the board. Cunningham is more concerned about his job as CEO, and the chairmanship is becoming perfunctory and strictly secondary in his mind. This becomes reflected in the way the board functions and how the relationship hardens into a routine and nonproductive pattern. Directors become dissatisfied and grumble, but not sufficiently to mount an active campaign to change things as long as company performance is not too bad.

Our experience as directors indicate that this common pattern shows signs of danger; it is one that can and should have been avoided, and one that has proven costly to many corporations.

THE CHAIRMAN HAS ULTIMATE RESPONSIBILITY

Deriving from the firm principle that the board's role is supervisory, with operations delegated to management, the person with the ultimate formal authority and responsibility for overseeing the management of any company is the chairman, not the CEO. This is so because the legal governing body of all corporations is the board, and its chairman is the person who, by appointment or election by the directors, presides over the board and through it, the company. (See Exhibit 9.1 for a general outline of the chairman's job.) The CEO is essentially a creature of, and reports to, the board.

It is the chairman who has the most influence on how effectively the

Exhibit 9.1

CHAIRMAN OF THE BOARD
OUTLINE FOR A JOB DESCRIPTION

1. **Managing the Board**
   a. Chairing meetings of the board
   b. Setting meeting schedules
   c. Setting meeting agendas
   d. Managing directors' performance
   e. Communicating with directors between meetings
   f. Controlling meeting attendance
   g. Determining board information packages
   h. Helping appoint committees
   i. Attending committee meetings where appropriate
   j. Determining director compensation

2. **Developing a More Effective Board**
   a. Determining board contribution
   b. Planning board composition and its succession
   c. Ensuring the recruitment of new directors and the "retirement" of those who are ineffective

3. **Working with Management**
   a. Monitoring and influencing strategic management
   b. Building relationships
   c. Helping define problems
   d. Monitoring and evaluating performance of the CEO and senior officers
   e. Representing shareholders and board to the management
   f. Representing management to the board and shareholders
   g. Maintaining accountability by management
   h. Ensuring succession plans in place at senior management level

4. **Managing Shareholder Relations**
   a. Chairing annual and special meetings of shareholders
   b. Meeting with major shareholder groups
   c. Meeting, accompanied by the CEO, with financial analysts
   d. Meeting, accompanied by the CEO, with financial press
   e. Meeting, accompanied by the CEO, with potential sources of debt and equity capital
   f. Communicating with shareholders and potential shareholders

5. **Liaison with Other Parties**
   a. In conjunction with the CEO, representing company to public, suppliers, customers and staff
   b. In conjunction with the CEO, developing relationships and representing the company with governments, regulators and government agencies
   c. As requested by the CEO, working with competitors on industry problems
   d. Liaison with CEO and management
   e. Representation on other boards
   f. Public service and a leadership role with the CEO in charitable, educational and cultural activities

board operates and whether it works as what we term an ''old-style'' board (perfunctory, superficial, and impotent) or as a ''new style'' board (vigorous, creative, and empowered). The chairman therefore has a major influence on the relationship that develops between the board and CEO. In many widely-held companies, where the chairman is also the CEO, the chairman's power is so great that it is ordinarily unassailable. The exceptions are in subsidiaries, joint ventures, or situations where the chairman is appointed by owners with a control block or shareholders' agreement.

If, then, as reported daily in the media the performance and competitive ability of many North American companies is unsatisfactory, who should be held accountable? If, as many insiders and informed observers contend, boards are seriously underperforming, who bears the primary responsibility? If, as many argue, corporate performance and board effectiveness need to be greatly improved, who must take the initiative? Clearly, the chairman. As water will not rise higher than its source, so in a corporation the quality of governance will not be better than the quality of the chairman.

This is not to say that other factors are not important, nor that individual directors cannot make a difference in the way a board operates. They can and do. But the first among equals in any board is the chairman. In most cases, what the chairman wants, the chairman gets. It is the chairman who is at the eye of the storm that is building around our system of corporate governance and who must answer for its not performing as it should. Both the problem and the solution inevitably begin with and centre on the chairman's competence.

In a large majority of North American companies, the jobs of chairman and CEO are combined. In Canada, the jobs are combined in three-quarters of the *Financial Post* 500; in the U.S., the chairman is also CEO in roughly 80 percent of the *Fortune* 500 companies. This is not the case in other countries; in the U.K., for example, the tradition of non-executive chairmen is much more prevalent. This North American pattern is interesting because it means that two clearly and distinctly different jobs, embodying unavoidable conflicts of interest, are combined.

THE JOB OF THE CHAIRMAN: MANAGING THE BOARD

For a definition of the job of the chairman we must go back to the rules governing the limited liability company, an autonomous legal entity which has its origins in eighteenth century British statute. In this well-known model the logic is simple and straightforward. The shareholders own the company. They elect a board of directors to ''manage or supervise the management'' of the corporation. Since in law all directors are considered equal and there is no mention of a chairman, the position arises from the detailed bylaws enacted by the directors to regulate the ''transaction of the business and affairs'' of the corporation. Ordinarily such a bylaw states simply that ''except for the election of a chairman, the chairman of the board. . . shall be chairman of any meeting of the board''.

So much for legal theory. The reality of the chairman's job is very different and much more complex. Stripped to its bare essentials, the job of the chairman is to manage the board so that it performs effectively. Hence, the first requirement for a chairman is to have a clear view of what the board must do to be effective. The chairman's job, in other words, is defined by the job of the board and the realities of the organizational context in which it works. In actual practice, except for a few required formalities, the chairman's job is undefined and open-ended; no standard job description exists. Most chairmen learn the role by observing other chairmen.

THE CHAIRMAN'S JOB VARIES FROM FIRM TO FIRM

The chairman's performance requirements and response are contingent on several key factors that differ from company to company. The major determinant of the chairman's job is the company's ownership pattern (see chapter 5). The basic functions required of the board are performed, or not performed, to widely varying degrees depending on the ownership structure.

Other key factors determining how a board works include the scope of the job and title of the chairman, whether the chairman is also CEO, the relative competence, experience, and roles of the chairman and the directors, whether the board is influenced by what we have termed the ''old-style'' or the ''new-style'' culture, company circumstances and performance, the chairman's relationship with directors, the time the chairman has spent and intends to stay on the job, and whether a successor is being groomed. All these factors influence the roles the chairman plays and the challenges that must be met. The many variations in these factors mean that except for the general responsibility to manage the board, the job of chairman is unique to any specific company.

THE JOB OF THE CHAIRMAN: TASKS AND CHALLENGES

The chairman is required to play a wide variety of roles that are variable, complex, open-ended and dependent on the personalities and circumstances involved. These roles must be performed well to achieve success; as one chairman put it, ''Here's what I have to do to get the wood chopped.''

Understanding the Job

Because of the importance, complexity, sensitivity, organizational dynamics, and open-endedness of the chairman's job, it is difficult to define in detail, and no inclusive or definitive formula can be laid down. Although informal counsel is available from experienced chairmen, there is no book or course on the full scope and requirements of the job as it should be performed in any specific situation. Moreover, even if there were, chairmen would have to adapt it to their own personality, history, strengths, weaknesses, style, and the needs and expectations of the very large formal and informal network of people for whom the chairman becomes a critical centre and reference point.

The first step, then, is to understand the specific job at hand — how to perform the required routine, what needs to be changed, what should be left alone, action priorities, process and style. This review should begin with a discussion of expectations and ideas with key reference people including, as appropriate, major shareholders (especially if there is a control block), predecessors, and the most influential directors and managers. These discussions should be aimed at exploring, understanding, and agreeing on fundamentals of problems, actions, priorities, and expectations. Based on these discussions, the chairman can begin implicitly or explicitly to map the influence and accountability network that forms the organizational context for the job and to formulate guiding agendas — strategic, tactical, and personal.

The job of sizing up the roles and how they should be performed is basic to all that follows. Indeed, in many cases, this size-up should pay special attention to the differences the chairman intends to incorporate from the ways in which others have performed the job. Without this kind of review and analysis, it is easy to get off on the wrong track and, in many cases, never to be able to begin again in the right way.

Learning to Perform the Roles

The next requirement of the new chairman is learning how to perform the required roles competently, confidently, and with character. Since the job is always changing, there are invariably new challenges, many of which can never be totally mastered. Before long the chairman may be called upon to act convincingly in the roles of discussion leader, spokesman, referee, strategist, politician, decision maker, leader, follower, motivator, teacher, cheerleader, disciplinarian, moralist, confidant, father confessor, personal counsellor, coach, friend/enemy, and a dozen more. The job soon challenges the role repertoire of even the most able and experienced manager and leader. Since no one can effectively be all things to all people, part of this experience is understanding and getting to be at peace with "playing yourself" — leading from strengths and character, and minimizing weaknesses.

New chairmen start with all the obvious high-profile tasks that they alone can do: chairing regular board meetings and annual and special shareholders' meetings, (and in the process, learning some of the fine points of rules of order and how to keep a meeting on track); speaking for the company in a variety of different meetings together with or without the CEO; representing the company as appropriate in industry circles with competitors, customers, suppliers, government, and other organizations; acting as the company patriarchal figure at retirements, funerals, weddings and other special occasions; and other similar tasks that quickly fill all the working days and many evenings. When these routine tasks have been met and mastered, time and attention can be freed to attend to the endless stream of other duties.

Pushing for Top Corporate Performance

The chairman's most important single responsibility is to ensure that management, led by the CEO, delivers satisfactory performance for the board and shareholders. While satisfactory performance must be defined in detail and worked out as a clearly-understood contract between the board and management, it begins at the very minimum with increasing shareholder wealth by earning profits over time that are greater than the cost of capital, and improving the company's competitive position in all its businesses. From this beginning point, satisfactory performance should include the realization of improved benefits for all the stakeholders on whose support the company must rely. This job never ends and no matter how much time chairmen spend with individuals and groups on formal and informal planning, budgeting, organizing and reviewing, they could always spend more. In this area the chairman must obviously work primarily through the CEO and hold him or her responsible. If the two jobs are combined, the issue of separating them must be faced, especially when operating performance is unsatisfactory.

Handling Tough and Sometimes Nasty Problems

Few chairmen are on the job long before testing problems and unpredictable emergencies arise in which they are unavoidably required to play high-profile roles of wise man, negotiator and judge. Whatever the "hidden horrors'', personal or business, they must be treated with great care because the chairman's role in dealing with such problems has high visibility and consequently a significant effect on the chairman's power base and reputation, both inside and outside the company.

Working With Other Key Managers Individually and Collectively

The chairman has the primary responsibility for communicating and bridging between the board and management. As a result, the chairman is heavily into coaching and team building. Handling all the key players with respect calls on human resource management skills to a high degree. While these relationships are of great importance, they are also very sensitive. A chairman needs to be open, supportive, friendly and cooperative, but tough, demanding and professional as well. The chairman must avoid being coopted by management and losing objectivity in the evaluation and accountability to shareholders for the results achieved by the organization.

Developing and Managing the Board's Supervision of the Company's Strategic Agenda

The chairman must size up the company's situation, decide what needs to be done and supervise the development and implementation of a clear vision and strategic agenda. If his agenda differs from the views of management, a major shareholder or the board, the chairman needs to seek consensus; get management, owners, and the board to buy in; see that the tasks involved are completed in a reasonable time frame; and keep the agenda turning over so that closure and progress are satisfactory. Mutual agreement between the board and the CEO on the implementation of the company's strategic agenda should be the base for evaluation and compensation of the entire top management team beginning with the CEO.

Managing the Board

As the person whose primary job is to preside over the board, the chairman must spend much time planning, organizing, attending, and following up on the meetings of the board and its committees. In fact, the ongoing agenda of board-related activities is the hub and integrating factor of all the chairman does. These tasks can be outlined as follows:

(1) *Managing board meetings.* Although board business is increasingly being conducted in committees, the formal board meeting is still the principal forum for the transaction of board business. Telephone or video

conferences are a poor substitute for the full-fledged, in-person board meeting. For most directors, the board meeting is where their major contributions are made. Preparation for, and management of, board meetings is a major part of the chairman's operating routine. Scheduling well in advance; working around conflicts; ensuring the proper flow of agenda topics; allowing adequate time for discussion; minimizing set-piece, boiler plate presentations; knowing how to pace the meeting and when to call for a vote — all are important elements in making board meetings productive. A most critical judgment call comes in managing the information that goes to directors. The chairman must manage the fine balance between sending out too much and too little information. Neither overloading directors nor failing to provide them with essential material is conducive to effective board operation.

(2) *Preparing for meetings.* Since there are usually some 20 to 30 meetings annually of a board and its various committees, preparing for them can be an almost continuous and extremely time-consuming job if it is done well. The first task is making up the agenda and planning the outline of meetings. While much of this work will be delegated and influenced by legal requirements and company routines, the chairman nevertheless needs to shape and form the agendas so that they are integrated with the management problems of the company and the chairman's idea of where the company should be going. Much time is spent planning and reviewing reports, presentations and activities, integrating committee work and reports and making sure that all will go well, that transportation and hotel arrangements are correct and so on. The work of many boards and committees has a systematic annual schedule of reviews, tasks, reports and meeting locations that must be managed and integrated. All of these activities require much personal interaction, influence, negotiation, and attention to make sure they are right.

(3) *Staying in touch.* The oil necessary to make any board function well is communication, especially one-on-one conversations that enable the chairman and directors to share concerns, trade ideas, keep up to date, offer advice and counsel, avoid misunderstandings and build positive relationships. The sheer time demands of the job provide a compelling reason for having a substantially full-time chairman.

(4) *Working with board committees.* With the work of many boards now structured around several continuing committees, board chairmen, regardless of the effectiveness and responsibility of committee chairmen, must spend significant time and effort planning and integrating committee chairmen's work and guiding their agendas and reports as necessary. In

many cases, the chairman's personal presence is required at committee meetings, requiring considerable time and preparation.

(5) *Managing board performance.* This task requires the chairman to step back and evaluate the effectiveness of the board and to plan and implement improvements in its function. Since the cause-effect relationship of the board to actual annual company performance is indirect, complex and conjectural, evaluation of any board is a sensitive judgment call. The chairman must assess directors not only individually and collectively, but also leadership, management, committees, relationships, operations, and results. The chairman must then systematically shape and implement the never-ending improvements without which progress will stop.

(6) *Developing the board.* This job involves all the activities necessary to upgrade the board. It is based on implicit if not explicit evaluation of directors individually and collectively, and a plan to upgrade through recruiting, retirement, and improving operating effectiveness. Although board appointments are made infrequently, the task of succession planning is no less critical to long-range effectiveness. In our opinion, this is not usually done well.

This brief outline of the basic roles and responsibilities of the chairman makes it obvious that doing the job is an open-ended challenge. While many incumbents perform the function, relatively few do it well and fewer yet ever master it.

CHAIRMAN PERFORMANCE: THE REALITY

Having outlined the job and tasks of the chairman, let us look at how the job is done. By comparing the ideal with actual practice, we are led logically to a number of recommendations for improving the effectiveness of chairmen and through them the boards and companies for which they are responsible.

First, any overall assessment of chairmen based on the effectiveness of boards as indicated by company performance, and the many cases that we have seen first hand of director dissatisfaction with the system, point to a general overall rating of chairmen as mediocre at best, and frequently poor, with individual chairmen ranging from terrible to excellent. While there are a few companies that are successful in terms of earnings, growing shareholder value, meeting basic internal goals and performing well compared to competitors, many are not.[1] On these basic measurements alone many boards and, therefore chairmen, rate as unsatisfactory. Our research indicates that their main problems can be divided usefully into three categories: (a) visible problems in regard to poor management of the board, (b) underlying problems related to a lack of understanding and ability to perform the job, and (c) basic problems stemming from personal weaknesses and lack of leadership ability.

The most obvious surface problems are as follows:

Unproductive meetings

Although board business is increasingly being conducted in committees, the regular, full board meeting with personal attendance is still the principal arena for discussing and voting on board decisions. It is in these meetings that the sins of commission and omission that lead to poor performance are made or ratified. Some of the most obvious problems of poor meetings are:

- Poor agendas. Too much time is allocated to routine, unimportant items and too little to important items.
- Much reporting and repetition of material that has been sent out in advance and has been carefully studied by all conscientious directors.
- Too much disorganized and undigested information.
- Focusing on issues when they have developed so far that positions have jelled, decisions have been made and it is too late to benefit from penetrating, helpful questioning and counsel.
- Meetings that turn into management discussions of operating problems.
- Meetings that are too long or too short. Ordinarily a good average length of time is about three or four hours. Much less means too much haste or superficiality; much more means that they are poorly organized and deteriorate into management discussions.
- Closing off discussion and debate prematurely and cutting off dissenting analysis. Many major debacles could have been avoided if chairmen really heard and took seriously the concerns and polite opposition of directors.
- Process without substance: carrying on with set administrative routines that preclude productive dialogue on more important problems; ritual that avoids substantive issues.
- Too many meetings or too few.

Inadequate board management

Many chairmen let boards muddle along without definition of their role, standards of effectiveness, measurement and appraisal of performance, feedback and positive or negative reinforcement of effective and ineffective participation.

Many chairmen do not take positive initiatives to break the "old board" syndrome and make progress to implementing the "new board" culture. Some chairmen do such a poor job of communicating and interacting with directors individually and collectively that meetings are almost a get-together of strangers who understandably almost never work effectively as a team.

Failure to upgrade and develop the board

Many chairmen, especially those who purposely manage the board by the old style, live with a low quality board without making a plan and taking the action to improve it. In these boards it is assumed that the *status quo* should be continued, the only turnover is by retirement and no one would dare change some of the outdated traditions. As a result, the chairman lives with low quality directors who are noncontributors and who bring the whole board down to their level. Some chairmen, who are notorious for removing anyone who thinks independently, silence or push out any really competent members they may have, and find their boards loaded with directors who are impotent, poorly motivated, incompetent, or unprofessional.

Unwillingness to encourage full contribution from the board

Perhaps as a result of bad attitudes, insecurity, and suspicions, some chairmen neither want nor get full value from directors. Some do not listen to the message that directors are trying to give. Lack of sensitivity in human relationships very quickly turns off a board because directors are not going to force their way in where their counsel is not really wanted. Some chairmen do not adequately challenge the board, perhaps because they think that would be asking too much; some are too proud to admit that they have problems, and consequently cannot relax, admit they are human, and accept help. Hubris, an attitude of complacency, and lack of tough-mindedness often makes it difficult to face unpleasant realities that need to be addressed. The result is that some chairmen deliberately ensure that the board is much less than the sum of its parts.

Underlying problems

Some of the underlying problems are a lack of understanding of the job of the board and hence the chairman, lack of widely-accepted standards of performance, defense of the ''old style'' board culture, unwillingness or inability to change the *status quo*, lack of pressure to improve and upgrade boards, lack of concern and clarity of the effect of boards on company performance, lack of public focus on boards and their accountability for results, and passive acceptance of unsatisfactory and mediocre performance of boards by all involved.

Basic problems

Basic problems, the deepest and most difficult, cause of the poor performance of some chairmen, include personal weaknesses that prevent them from being more effective. Those weaknesses most commonly reported in the business press include negative attitudes to boards, greed, hunger for power, insecurity, lack of integrity, stubbornness, complacency, risk aversion, bad judgment, lack of vitality, excessive self-interest, bureaucratic behaviour, isolation, unethical or immoral behaviour, inability to foster positive relationships and, in some cases, deep-seated neuroses. Unfortunately, some chairmen have serious character flaws, lack ability as leaders, have no vision or mission and are unable to recruit, develop, and coach a strong team of able managers. When such character defects are combined with virtually unlimited power, it is hardly surprising that crises of leadership failure are commonplace.

HOW CHAIRMEN CAN BE MORE EFFECTIVE

If board effectiveness and company performance are to be improved, chairmen must take the initiative to lead the process. Here is what chairmen need to do:

Change Their Attitudes To Their Boards

The chairman's attitude to the board is the most fundamental determinant of board quality and effectiveness. While some chairmen view their board positively as an asset, others view it negatively as a liability: herein lies the critical difference. Chairmen who see their boards as an asset typically work to enhance and utilize that asset. Chairmen who see their boards as a necessary evil, potential nuisance and/or threat, circumscribe their board, do the least necessary for it and use it as little as possible.

Logically, it seems odd that most boards could be seen as anything other than an asset. A typical board consists of 12 to 15 widely-experienced individuals, most of whom are not employees, who bring judgment and a variety of skills to the company and who generally are drastically underpaid by the standards of their other activities, especially in light of their potential liability as directors. Harnessing the talent of such a group can be of immeasurable service to the company. Many CEOs, however, identify more with management than shareholders and are nervous about, and suspicious of, their boards. They see outside directors as amateurs, meddling in management's rightful jurisdiction. They see the work involved in preparing for and reporting to the board as a bother and distraction from their more important tasks. The directors may have some peripheral value in generating business or providing a public profile, these CEOs believe, but generally directors should be seen and not heard. They are viewed with the suspicion of an opposition party that could reduce the power and freedom of the chairman. Many, if not most, of the other obvious and underlying problems of poor chairmen follow directly from this unfortunate mindset.

Develop A More Effective Board

Managing the board, like managing anything else, involves setting goals for performance and improvement, developing and implementing plans, and following up. The chairman's job as manager requires:

- Determining what sort of board the chairman wants to have and identifying the gaps between the existing and desired boards.
- Developing a plan to get from point A (what we have now) to point B (where we want to be). Implementing the steps necessary to make the plan work.
- Correcting the plan, as necessary, in the light of later experience.

There are a number of examples of effective chairmen and boards; they follow the pattern of the "new-style" board and are open, constructive, and challenging. Directors walk out of good meetings feeling renewed and invigorated, having learned something and having made a contribution to something important.

Through careful planning and execution chairmen can achieve this kind of board, no matter what they have inherited. The first and most basic step is to define the profile of the "ideal" board: how big a group, what mix of contributions and qualifications, expertise, experience, age, location, nationality, race, and gender. Diversity is normally a strength; a board made up entirely of businessmen from one part of the country may not provide all the points of view desired.

Then, by contrast, the chairman can identify the profile of the existing board. The difference between the ''ideal'' and existing profiles helps to define the characteristics of new appointees to the board. A simple time chart indicating normal retirement ages for individual board members provides a rough timetable for either downsizing the board or making new appointments. If the normal pace is too slow, other steps will have to be contemplated. Over time, piece by piece, the new and better-qualified board can be put in place.

BOARD PERFORMANCE SHOULD BE MEASURED REGULARLY

Since the job is to manage the board so that it performs its role more effectively, the chairman needs to define (a) what the board's role is; (b) how to measure its effectiveness; and (c) how to reward effective (and discipline ineffective) performance. What is needed is a standard, a measure of performance against the standard and a program of action to follow up.

Because directors are normally given only a minimal legal description of their duties and responsibilities, the performance standard that results is often minimal, ill-defined, vague, and legalistic. Measurement without a well-defined standard is very difficult, if not impossible. Consequently, for most boards, virtually no appraisal is made of overall performance, and only very obvious measures are applied to individual directors: Did they attend meetings? Did they make fools of themselves? Did they antagonize other board members? Without any serious and systematic attempt to measure and critique board contribution, it is scarcely surprising that, except for gross misconduct or nonattendance, directors tend to have a form of tenure in their positions; turnover is very low.

This cycle tends to become demoralizing and debilitating. Otherwise-good directors either quit in frustration, or fall in with the sloppy but comfortable norms of the board, make a minimal contribution, and accept their director's fees and perks. The chairman must break this vicious circle. Developing a position description and performance standard, preferably with active board or committee participation, is a good first step. From there, it is possible to proceed to some form of performance evaluation, whether formal or informal, leading to action in the form of retention of the individual on the board or not, as the case may be.

Review of an individual's performance needs to be done regularly and informally. The best chairmen we know have an annual get-together, usually at lunch and always one-on-one, with each director. Discussion can be quite unstructured and two-way in its evaluations — the chairman can be as much under examination as the director. Often, small but important improvements can emerge from such discussion. Obviously the discussion must be frank and constructive.

Developing standards and measuring performance are of little use if they are not followed up by action. Dealing with the consistently nonperforming director is one of the most difficult issues faced by a chairman. Because it may involve personal friendships, strong past contributions or high public profile, chairmen often simply do not face the issue and carry the nonperformer. This can seriously erode — or indeed destroy — the very thing the chairman is trying to achieve.

CHANGING THE CULTURE

Changing the culture of a board often means that the chairman needs to raise the degree of creative tension in board operations. This means leading by example to encourage a psychological climate that is stable and supportive but relentlessly demanding of continuous upgrading and improvement of all aspects of board functions. Tuning up awareness and concern must be constructively managed and focused on positive ideas and results, as in athletic coaching at high performance levels. A most important requirement is that chairmen must improve in disaster avoidance. Boards must avoid major blunders, such as not understanding the problems of changing markets, letting the design — strategy, organization, systems, and operations — of a company become outdated and noncompetitive, organizational calcification, leadership failure,[2] gambling the company on excessive risks and disastrous diversifications and acquisitions. The billion-dollar screwup syndrome with its huge losses for shareholders must be eliminated.

THE CHAIRMAN MUST BE A LEADER

It should be clear from all of the above that competent chairmen must also be leaders. Their position of being first among equals on their boards requires that they set the tone and pace for the entire organization. To perform satisfactorily in this role, the chairman must develop an inspiring but credible, and overarching but practical, vision for the organization and demonstrate the ability to help managers to become and accomplish more than they could on their own. The essence of this challenge is to work on the mission and culture to make the whole more than the sum of its parts. Because of the great power and influence of the position, the related risk for any chairman is that through lack of knowledge, skills and proper attitudes, he or she behaves in a way that results in performance falling far short of its potential.

CHAIRMEN NEED TO GET TOUGHER WITH THEIR CEOs

Chairmen need to be much more professional in their dealings with CEOs, an obviously impossible undertaking when the two jobs are combined. This improvement is especially needed in two critical areas. First, chairmen should be much more forceful in negotiating an explicit performance contract with their CEOs. This contract should be based on a realistic and mutually acceptable agreement, reviewed and ratified with the board, perhaps through the human resource committee, covering performance expectations and requirements. Job compensation and tenure should, of course, be tied to CEO job performance measured against this agreement. Many CEOs have been left on the job years after they should have been replaced because this kind of performance requirement has not been enforced. Second, chairmen need to take the lead in ensuring that CEO compensation is reasonable, relating it to job performance, profitability, and increase in shareholder wealth, rather than company size and CEO tenure. Only the chairman can take leadership in correcting these problems.

SHOULD THE CHAIRMAN BE CEO?

By now, our position on the issue of whether the positions of chairman and CEO should be combined (unitary leadership) or separated (dual leadership) should be clear. This has been a long-standing major issue, with strong arguments advanced on either side. Those advocating the separation of the jobs argue that in any major company the chairman's job requires full-time dedication, that there is a need for checks and balances between the two roles (if the chairman is also the CEO he is in effect "grading his own exam papers"), that there is a danger of the chairman/CEO dominating to the point of being authoritarian and dictatorial, that the self-interest of management needs to be better controlled, and that two heads are better than one.

Those favouring the combination of the jobs argue that this pattern has been the *status quo* for a long time, currently in three out of four North American companies, and if there were any competitive or survival advantage in dual leadership more companies would voluntarily adopt this arrangement. They also argue that implementing dual leadership has no significant effect on shareholder value; the costs of separation are larger than the benefits for most firms; the conflicts between management and the shareholders are less than commonly believed; there is a loss of incentive for advancement to new CEOs; leadership power is diluted; duality slows and complicates management; political problems arise from conflict between the two positions; it is more difficult to pinpoint the blame for poor leadership; and there is the extra cost of compensation for a separate chairman. In addition many firms use the sequence of positions of COO, president, CEO and chairman in a carefully planned ''passing-of-the-baton'' succession process.[3] Any or all of these arguments may or may not hold in any specific case.

Our position is that with today's business conditions and problems there is an increasingly obvious, fundamental conflict of interest between the chairman and the CEO that the remaining members of a board will, for many reasons, often be unable or unwilling to police and arbitrate. The crucial difference between the two jobs is that the responsibility of the CEO is for the general management of the company and that of the chairman is for management of the trusteeship function of the board. Consequently, the two jobs have very different power, authority, responsibilities, purposes, activities, and time demands. With the board acting as an agent for the shareholders in hiring, directing, evaluating, and compensating management, there is unavoidable conflict of interest and tension between the mandate of the chairman and that of the CEO. With the expanding activities of the board; growing pressures from shareholders, the courts and lawmakers; and increasingly competitive business conditions, the board's (and hence the chairman's) job has been expanding exponentially. Today in any sizeable public company the chairman's role is almost certainly shortchanged unless it is virtually a full-time job. Lacking this kind of necessary dedication, many boards have defaulted on the task of providing checks and balances to control management and curb serious wrongs, including mismanagement, loss of shareholder wealth, erosion of competitive position, and excessive compensation. A valid exception to this general conclusion is, of course, when the company is in a crisis that calls for unitary command, as in the case of Chrysler in its turnaround from failure under the leadership of Lee Iacocca.

When an incumbent has both titles, self-interest, operating pressures, and time limitations all dictate that the CEO job gets top priority; almost inevitably the chairman's role receives short shrift. The pressures on a CEO for performance and the continuous, grinding pressures of the CEO's job mean that the chairmanship functions get pushed aside, to be performed when necessary, but not in a fully dedicated, creative and planned sense. When the chairman's job is consciously or unconsciously subsumed, the critical accountability of the CEO to the chairman and the board is seriously reduced, if not eliminated. Whatever may have been the case in earlier and easier times, the job of chairman of any sizeable public company today is not one that should be combined with and superseded by that of CEO. For the board system to work as intended, the CEO should report to the chairman and board, not vice-versa.

We fully recognize the difficulties that can be created when the positions are split. Two individuals — each a power centre, each with strong personal views and accustomed to being in control — are asked to share power. Conflict often results, but then, in many cases perhaps it should. The relationship issue is never easy, and with the jobs split, there is more potential for high visibility conflict and disagreement, something that most companies seek to avoid, often to a fault. On balance, however, we are convinced that, for most large, publicly-held companies, the case for splitting the jobs is persuasive. No doubt this suggestion will be controversial, especially among present chairmen and CEOs, many if not most of whom have a vested interest in the *status quo*. But otherwise, we see little hope for substantive improvement in the performance of many corporate boards, which, without clear focus of responsibility, will remain the weakest link in the chain of corporate governance.

NOTES

This chapter is based on our article ''Improving Board Effectiveness: The Problem and Solution Begin with the Chairman'', *Business Quarterly* (Summer, 1992).

1. See, for example ''Shareholder Scoreboard'', *The Wall Street Journal*, February 29, 1996, Section 12.

2. Benson P. Shapiro, Adrian J. Slywotsky and Richard S. Tedlow, ''Why Bad Things Happen to Good Companies,'' *Strategy & Business*, Second Quarter 1996, Booz-Allen & Hamilton, p. 16.

3. James A. Brickley, Jeffrey L. Coles and Gregg Jarrell, ''Corporate Leadership Structure: On the Separation of CEO and Chairman of the Board,'' November 29, 1994, (unpublished draft paper, William E. Simon Graduate School of Business, University of Rochester, Rochester, N.Y).

Chapter 10

BUILDING LEGITIMACY AND POWER

"Management has power. Indeed, to do its job, it has to have power. But power does not last, regardless of its performance, its knowledge, and its good intention, unless it be grounded in some sanction outside and beyond itself, some 'grounds of legitimacy'."
(Peter Drucker)[1]

"Power tends to corrupt; absolute power corrupts absolutely."
(Lord Acton, 1887)[2]

Governance is all about power and authority, its distribution and use within the governing system. Legally, the ultimate source of power is ownership, and for a business corporation ownership rests with the shareholders. The corporation is the property of the shareholders, and it is their right, within legal and social limits, to run the corporation as they wish. They delegate some, but not all, of that power to a board of directors, retaining the right to elect directors, appoint auditors, and to approve other major actions, such as the sale of the company or major parts of it. In return they require regular accounting from the board on the exercise of the power that has been delegated to it. The board is supposed to be the agent of the owners. The board, in turn, delegates the power to manage operations to management, retaining a number of powers to itself, such as declaring a dividend, approving major decisions, and appointing officers. Management must give the board a periodic accounting on its exercise of the delegated power. So goes the theory: legal power to decide and act is delegated down the line, accountability flows back up. The system, to work, requires a balance of power; it is based on checks and balances.

Building and maintaining legitimacy in the use of power requires an understanding of the source and scope of authority. Legitimate power is derived from the delegation from and consent of those with ultimate authority: in a democracy, the voters; in a corporation, the owners. Illegitimate use of power never lasts, unless imposed by force. Much of the growing criticism of corporate boards in this century stems from their lack of legitimacy and power. Legitimacy means the possession of real, genuine power to act, and authority from the owners to continue to use that power. In the board system, as in all other institutions of a pluralistic democracy, legitimacy and power are inseparably linked: strength in one supports the other, and weakness in one diminishes the other. Without the support of the owners, the board that attempts to exercise power is building on a foundation of sand.

These issues were apparent in the cases of two contrasting companies: one, a widely-held bank; the other, a large manufacturing company.

THE MAGNUM BANK

The Magnum Bank was well known in financial circles for its large, prestigious board numbering 29 members. Although many of their names were unknown to the general public, the directors were carefully chosen by the Chairman and CEO from the elite inner circles of business and society, primarily in terms of their compatibility with the incumbent members of the board, expected support of the management, and ability to bring business to the bank. With a prodigious work load of routine loan approvals, the board relied on a hard-working, five-man executive committee, three insiders and two outsiders, that met weekly to get through all the work of formally reviewing and approving credit decisions processed at the customer contact levels of the organization. The full board compliantly rubber-stamped the executive committee's decisions at its poorly-attended monthly meetings. Several of the directors had never spoken in any meeting, other than seconding the occasional routine motion. One of the leading directors had half-jokingly confided in a friend that three of the directors were not qualified to be hired to handle even an entry-level job in the bank.

For many years, the bank's performance had been mediocre; it was periodically criticized by investment analysts for major loan losses and problems that had been largely avoided by competitors. In light of the relatively meager wages paid by the bank, and two large layoffs in a downsizing program, the seven-figure compensation package of the three top-ranked managers had been widely criticized in the media, and morale was low. The chairman/CEO, little respected either inside or outside the bank, was widely regarded as arrogant and authoritarian. Well-known for his opinion that it was difficult, if not impossible, to find candidates who were adequately qualified to be directors of the bank, he viewed his board as a burden with which he had to live. Reflecting on the progressive changes made by the chairman of a competitive bank to involve and empower his board, the chairman was reported to have said, "He's going to create a Frankenstein monster, and he'll regret it".

* * * * *

THE CHEMCO CORPORATION

When the directors of the Chemco Corporation gathered for a regular meeting in New York, they little suspected that it was to be a watershed event in the history of the company. Normally based in Toronto, this was the first time that they had met outside the company headquarters. James Bryson, the company's high-profile chairman and CEO had suggested the change in venue so that the directors could meet with the leaders of the company's largest shareholder, the Brooks Fund, a large, long-established, and highly successful investment fund which held close to 30 percent of Chemco's shares.

Several of the directors came early, and arranged an informal dinner two days prior to the meeting. During the course of the dinner, Daniel Durgin, a long-time, highly respected director of Chemco, commented that he was thinking of stepping off the board. Pressed to give his reasons, he said for some time he had been getting increasingly uncomfortable at the way things were going, and particularly with the way Bryson was running the board. He mentioned a recent compensation meeting where Bryson had "bullied" the committee, and berated the Brooks Fund's highly-respected CEO, who was a member of the committee. He felt that Bryson had for some time been acting in an irrational and domineering manner, not listening to other board members and pushing his own strategic plan, against the majority of the board. "He's become a megalomaniac. I'm getting close to retirement, and life's too short to have to put up with that kind of nonsense", he said.

Durgin's remarks triggered a lengthy discussion and opened a floodgate of comments and criticisms of Bryson and his behaviour. "I had no idea you felt that way," said one board member. "I've been feeling much the same, but I thought that because the company was doing pretty well and nobody said anything at the board meetings, I must be the odd man out." Others echoed his sentiment, and the group realized that they had all been harboring similar reservations about Bryson, but had never had any opportunity to meet without him present. The company had been doing reasonably well financially, at least on the surface. The two Brooks representatives on the board had never indicated displeasure. As the dinner broke up, the group asked Durgin to approach the Brooks people, indicate their unhappiness, and sound out Brooks as to their position.

The next day Durgin made an appointment to see Brooks' CEO and described what had happened at dinner. The CEO clapped his hand to his forehead, and replied: "This is amazing! We've been assuming all along that you folks were happy with Bryson. We've been fed up for some time, but we weren't about to do battle with the rest of the board, whom we respect. This is serious stuff. We've got to do something about it." After further discussion, it was agreed that Durgin and Brooks' CEO would have a private meeting with Bryson before the board meeting the following day and ask for his resignation.

At the beginning of the board meeting, Bryson announced from the chair that he was resigning effective immediately, and left the room. The board spent considerable time discussing the sudden turn of events, including severance arrangements, plans to replace Bryson, and other matters related to the changing of the guard. In the course of the discussion, it emerged that, unknown and unreported to the board, Bryson's brother had once bought shares in a company that was the target of a Chemco takeover, and had profited handsomely from the deal. Bryson had also ordered staff to manipulate elements of the company's stock option plan to his personal benefit. He had gathered power to himself by carefully controlling the board and the information it received. It appeared that Bryson's firing came as a considerable relief to the staff, who had put up with his domineering tactics in silence for several years. As the stories piled up, one board member commented: "This is astounding. How could we have been so misled over all this time? If we'd never had that dinner Bryson would still be running the company!"

* * * * *

These cases provide vivid insights into issues of legitimacy and power in governance. For power to be legitimate and effective, it must satisfy several accepted standards.

1. LEGAL AUTHORITY

Is the company operating within the laws that govern it? Does it meet the requirements for reporting to shareholders, for meeting with shareholders at least annually, for election of directors, and for appointment of independent auditors? Most corporations acts require these essential steps as a means of providing a minimum degree of legitimacy for business decisions. They are intended to provide a framework for corporate democracy, but in practice often result in more form than substance and a cynical attitude towards their use. Operating *legally* and operating *legitimately* are not the same thing. From the viewpoints of all the corporate stakeholders involved, legitimacy usually demands a much higher standard of behavior than simply not being illegal.

In any democracy, there is a major concern that people in positions of power be elected and/or appointed by a process based on openly-conducted tests of merit and capability. Until directors are evaluated and elected by a process that is more open, less under the control of incumbent management, subject to review and improvement, fair and in the public interest, the mandate and authority of directors will fail to have widespread support; directors will serve at public sufferance but without willing and active endorsement.

2. ACCOUNTABILITY TO SHAREHOLDERS

The board system rests on the premise that the directors and through them, management, are accountable for serving as agents of the owners of the business. In the case of the Magnum Bank, the board was largely impotent, and the company was being run by the chairman/CEO and the executive committee; continuing mediocre performance and poor morale had so far failed to trigger action from the widely-dispersed shareholders. At Chemco, the chairman/CEO had cleverly played the game of ''divide and rule'' with the board, keeping information from directors and carefully controlling their agenda. In neither case was the board fulfilling its role as steward of the shareholders' interest, at least until late in the game in Chemco.

3. PERFORMANCE FOR STAKEHOLDERS

Ultimately, the private enterprise system depends on the acceptance and support of the general public, particularly the stakeholders of business — consumers, employees, customers, creditors, suppliers, communities, and governments. They look to the business system for effective, efficient, and honest performance in serving their needs, and when this is lacking the scene is ripe for political action demanding increased government surveillance and regulation. The continuing unsatisfactory performance of Magnum, coupled with the problems of low morale and public criticism of excessive executive compensation, all suggest that trouble is ahead for management. Aggrieved stakeholders eventually reach their limits of tolerance for those who are contemptuous of or threaten their interests.

4. MORALITY AND ETHICS

Dishonest and/or questionable behaviour by the major players in both these cases is clearly offensive to public standards of morality and accepted ideas of what is right and wrong. Public exposure of such behaviour creates a cynical attitude towards business generally, and a climate that favors steps to circumscribe the use of corporate power.

If indeed we are "to restore an independent and strong board of directors", as Drucker has advocated,[3] we must restore its legitimacy and power. While leadership is a make-or-break factor in board effectiveness, it is highly dependent on the degree of power granted by, earned from, or taken from the shareholders: without recognized legitimacy, leadership is, sooner or later, impotent. Taking steps to upgrade the power and effectiveness of a board of directors must be built on a base of knowledge and approval from the shareholders.

Legitimacy is political support from the major sources of power, usually large shareholders. It comes from being perceived as doing what is best for the shareholders (optimizing shareholder value), and other stakeholders, and conforming to laws, agreed principles, and accepted standards of the majority of owners.

Power, on the other hand, is the control of resources and the capacity for decision and action to cause or prevent action through the control of others. It is the necessary ingredient in managing a business; without it, management cannot function. The governance system is designed to see that management exercises its power legitimately in the interests of the owners, and the board is the key agent of the shareholders in making that happen.

There are two major reasons why corporate boards have failed the test of legitimacy:

1. Shareholders have abdicated their rights and responsibilities as owners;

2. Management, or in some cases a major shareholder, has moved into the void, and taken control of the governance process.

SHAREHOLDERS HAVE ABDICATED THEIR OWNERSHIP ROLE

Shareholders are the foundation of the governance system; for it to work, they must act as owners, informing themselves about the company, exercising their right of ownership by monitoring and calling those to whom they have delegated authority to account for the stewardship of assets under their control, and by acting to withdraw that power from individuals and groups when they are displeased with their actions and/or results.

Over 60 years ago, Berle and Means[4] drew public attention to the fact that shareholders were not, in fact, acting as owners. The development of markets for the transfer of shares had made it easier for many investors, especially small investors, to "vote with their feet" rather than attempt to exert their will through the governance system.

The continuing evolution of markets for shares has unquestionably enhanced the ease with which investors can acquire or dispose of their holdings. When much of the framework of corporate legislation was put into effect it was built on the concept of shareholder democracy. At that time the world was a much different place. Stock markets were rudimentary; ownership of shares and trading was done by a relative few, mostly individuals; communication was difficult and modern management methods and institutions had not yet evolved. Legislators and lawyers could scarcely have foreseen the development of today's sophisticated markets, their global reach, and computerized trading, much less the elaborate infrastructure and incredible resources of the financial institutions using the system.

The mobility of investment in this system is remarkable, even for the small, individual investor. Today, he or she can buy or sell shares almost instantaneously as part of the much-touted "information highway". Why bother to invest the effort, expense and time to evaluate the job being done by management or the adequacy of the board when with a phone call, fax or personal computer that individual can switch his or her investment to another company that seems to be doing better? Especially when he or she is being exhorted to do so by an investment adviser/salesperson, who incidentally happens to earn a commission on every trade? Better still, why not put all of his or her investments in a mutual fund, where a presumably knowledgeable investment manager, for a fee, will relieve the individual of all the work and decision making?

The net result of such pressures is to create an investor completely disconnected from the process of corporate governance, who is interested in short-term performance, and who generally cares not a whit about "shareholder democracy" in the companies whose shares he or she temporarily holds. The undoubted existence of a large body of such investors, and the mobility of the market that has helped create it, has seriously challenged the cornerstone of our corporate governance system.

> . . . Limiting owners' liability to the extent of their investments, combined with the development of liquid markets, has changed the essential character of shareholders. Having only a day-to-

> day interest in the value of a piece of paper, they have lost any long-term interest in the value of the company and now bear little resemblance to the owner so venerated by tradition and law.[5]

Fortunately, perhaps, a more recent development has given some hope for a restoration of the balance: the emergence of large institutional investors, particularly pension funds, as major owners of American business.

THE GROWTH OF INSTITUTIONAL INVESTORS

In 1976, Peter Drucker began his book, *The Unseen Revolution*, with the following observation:

> If socialism is defined as ownership of the means of production by the workers — and this is both the orthodox and the only rigorous definition — then the United States is the first truly socialist country.
>
> Through their pension funds, employees of American business today own at least 25 percent of its equity capital, which is more than enough for control. The pension funds of the self-employed, of the public employees, and of the school and college teachers own at least another 10 percent, giving the workers of America ownership of more than one-third of the equity capital of American business. Within another 10 years the pension funds will inevitably increase their holdings, and by 1985 (probably sooner) they will own at least 50 percent — if not 60 percent — of equity capital. Ten years later, or well before the turn of the century their holdings should exceed around two-thirds of the equity capital . . . plus a major portion — perhaps 40 percent — of the debt capital (bonds, debentures and notes) of the American economy. Inflation can only speed up this process.[6]

Twenty years after it was chronicled by Drucker, the unseen revolution has arrived with a vengeance, both in Canada and in the United States. This ''revolution'' has transformed the business world, because the pension funds have become, willingly or not, long-term investors. Yet the increase in the ownership of North America's public companies by pension funds has not yet been mirrored by a similar growth in the power to influence their investments, nor has it yet been balanced by an appropriate voice in corporate governance.

Institutional shareholder ownership has been likened to property without rights, because institutions like pension funds face many impediments that inhibit their ability to exert control over their investments. They manage other people's money, and consequently hold a fiduciary duty under law to protect their beneficiaries' investments. In the case of mutual funds and many money managers, this may lead to relatively short-term equity investing in an attempt to "beat the market". Pension fund shareholdings, however, are so large that they cannot readily move in and out of the market, and have indeed become the market, forcing them to resort to indexing or other strategies that have made them, for all practical purposes, captive, long-term investors. Because their membership is so dispersed, this has left many of the responsibilities of ownership in the hands of the pension fund managers.

Pension fund managers have generally been reluctant to take an activist position with respect to the governance of the companies whose shares they hold. Many have lacked the background or training, and felt incompetent to judge the management of large corporations. The time requirements and administrative costs involved in managing substantial investments have further discouraged taking an activist stance. But the tremendous growth in the size and power of pension funds has meant that they have had little option but to exercise that power responsibly, and become involved in issues of governance. Today, we increasingly see pension fund managers not only voting their shares independently, but some are taking seats on the boards of investee companies.

Some commentators have seen the growth of pension fund power as the hope of the future for restoring accountability to corporate governance. A relatively few well-financed and well-informed long-term investors, taking an activist role in voting their shares, are seen as the potential vehicle for transforming and revitalizing the board system, and restoring balance to the relationship between the owners and the managers of business. On the other hand, if institutional investors lack the resources, organization, ability and will to play an active role in corporate governance, their influence will be muted and ignored.

THE MECHANICS OF GOVERNANCE

Throughout the history of the modern corporation, the mechanisms of corporate democracy — the annual meeting of shareholders, the voting/proxy process, the flow of information to shareholders — have been heavily weighted on the side of corporate management, not the owners. Denied simple access to the process of director election, and seeing the difficulties involved in changing that process, many stockholders have resigned themselves to nonparticipation and abdicated their rights and responsibilities as owners. Reform of the system depends on their preparedness to exercise their ownership rights. Over time, and in response to widespread abuses, regulators have liberalized the system so as to partially rectify the balance. But the pace of reform has lagged behind the needs of the system.

In their important book *Power and Accountability*,[7] Monks and Minow describe the complex process by which proxies are solicited by companies and voted by shareholders. They conclude that the system is ''great for making it easy to buy and sell stock, but (makes) it even harder to exercise the other rights of share ownership, and by doing so, created something of a vacuum.'' In fact, concern over management control over the proxy process led the U.S. Securities and Exchange Commission in the early 1990s to institute a number of reforms designed to make it easier for shareholders to communicate with each other and mount concerted cooperative action. These moves may be followed by similar actions in Canadian jurisdictions.

Annual meetings — a basic element in the concept of shareholder democracy — remain a bad joke. Mandated by corporate law, these meetings are regarded by many chairmen as a necessary evil. Armed with military-drill like preparations, a majority of proxies, with pre-arranged movers and seconders for all their desired motions, and with control of the microphones, chairmen compete to see how quickly the meeting can be steered through the necessary reports and resolutions. Genuine discussion of issues is discouraged. Shareholders are often treated with scarcely concealed disdain. Depending on the company's most recent results, the meeting may then be turned into a public relations exercise, with sound and light shows and even a meal thrown in.

A third key element in shareholder democracy — the provision of relevant and timely information in a form that can be readily handled and understood by busy shareholders — gets at best a mixed report. Recent years have seen a rapid increase in the flow of mandated disclosures to shareholders; financial reporting is increasingly on a quarterly basis, annual reports are more comprehensive, detailed and informative; and annual information forms, proxy solicitation statements, and Securities Commission filings are generally available. With the initiation of corporate web stations on the Internet, this rapid flow of information promises to become a flood. There is often so much information, a great deal of it irrelevant to the committed shareholder, that he or she has neither the time nor the inclination to dig in and do the necessary homework. At the same time, information highly relevant to doing the shareholder's principal task — evaluating the work of the board, and of individual directors, in carrying out their mandate to represent the owners' interest — is sketchy at best. Data on executive compensation, for example, has only recently become available in useful and complete form in Canada.

Into the breach have come the analysts, employees of the investment houses who make their money by underwriting and selling shares. The analysts are paid to sort through all this data, analyze the strength of management, assess their performance, and make recommendations to shareholders or potential shareholders as to whether to buy, sell, or hold shares. Unfortunately, to the extent that most analysts work for the seller of the stock, their independence and objectivity are suspect.

Action to redress many of these weaknesses in the system is being pursued vigorously by a growing number of groups representing shareholders, and by some of the larger public pension fund managers. Improvement in shareholder relations can and should come primarily from within — from enlightened chairmen, directors, and managers who understand the importance of restoring the essential link between the owners of the business and those who manage it. But such a perspective by management is far from being universal, and there is still the need for progressive and timely regulation, much of it the responsibility of securities commissions.

MANAGEMENT CONTROL OF THE BOARD

In addition to controlling much of the process by which shareholders acquire their information, make their judgments, and are supposed to hold directors accountable, management of many public companies has also taken control of the internal processes by which directors are selected and boards do their work.

As we saw in the last chapter, the widespread practice of combining the jobs of chief executive officer and chairman effectively vests the responsibility for running the board in the person who is supposed to be accountable to the board for company performance, an undeniable conflict in which the chairman is expected to pass judgment on how good a job he has done as CEO. This organizational arrangement appears to have grown out of the philosophy of "corporate capitalism" espoused by many company leaders half a century ago, and continues despite the obvious illogic and growing criticism by most business commentators. It certainly represents a denial of the basic concept of corporate governance represented in most corporate law.

The chairman/CEO combination clearly gives management the opportunity to run the corporation for its own benefit, and not necessarily for the benefit of shareholders. Control over the entire board process — the size and composition of the board, the information provided, the conduct of board meetings — falls largely under the company's senior manager, who also controls the strategic agenda. Power is not balanced, it is focused on one person. In extreme emergency, when the company's back is to the wall and its very existence is at stake, there may be some justification for such a concentration of power. But such an arrangement in normal times invites abuse.

The wave of mergers and takeovers that characterized much of the 1980s forced boards and management to face their own fallibility. The prospect of losing their jobs to raiders and takeover artists led many managements to erect a host of barriers designed primarily to preserve their autonomy. New and catchy terms — golden handshakes, parachutes, poison pills, shark repellents, white knights — became part of the everyday jargon of business. Shareholder democracy was usually the loser.

In Canada the existence of restricted shares poses a similar barrier. Some 15 percent of the shares listed on the Toronto Stock Exchange have either limited or no voting rights attached to them:[8] the owners provide equity, but forego some degree of voting privilege. Designed mainly to allow voting control to remain in limited hands, restricted shares have been used as method of broadening the ability of companies to raise capital. As a result of several widely-publicized abuses of minority shareholders, regulators have required so-called "coattail" provisions to protect the equity interest of holders of restricted shares.

By and large, shareholder groups and many institutions have expressed strong opposition to devices such as poison pills, and in some cases have counseled investors to avoid companies which use them. Boards have attempted to justify their use, arguing that they discourage "creeping takeovers", force bids into the open, and provide directors and management with the time to evaluate them and seek other bidders. Although there is some validity to this argument, there is no doubt that these manoeuvers represent barriers to the exercise of shareholder democracy, and can as easily be used to protect irresponsible boards and management as to preserve shareholder interests.

RESTORING LEGITIMACY AND POWER TO THE BOARD

The failure of corporate governance in North America has been, at root, a failure of shareholder democracy and the failure of directors to live up to passable standards of competence, responsibility, morality, and public service. Restoring legitimacy and power to the board of directors is a fundamental step in building an effective, competitive enterprise, able to compete with the best in the world. To regain their power boards must aggressively pursue their prerogatives and exert their authority. In the current board power structure and "don't-rock-the-boat culture," this will require much drive and determination.

Shareholder democracy must be understood in the context of the *accountability framework* for directors and boards. In any open political system, having authority and responsibility demands accountability. However, accountability is meaningless without good answers to fundamental questions: Accountability to whom? For reporting on what? With what rewards, punishments and sanctions attached to judgments of what is reported? Nowhere in the governance literature have these questions been satisfactorily addressed. Not surprisingly we lack clear, practical and widely-accepted answers. In reality directors are not directly and explicitly accountable to anyone. Indirectly and implicitly they are accountable to (a) the chairman or controlling shareholder who led in their appointment and can influence their status and retirement and (b) to each other for their contribution and behaviour. As a result, the requirement of accountability raises all-important, unavoidable, disconcerting and as-yet unanswered issues that merit much more careful consideration and analysis than they have so far been given by those concerned with governance.

The main hope for restoration of the balance is in the rise of large institutional investors, in for the long haul and conscious of their rights and responsibilities as owners. Institutional investors may well be the only source of power with enough clout to stiffen the backs of timid directors and leverage the drive of boards to regain their power over management. Already we are seeing this happen, with what appears to be, even at this early stage, positive results.

Some of the implications are clear. Corporate boards must establish lines of communication with the principal institutions, and regular reviews must be held on matters of corporate strategy, organization, and performance. There is, however, a difficult line to walk: privileged or advance information cannot be disclosed unless it is made available to all other shareholders at the same time. Otherwise the institution given privileged information becomes an insider unable to buy or sell the company's shares. Sheer magnitude of holdings should not give the institutional shareholder any special right or privilege. This makes for some tricky ethical issues for company directors who are representatives of large institutions: the rule is that, as directors, they are responsible to all shareholders of the company, and must act in the best interest of all shareholders, not just their institutional sponsors. Yet, at the same time, fund managers have a fiduciary responsibility to their members. Many pension fund managers do not want to be put in this position, and have opted to limit their interest in governance.

"Management needs to be made accountable to someone who has the power, the motive, the perspective, and the ability to represent the public interest effectively. We have in the pension fund system the necessary core of long-term shareholders. . . . Once there is agreement on the ultimate use of fund assets, appropriate institutional development will be forthcoming."[9]

Until directors individually and boards collectively are seen to live up to the tests of any important institution in an democratic society — not only fulfilling their legal obligations but serving constituents and the national interest, and demonstrating openness and accessibility — the board system will lack legitimacy, and as a result, power. Clearly, if the board system is to be renewed and empowered the most obvious first task of board leaders and members is to meet this challenge.

NOTES

1. Peter F. Drucker, *The Frontiers of Management* (New York: Harper & Row, 1986), pp. 251-52.

2. John Emerick Edward Dalberg, Lord Acton (1834-1902), *Letter to Bishop Mandell Creighton, 1887*. Certainly one of the most quoted sayings on the subject of power.

3. Drucker, *The Frontiers of Management*, p. 252.

4. Berle and Means, *op. cit.*

5. Robert A.G. Monks and Nell Minow, *Power and Accountability* (New York: Harper Collins, 1991), pp. 17-18.

6. Peter F. Drucker, *The Unseen Revolution* (New York: Harper & Row, 1976), pp. 1-2.

7. Monks and Minow, *op. cit* p. 29.

8. Brian Smith, Ben Amoako-Adu, and Jacques Schnabel, ''Characteristics and Trends of Restricted Shares Listed on the Toronto Stock Exchange,'' *Working Paper NC 89-10*, London, Ontario, The National Centre for Management Research and Development, 1989. Smith and Amoako-Adu have two other working papers (NC 89-24 and NC 89-25) outlining their extensive research on this topic.

9. Monks and Minow, *op. cit* p. 262.

Chapter 11

DEFINING THE DIRECTOR'S JOB

"I wonder what all these visiting geniuses are going to try to lay on us today?"
(Comment of one inside director to another as they got off an elevator on the way to a board meeting.)

PETER FRANCIS AND HIS BOARD

Peter Francis led the way as the foursome walked in to the men's grill and ordered refreshments. As he took his chair and stretched out, Peter addressed himself to the other three, all business friends:

"You know, until they made me CEO last year I had no idea how tough it is to run a major company like mine. Until you've done it, you can't really understand all the demands of the job. Your life changes completely. Instead of being part of a team and answering to someone else, you're now the end of the line. Everything ends up on your desk, and there aren't enough hours in the day to deal with it. Almost all your waking thoughts, and many of your subconscious concerns while you're asleep, are focused on the company. Even while I'm lining up a putt out there, I've got something else on my mind concerning the company.

That brings me to the board. I've worked most of my adult life for this company, and I know where it has come from, who the major players are, their strengths and their weaknesses. I know the competition, and where we have opportunities to beat them out. The board knew all that when they appointed me, and it was the reason why they picked me. I have proved many times that I can deliver.

For them to look over my shoulder and tell me how to do the job is ridiculous. They're all part-timers, they have other interests and different backgrounds. With respect, none of them know as much about this business as I do and if they did they should be the CEO, not me. They rely on me for much of their information about what's going on. They're good people on the whole, and I appreciate the vote of confidence, but it's simply laughable to think that they could run this show.

From where I sit, the board should butt out and let me do my job. I don't need a bunch of back-seat drivers. They fulfilled their responsibility when they selected me, and they can keep tabs on how I'm doing by looking at the bottom line. If they're unhappy about our performance, they can always fire me. But in the meantime, they should get out of my hair — or at least what there is left of it!"

* * * * *

What *is* the director's job? Is it, as Peter Francis says, "to butt out and let me do my job"? Is it to be more involved in running the company? Or is it something else?

The board's performance requirements and possibilities are contingent on several key factors that differ from company to company. The first factor is variations in board functions — boards vary widely in what they do and how they do it. The law emphasizes three points on board responsibilities: (a) the job is "to manage or supervise the management" of the company; (b) directors are required to "act honestly and in good faith with a view to the best interests of the corporation" and "exercise the care, diligence and skill that a reasonably prudent person would exercise in similar circumstances"; and (c) to fulfill their duty, directors should have sufficient information to enable them to make knowledgeable decisions on matters coming before the board, and should be generally familiar with all aspects of the business and affairs of the corporation.

THE BOARD HAS FIVE BASIC RESPONSIBILITIES

In any board that is adequately fulfilling its responsibilities, these general requirements are carried out through five basic tasks, which although they overlap and must be totally integrated, can be described as below.

1. The most important overall responsibility of any board is directing and supervising strategic management, the integrated planning and implementation of the major changes needed to improve corporate performance. The board should oversee a strategic action program that will take the company from where it is to where it should be in terms of profitability, growth and competitive strength. Supervision focuses on keeping management accountable for performance in defining purpose and strategy, organizing, implementing plans, meeting objectives, competing successfully and satisfying the requirements necessary to

merit the continuing support of shareholders and other non-owner stakeholders.

2. Appointing and overseeing the CEO and other officers. This task includes appointing, setting terms of employment, supervising, evaluating, compensating and, if necessary, removing all corporate officers, beginning with the CEO. It also involves approving major organizational changes, and ensuring that adequate plans are in place for management succession.

3. Representing shareholders and maintaining shareholder relations. These tasks include representing their interests in management and board councils; reporting to shareholders as legally required, and otherwise communicating to them directly or indirectly through the financial press, analysts, and others as to plans, decisions, prospects and results; and reflecting shareholder concerns to management.

4. Protecting and enhancing the company's assets. When major issues arise in management, ownership, investments, acquisitions, divestments, raids or insolvency, the board must be fully involved, in some cases even to the extent of taking over the decision-making role.

5. Fulfilling fiduciary and legal requirements. The board is responsible for adherence to the laws, payment of taxes, regulatory requirements, and the preparation and maintenance of necessary minutes, documents, contracts, and records.

COMPANY OWNERSHIP AFFECTS BOARD FUNCTIONS

In actual practice, the above five basic functions are performed (or not performed) to widely varying degrees, depending on the pattern of ownership (see Chapter 5).[1] Companies for which there is a single shareholder typically use boards in an advisory capacity, and the director's responsibility is largely what the shareholder says it is. In companies that have minority shareholders, both the law and increasingly accepted practice require directors to represent the interests of the minority as well as those of the controlling shareholders. In widely-held companies, with no clear control block, management may tend to predominate over shareholders' interests, and the directors must strive to keep the shareholders' point of view in clear focus. These roles can be conceived of as consulting (advisory) and trusteeship (fiduciary), and the mix of roles can be pictured as shown in Exhibit 11.1. Even in privately-owned corporations, where directors are appointed by the owner primarily for advice and/or business development reasons, directors retain some fiduciary responsibilities. In widely-held corporations, boards play a much greater trusteeship role, and their consulting responsibilities typically form a less important part of the mix of duties.

Exhibit 11.1

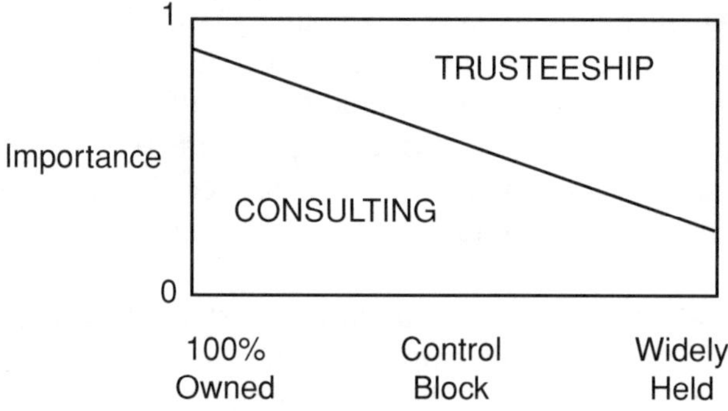

THE JOB OF THE BOARD

Given that the legal duty of the board is to act as agent for the shareholders in overseeing the affairs of the corporation, how do the five responsibilities translate in managerial terms into a practical job description? As legally-empowered intermediary between shareholders and management the board must relate to both of these basic groups in the political structure of the firm. On behalf of the shareholders, the job of the board is fiduciary, acting as stewards for the shareholders in safeguarding and maximizing the value of the company's assets. For management, directors should offer high-level advice (consulting) in terms of advice and guidance in regard to the strategic management of the corporation. For directors to govern means to take responsibility for the big issues and problems and to lead in taking decisions and initiatives as necessary to make things happen as required for the success of the firm.

1. Overseeing Strategic Management

As explained in Chapter 7, the first responsibility of directors is to ensure that the highest possible standards of strategic management are developed and followed in the firm. The day-to-day work of strategic management is, of course, delegated to management. However, translating the directors' duty into practical, operational, business terms means nothing less than overseeing — understanding, monitoring, evaluating, controlling, and guiding — the strategic management factors and processes of the firm. The board's responsibility is to ensure that the company has a coherent, effective and competitive strategy and is successfully implementing it. Anything less means not understanding or turning a blind eye to its fiduciary obligations, current standards of care and reasonable business competence.

2. Management Selection, Supervision, and Upgrading

The second most important task of any board, a critical element in strategic management, is to develop, empower, and oversee the best possible top management team. In down-to-earth working terms, this means to hire, appoint, monitor, evaluate, counsel, discipline, support, pay and, if necessary, fire and replace the CEO and other top officers of the firm. For obvious organizational reasons — the rest of the top managers all report to the CEO, and in dealing with them the board acts on his or her advice — the CEO is the primary focus in carrying out this responsibility. The supervision of strategic management and development of leadership in the CEO and top officers are inextricably related and mutually reinforcing, either positively or negatively. Overseeing the development and implementation of strategy and ensuring excellent management are the twin foundations on which all the other duties of directors are based.

Peter Francis' discourse reflects a common attitude in business towards the board's role and relationship with its CEO. Most board job descriptions — where they exist — lead off with the task of selecting and monitoring the company's chief executive officer. Most directors regard the selection of a new CEO as their single most important responsibility, followed closely by the continuing task of monitoring performance, determining compensation, and, if necessary, removing him or her from the job.

In theory this makes a great deal of sense, but in practice there are serious difficulties. Most directors have trouble making the decision to discipline or sever their most senior employee, who is usually a fellow board member. It is easy to say "fire him if the results are lousy", but often results are mediocre, not good but not bad enough to warrant termination. There are always excuses for why results are not outstanding — the economy was bad, a key manager was unable to deliver promised results, the competition acted irrationally, there was an unexpected glitch in the market. It is easier for the board to accept a revised plan, to wait until more evidence is in, before taking the unpleasant step. Time passes, and by the time the evidence of poor performance is overwhelming, years may have passed. GM's board, reluctant to rock the boat, was not stirred into action until the evidence could no longer be denied and the outside pressure became irresistable; the cost to shareholders was enormous. The problem with the philosophy of "leave me alone, and fire me if the results are bad" is that the process is usually too slow, the results often too ambiguous. When the evidence is clear, it is too late, and serious damage has been done to the organization that will be difficult and costly to rectify.

The solution is for the board to be actively (not passively) engaged in supervising the process of strategic management. It is clearly important for the board to take the lead in appointing a CEO. But this process does not take place in a vacuum. The CEO is chosen to contribute to, and to lead management in evolving and implementing, a strategy. The qualities sought in a prospective CEO are to a large extent determined by the company's strategy and future direction — if that strategy calls for vigorous overseas expansion, then the CEO chosen should have international experience and capability. If the company is facing major financial obligations, the CEO will need to have a good grasp of finance. And so on.

By the same token, the strategic direction of the company provides a framework for evaluating the performance of the CEO; without a clear strategy, it becomes almost impossible to monitor and evaluate performance on a continuous basis. The board cannot be passive in this. It cannot leave to the CEO the development of strategy; the board's job is not only to see a strategy is in place, but that it is one that has been developed by board and management together, and is wholeheartedly subscribed to by both parties. Monitoring the CEO's performance is the means by which the board carries out its duty of due diligence in ensuring the implementation of that strategy, and its amendment as necessary.

3. Maintenance of Good Shareholder Relations

As agent of the shareholders in dealing with management, the board is responsible for maintaining two-way communications between the shareholders and management. In a company with a controlling shareholder, representing and protecting the minority shareholders is especially important. The board must ensure that external reporting is optimal — timely and fully adequate — and that shareholders' views and wishes are communicated to management. Under all Business Corporations Acts the main accountability event is the annual shareholders' meeting and the main accountability document is the published annual report disclosing required comparative financial statements, management's discussion and analysis of financial condition and results of operations (''MD&A''); the auditor's report; and any other information demanded by the company's articles, by-laws or any shareholder agreements.

Management treatment of these major requirements varies widely. Many companies view the annual shareholders' meeting as a bothersome legal ritual and run through a tightly-scripted hollow routine in the shortest time possible. Many annual reports provide no more than the minimum of legally-required information and are designed primarily as public relations propaganda. In general, many companies do not treat shareholders as anything more than faceless transient investors without any long-term proprietary involvement.

Ideally the company-shareholder relationship should be much better than this, and some companies and investor relations professionals, no doubt spurred on by the anticipation of more aggressive institutional investors, are trying to do better. There can be no doubt that mutual and pension funds and other institutional investors are awakening and beginning to flex their muscles, primarily in pressuring the management of companies that are not performing satisfactorily in increasing shareholder value. Nevertheless, until the fundamental differences between ''investors'' and ''owners'' are reconciled, no clear new requirements or definitive action are likely to appear for most companies.

4. Protecting and Optimizing Company Assets

This responsibility is fulfilled primarily by the review and approval of all material decisions, actions, policies and functions. Board approval is required for any material ''act or omission'' (''the oppression remedy'', section 247, Ontario Business Corporation Act) that affects the interest of any ''security holder'' of the corporation. This means that board approval is required for all material capital expenditures, acquisitions, divestments, or other acts or omissions that affect the purpose and strategy of the business. In this context, ''material'' is usually defined as a proportion of total assets, ordinarily one or two percent, or as affecting investors' decisions to buy or sell a security of the corporation. Monitoring and strengthening the finance function and increasing shareholder value are of particular importance in discharging the fiduciary duties of all directors.

Also to be singled out for special emphasis and importance to boards of directors in supervising the monitoring, evaluation and approval of the management of the firm are the following functions:

- Environmental responsibilities
- Competition law compliance
- Securities offering requirements
- Mergers and acquisitions
- Pension plans
- Insolvency and reorganization procedures
- Financial and treasury risk problems
- Occupational health and safety regulations

5. Fulfilling Fiduciary and Legal Requirements

This means ensuring that the company acts at all times in accordance with relevant laws and regulations and adheres to high ethical and moral standards. Legal requirements include the administration of all necessary minutes, records, contracts and documents. In addition the board is responsible for acting as necessary in unusual circumstances. In emergencies or crisis situations such as raids, severe financial troubles, insolvency, death or removal of the CEO and chairman and so on, the board, or a special committee, may have to take direct control, make major decisions and take action for the company.

Lastly, it is important to note the board's responsibility for the management of corporate governance. Only the board is qualified to manage its own function. In order continuously to upgrade the work and performance of the board it is necessary to define the job; implement in practice the job definition; monitor, assess and evaluate the work and process of the board and its members individually; and do all that is necessary to ensure the competent performance and upgrading of all its duties.

DIRECTOR AND BOARD PERFORMANCE SHOULD BE MEASURED

Performance appraisal can and should be carried out at two levels: at the level of the board as a whole, and at the individual director level. The first involves all the directors in a review and appraisal of how well the board is doing *as a team* to meet its evaluation criteria, and what can be done to improve each separate dimension of performance. The second involves *individual* appraisal, a much more difficult and sensitive area fraught with potential difficulties. Speaking on the subject of formalizing individual director appraisal, one major bank chairman described this latter process as ''intellectually appealing, but practically unworkable''. We agree there are problems involved, but hasten to add that the problems that arise from not appraising individual directors in some form are even worse.

Board self-appraisal can be a useful process but, like any other useful exercise, can be overdone. Annual self-appraisal retreats generally focus on such topics as size and composition of the board; the company's strategic plan and the planning process; the effectiveness of committees; management succession and compensation; the frequency, administration, and conduct of meetings. Questionnaires probing directors' reactions to sensitive issues can be used to deepen, explore, and structure responses and subsequent discussion. Outside consultants are often used to administer and interpret results.

Individual director appraisal is something else, and few companies have even attempted to pursue this course... ''boards are finding and will continue to find it difficult to evaluate individual members' performance. Human nature being what it is, directors find it very uncomfortable to make judgments about each other's performance.''[2]

If the purpose of appraising individual directors is to weed out those who are not performing, this is a judgment call that is relatively easy for a chairman to make, and surveys of other members don't add very much that is useful. The reluctance of many chairmen to make such a judgment on their own may explain well-meaning but misguided attempts to enlist other board members in the exercise. The fact is that making and acting upon such judgments is a key item in the chairman's job description, and he or she alone must ultimately be responsible for board performance. This is not something that should be delegated.

If performance is to be improved through the applications of the fundamentals of management control, it is essential to have some yardsticks against which to measure the contributions of the board and of individual directors. Well-managed corporations today use some form of performance appraisal in measuring and rewarding its personnel at all levels. Not so its boards of directors. Very few indeed have reasonably clear-cut statements of objectives, position descriptions or standards of performance. Reviews of performance are rarely made, and directors are seldom if ever encouraged to improve their contribution or be replaced for underperforming. In effect, most have a form of tenure, continuing to be re-elected at annual meetings as long as they don't raise too much trouble at board meetings or otherwise embarrass the board.

Yet, until chairmen begin to implement a performance appraisal process analogous to that widely used at other levels, and this becomes part of the built-in, assumed culture of the board system, real improvement will not take place. Despite the difficulties involved in setting performance standards, there must be a process involving some rigor, coupled with action taken to reinforce desired standards through a sophisticated if informal reward and punishment system, including the turnaround or eventual dismissal of nonperformers from boards. Otherwise, there will be no disciplined, systematic progress.

Very few corporations — only about one in four — have formal position descriptions for directors, let alone standards of performance.[3] Most of those we have interviewed state that CEOs and board members alike have in the past rarely stopped to consider their functions, duties or roles, although recent attention to corporate governance issues has changed this somewhat.

Any evaluation system must be based on a set of objective criteria. These are hard to determine for directors, and executives we have interviewed agree that any type of formal evaluation of directors can easily lead to great confusion and dissatisfaction. Although it is simple enough to generate a list of desirable roles and behaviours for directors to carry out, it is very difficult to measure them. This, it is argued, is the main reason why most of those interviewed have never seen a set of written performance standards for directors or boards.

One must also be aware of the difficulties of measuring performance even when clear standards have been enunciated: Who shall do the measurement and evaluation? Should it be done formally or informally? How often? With what consequences? It is important to remember that although directors act as individuals, optimal performance will be achieved only when individual directors act collectively as an effective group or team. It is therefore important to determine the individual director's contribution to the overall task of the board as a whole over time.

A POSITION DESCRIPTION FOR DIRECTORS

The first step towards an evaluation system for directors is the development of a position description (see page 197-99 for a sample). This is not the same as a director's manual, or a description of directors' legal duties and responsibilities. Most companies have these now — or should have. What we are talking about goes beyond legalities to outline the principal management activities of the Board — approval of strategy, CEO succession, and so on, and the director's individual responsibility for each. The analogy is to management job descriptions. And, as with management job descriptions, the process of preparing such a statement can itself be valuable and instructive to those participating. The final result should be discussed and approved by the whole board.

The content of the job description will vary from board to board. A major factor influencing the director's job is the pattern of ownership of the company. Clearly, the "position description" for a director of a widely-held corporation will be different from that of either the director in a privately-held corporation, or one with a clear control block. The degree of public responsibility and exposure to liability also varies considerably by ownership pattern. And the kinds of issues that the board concerns itself with will vary by ownership pattern. The director is, after all, the representative of the shareholders, and priorities and emphases will depend on who the shareholders are.

Standards of Performance (Exhibit 11.2) are not the same as a job description, but should flow from it. A standard of performance attempts to express a measurable target, either quantitative or qualitative, against which the director can be rated. It is easy to measure whether a director attended a meeting. And one can argue that attendance is pretty basic — it is difficult to carry out one's responsibilities without being present at meetings. But even so, we can recall cases where directors have had a major impact on the company in spite of poor attendance, through their contacts with major shareholders, the CEO and management, and contributions outside formal meetings.

The quantitative measures most commonly used to evaluate directors are:

1. *Attendance* at meetings, both board and committees.

2. *Preparation* for meetings, admittedly a judgment call, but usually pretty obvious to a perceptive observer.

3. *Participation* in meetings, not necessarily in quantity but with a qualitative element as well. Too much participation can be a negative.

Most chairmen and directors can and do make implicit if not explicit judgments of each other based on these relatively crude criteria. Collectively, they provide some measure of the contribution of the individual to the group. And they provide a kind of fitness test for board members — if a director skips meetings, is ill-prepared, and contributes little, there is clearly not much justification for keeping that individual on a board.

For the director who passes this first hurdle — who attends, is pre-

Exhibit 11.2

STANDARDS OF PERFORMANCE OF DIRECTORS: AN EXAMPLE

The job of the board has been properly done when:

1. There has been prepared a written statement of broad corporate policy, including definition of what businesses the company is in.
2. Long- and short-term objectives have been established for the company that reflect shareholder expectations.
3. A specific plan has been established for meeting objectives.
4. Standards of performance are in place and have been communicated to management.
5. The job of the CEO has been defined.
6. A CEO who has the confidence and support of the board has been appointed.
7. The problems and needs for succession to the CEO have been recognized and planned for.
8. The board has adequately supported the CEO through assistance and counsel.
9. Issues have been identified, solutions determined, and action taken on all major problems facing the company.
10. The duties and responsibilites of the board and its committees have been defined and are being carried out.
11. A procedure has been established for recruiting and compensating directors.
12. Provision has been made for perpetuating a sound board, including a retirement plan.
13. Provision has been made for constructive board meetings, including an adequate flow of information for the board to carry out its duties.
14. There is adequate staff support for the board and its committees.
15. The affairs of the company have been fully and fairly reported to the shareholders.
16. The required legal documentation is proper, complete and up-to-date.

Source: Adapted from *The Corporate Director* by Joseph Juran and Keith Louden, published by the American Management Association (New York, 1966). This version has been implemented in a large publicly-held corporation and is used here with permission.

pared, and participates helpfully — a second, more judgmental and qualitative, set of performance standards comes into play. These vary much more from company to company, and include:

1. Overall good judgment.

2. Compatibility with the group: independent, but also a "team player".

3. Major contributions in the past.

4. Special skills or experience, such as technical, legal, marketing, financial.

5. Public profile and prestige.

6. Contacts, business generation, or special contributions.

7. Overall value of contribution in fulfilling the board's duties.

Then, too, there is the need to maintain some balance or mix on the board — by occupation, experience, region, gender, race, or other criteria. Diversity is a strength which may in some cases mean carrying a director who is otherwise weak in performance.

The weight to be attached to each criterion will vary from company to company. But they can and should be considered, and some sort of overall assessment made, no matter how crude. One form of "report card", or "evaluation guide", is shown in Exhibit 11.3.

WHO SHOULD DO THE EVALUATION?

Clearly, the chairman is the central player. It is — or should be — in the chairman's position description that he or she is in charge of managing the board, and will be measured in part by how well the board as a whole performs. To carry out parts of this task, the chairman may well want the assistance of a few senior and respected outside directors. This could be accomplished through an expansion of the duties of the board's nominating committee, where there is one. Evaluation of existing director performance and the termination of unsatisfactory directors would seem a logical extension of the nominating committee's traditional role in helping screen and select new directors. And it may help take some of the pressure off the chairman in cases of personal friendship with nonperforming directors.

Exhibit 11.3

A "REPORT CARD" FOR DIRECTORS CLASSIFIED BY EFFECTIVENESS

Ratings	1 Unsatisfactory	2 Poor	3 Average	4 Good	5 Excellent
Skills/Ability	Seldom, if ever contributes	Marginal	Occasional contributor	Strong, consistent performer	Outstanding leadership capabilities
Knowledge	Incompetent	Weak	Reasonable	Well informed	Comprehensive, penetrating
Attitude/Values	Questionable	Follower	Unpredictable	Independent, positive	Responsible, ethical, congenial
Commitment	Weak	Limited	Generally good	Strong supporter	Totally dependable, "makes time"
Experience	Little, if any	Not much	Reasonable but limited	Wide, helpful	Extensive, varied, valuable, relevant
Overall	No added value, should be dropped	Under-performer Improve or resign	Weak supporter Some improvement needed	Strong contributor	Master professional, pillar of strength

But in the end result, it is the chairman's responsibility, and the way in which it is handled is all-important.

How is the process handled? Our experience and studies show that chairmen do one of two things when confronted with an underperformer — they either take the individual aside for a personal talk (which may or may not result in the individual not standing for re-election), or they duck the issue and live with the individual, and ''let age or time resolve the situation''. Over a third of the chairmen in one survey said they took the latter approach; a major indication that taking the easy way out often stands in the way of doing the correct thing.

The reluctance of chairmen to face up to the issue of nonperformance probably accounts for the growing use of fixed retirement dates for directors, now usually at age 70. Having an arbitrary rule provides an automatic cut-off and avoids any confrontation. It can also allow for special cases, where a director is still a major contributor although past retirement age.

The most common approach to corrective action is the one-on-one ''personal chat'' between the chairman and the director. Although still rare, these ''chats'' are in some cases becoming institutionalized — they are held regularly, say once a year, between the chairman and each director. This kind of review should generally not be seen as an inquisition, but a two-way discussion, with the director being invited to discuss any shortcomings he or she sees in the way the board is being run. After all, it is conceivable that perceived poor performance may in fact be due to the way the chairman runs the meetings, the scheduling of meetings, interpersonal dynamics, or personal problems that the director is reluctant to discuss with other directors. A change in the way the board is managed may well be the outcome of the discussion, rather than the director leaving the board. For a chairman who takes the job seriously and wants a more effective board, this process of one-on-one review should be welcomed and seen as an essential element in the job of managing the board professionally.

If it becomes apparent that the director cannot or will not change and must be terminated, the most usual way is to delete his or her name from nomination at the next annual meeting. This may involve the chairman having to bite the bullet, and tell that director that he or she won't be on the list. Having the backing of the nominating committee may make that job somewhat easier, less personal, and less arbitrary.

IMPROVED MANAGEMENT OF BOARDS LONG OVERDUE

This process — from job description, to standards of performance, evaluation, and action — seems to us to be long overdue in its application to corporate directors. Boards are too important a link in the chain of management to be left to the present haphazard and unsatisfactory, *ad hoc* methods of operation.

What is needed is better definition and evaluation of the job of the board. This is a function that falls clearly on the chairman, and it will never be carried out effectively without introducing some rigor into the process of evaluating director performance. To improve governance the effectiveness of directors must be upgraded, beginning more specifically with the drastic improvement or termination of the roughly 30 percent of directors whose current performance would be classified as unsatisfactory or poor.

The obstacles are admittedly large. But conceptually, the process is no different from evaluating management performance. All it takes is some leadership and some imagination. The importance of the goal merits the effort. Moreover, if it is not done through internal processes under the control of the chairman and the board, it will probably be imposed in one way or another by external forces, such as institutional shareholders.

NOTES

1. In Canada, unlike the United States, a number of companies are owned by the state, known as Crown Corporations. These represent a relatively small (5-10 percent) but significant part of the corporate world, and pose a number of unique issues of governance, with which we do not propose to deal.

2. Jay Lorsch, ''Performance Assessment in the Boardroom'', *Directors and Boards* (Spring, 1994), p. 12.

3. Notably Jonathon D. Kovacheff, ''Managing the Board: A Survey of Chairmen of Canadian Corporations'', *Working Paper NC 91-006-B*, National Centre for Management Research and Development, London, Ontario, February, 1991.

4. This Position Description, and the Standards of Performance statement were prepared for a major publicly-held corporation and adopted by its board. They are presented here unedited, with permission.

APPENDIX

SAMPLE BOARD POSITION DESCRIPTION FOR A LARGE, WIDELY-HELD COMPANY[4]

Preamble

The Board of Directors is responsible under law for the management of the company's business. It has the statutory authority and obligation to protect and enhance the assets of the company in the interest of all shareholders.

Although directors may be elected by the shareholders to bring special expertise or a point of view to board deliberations, they are not chosen to represent a particular constituency. The best interest of the company must be paramount at all times.

The involvement and commitment of directors is evidenced by regular board and committee attendance, preparation, and active participation in setting goals and requiring performance in the interest of shareholders.

Duties of Directors

The board operates by delegating certain of its responsibilities to management and reserving certain powers to itself. Its principal duties fall into six categories:

I. Overseeing and approving a strategy for the business,

II. Selection of the management,

III. Setting goals and standards for management, monitoring their performance, and taking corrective action where necessary,

IV. Approving policies and procedures for implementing the strategy,

V. Reporting to shareholders on the performance of the business,

VI. Approval and completion of routine legal requirements.

I. *Strategy determination*

1. The board has the responsibility to participate, as a whole and through its committees, in developing and approving the mission of the busi-

ness, its objectives and goals, and the strategy by which it proposes to reach those goals.

2. The board has the responsibility to ensure congruence between shareholder expectations, company plans, and management performance.

II. *Selection of the management*

1. The board retains the responsibility for managing its own affairs, including planning its composition, selecting its chairman, nominating candidates for election to the board, appointing committees, and determining director compensation.

2. The board has the responsibility for the appointment and replacement of a chief executive officer, for monitoring CEO performance, determining CEO compensation, and providing advice and counsel in the execution of the CEO's duties.

3. The board has the responsibility for approving the appointment and remuneration of all corporate officers, acting upon the advice of the chief executive officer.

4. The board has the responsibility for ensuring that adequate provision has been made for management succession.

III. *Monitoring and acting*

1. The board has the responsibility for monitoring the company's progress towards its goals, and revising and altering its direction in light of changing circumstances.

2. The board has the responsibility for taking action when performance falls short of its goals or when other special circumstances (for example mergers and acquisitions or changes in control) warrant it.

IV. *Policies and procedures*

1. The board has the responsibility for approving and monitoring compliance with all significant policies and procedures by which the company is operated.

2. The board has a particular responsibility for ensuring that the company

operates at all times within applicable laws and regulations, and to the highest ethical and moral standards.

V. *Reporting to shareholders*

1. The board has the responsibility for ensuring that the financial performance of the company is reported to shareholders on a timely and regular basis.

2. The board has the responsibility for ensuring that the financial results are reported fairly, and in accordance with generally-accepted accounting standards.

3. The board has the responsibility for timely reporting of any other developments that have a significant and material impact on the value of the shareholders' assets.

4. The board has the responsibility for reporting annually to shareholders on its stewardship for the preceding year.

5. The board has the responsibility for approving any payment of dividends to shareholders.

VI. *Legal requirements*

1. The board is responsible for ensuring that routine legal requirements, documents, and records have been properly prepared, approved, and maintained.

Chapter 12

THE COMPETENT DIRECTOR: Characteristics and Qualifications

Defining the competency requirements for a director and evaluating the qualifications of candidates get to the heart of board management. In the following case, the chairman of a board's human resource and nominating committee faces a sensitive problem in opposing a candidate for board membership.

TED BERNIER AND THE NEW BOARD MEMBER

A feeling of dismay and uncertainty flooded over Ted Bernier as he hung up the phone. He had just had a long conversation with Brian Trout, chairman of FTI Corporation, about the composition of the company's board, in the course of which Trout had proposed adding Alice Freeman to the board. Bernier, as chairman of the company's human resource and nominating committee, was convinced that this would be a mistake, and he had tried to dissuade Trout, but to no avail. Bernier knew that the Freeman family were large shareholders, and that Trout had been under pressure for some time from the family for direct representation. Bernier had no objection in principle to their representation, but what dismayed him was that the individual being proposed, with the family's backing, was Alice Freeman, 27, the eldest daughter. Bernier felt Alice had no qualifications for board membership, and that her presence on the board would undo much of the careful planning that he and Trout had done to ensure a strong and effective working board. Alice Freeman was a pleasant young woman who had yet to demonstrate her ability to settle down to anything. She had no real business experience, and had failed to complete a program in business administration at the nearby university. Her brothers and sisters were considerably younger, and had never indicated any serious interest in the company. Bernier felt that the existing board was an excellent one; small, vigorous, experienced and completely committed to the company and its goals. Financial performance had been very strong, thanks in no small measure to the guidance and leadership provided by the board. The board could "carry" Alice, he supposed, but the contribution would be entirely to Alice's education, and Alice had not demonstrated any real interest or commitment in the business before this. Bernier had an overwhelming sense that appointing Alice would not be a good move for FTI. What was he to do?

* * * * *

COMPETENCE FOR WHAT?

Competence, the possession of characteristics (and lack of disabilities) that enable a person to perform specified duties and responsibilities, is a critically important success factor for directors and boards. In fact, the successful performance of the entire board system depends on competence in the demanding job of overseeing the management of any corporation. Our purpose in this chapter is to examine the director's activities and roles in more detail, outline the specific competencies required by these roles, look critically at current levels of competence, and suggest how to upgrade these in light of growing demands on the board system.

One way of beginning to think about competence requirements for directors is to examine the functions and requirements of the job. Many observers of the corporate scene, convinced that boards are primarily figureheads or "rubber-stamps", think of the director's job as something that virtually anyone can do, and that it doesn't really matter much who is appointed to company boards. Others, seeing boards as a vehicle for some form of social engineering, propose requiring that board composition be balanced by gender, race, national origin, or other socio-demographic characteristics. Most such advocates have the attitude that "boards are of little use anyway, so why not put in anyone who will make it look better?", an obviously self-fulfilling prophecy.

The essence of our argument throughout this book is that boards have an important professional function to perform, and that appointing persons of competence to boards is a *sine qua non* for improving board performance. One way of beginning to think about competence requirements is to examine the functions and requirements of the job, to ground discussion in the realities of actual practice, to understand what directors are actually called upon to do.

JOINING A BOARD AND GETTING UP TO SPEED

A first step in joining a board is to respond to the initial feelers from the chairman or company spokesperson who approaches the potential director. This raises many questions for the individual in regard to sizing up and responding to the initiative that may lead to an invitation: What is the company all about? What business is it in? How is it doing? What is its reputation? What about its management? Is it a company that I would be proud to be associated with? Who else is on the board?

Then, from the point of view of his or her own situation: What will this mean to me? What will my contribution and role on the board be? What are the company's expectations and implied commitment? What are the time demands, and can I meet them? What is the meeting schedule? Travel requirements? Compensation? Perquisites? Stock ownership requirements and capital gains potential? Risks and possible hidden horrors? How does all of this fit with my present experience, know-how, activities and commitments?

What happens next? Introductions? Negotiations? Meetings? If the approach is mutually satisfactory, it will result in an agreement to take on a major commitment in which the director, for a fixed and usually modest fee, exposes his or her time, reputation and finances to potentially great demands and risks. The decision should not be made lightly.

Once the position has been accepted, considerable homework is required. The new director has a great deal to learn before he or she is in a position to contribute significantly to the work of the board. Preparation begins with reading and studying annual reports, directors' briefing books, by-laws, regulatory filings, analysts' reports, and a host of other documents. This is followed by meeting and sorting out a number of new people, requiring quick readings of character, competence and relationships, sizing up the power structure and pecking order in the company and on the board. What is the culture? What are the unwritten rules? Who can I rely on, and who must I watch out for? In some cases, there may be visits to company operations at both head office and in the field, to gain a better appreciation of the company, its business, its people, and its problems and opportunities. All of this is an important initiation ritual.

HOW TO FIT IN

After several meetings and enough opportunities to observe and evaluate the other members of the board, the new director begins to find a place among the cast of characters. Other directors, universal board characters, have already found their slots. There may be the non-participator, impeccably dressed, who seems only to sit, watch, and occasionally second the motion to approve the minutes of the previous meeting, whether or not he or she has actually read them. After two or three enigmatic comments delivered over five or six meetings, questions arise in the new director's mind: How did he get here? Why is he continued on the board? Of what use is he to the company? (Perhaps still waters do not run deeply!)

The board may also include the ready pontificator, complete with lengthy but shallow comments on any subject that comes up; the "we-are-here-to-support management" type who will vote yes to almost anything the CEO/chairman wants; the "penetrating-questioner" who can chip in with an unanswerable query on almost any topic; the "loose-cannon" who erupts periodically with loud and emotional outbursts that defy intelligent response and disrupt any attempt at useful dialogue; the Mr. or Ms. "Agin-the-government", with a negative and critical comment and position on any proposal, no matter how sensible or necessary. Most boards have in their numbers one or more "specialists", individuals who possess a great deal of knowledge and experience in a particular field, such as finance, banking, marketing, or government. Some of these directors never speak on issues outside their specialty but can be invaluable whenever such specialized knowledge is called for.

Then, there are the professional directors, usually solid contributors — experienced, qualified, competent, knowledgeable and committed, who do their homework, understand the issues, have a knack of getting to the point, and invariably make solid, wise and helpful contributions. They may not be — indeed they seldom are — the most voluble contributors, preferring to focus their efforts on matters of high priority rather than take up the board's limited time. In all the constellation of roles, with the wide variation that exists in each board of experience, intelligence, temperament, and helpfulness, each individual director must find a role to play, based on his or her own qualities and qualifications. Blending the roles to create an effective team is the job of the chairman.

DOING YOUR HOMEWORK

For most boards, every six weeks to two months a pile of material will be received which, along with previous material and notes, is required reading for an upcoming meeting. Included will usually be an agenda, minutes of a previous meeting, financial statements and information, operational reviews, and special reports on everything from hedging and capital appropriation requests to prospective acquisitions. Such material would take an hour or two to skim lightly, and five or six hours to study carefully. How is the director to handle all this material? Some directors, perhaps most, study it all conscientiously in advance, think about the issues and maybe even make a phone call or two for clarification beforehand.Others skim-read most of it on the way to the meetings, and sometimes focus on selected issues that seem important.

Knowledge is power. Thorough preparation for meetings is power in the hands of any director. Preparation gives the director confidence in addressing issues, in expressing views on these issues, and in debating issues with other directors or often better-informed management. Careful preparation gives the individual a considerable advantage in pressing his or her views in debate. Lack of adequate preparation leaves the director weak and impotent in discussion, asking redundant questions.

TRACKING THE STRATEGIC AGENDA

Good directors who take their duties seriously will, in one way or another, follow carefully and keep themselves well informed about the strategic agenda of the company (Chapter 7). They know that a director's central concern must be to monitor, evaluate and advise on the few most important problems and opportunities that are going to have a major impact on the company's success. They recognize that management has its own interests in this agenda, works at it every day, and is usually better informed on the technical aspects of strategic decisions. The director's job is to see the ''big picture'', anticipate issues from a wider perspective than management, and to bring his or her experience, wisdom, perspective and judgment to bear on any decision. This is surely the value-added by a competent and independent director.

Having the strategic agenda clearly in mind, the individual director has a framework against which to evaluate the many management-originated issues that will be brought to the board for decision: How does this request fit with the strategic direction of the company? Is the decision we are being asked to make consistent with the overall direction and goals in the strategic plan? If not, why not? Should we re-examine our strategy?

These questions are particularly appropriate in evaluating the regular capital appropriation requests that typically come before the board for approval. Often highly technical and involving significant sums of money, such requests are usually based on extensive management analysis, discussion, and approval prior to coming to the board. The board's approval is the last step in this process, and there is considerable pressure on the director not to question or delay approving the management recommendation. Ensuring that such decisions are congruent with the company's strategy, and that the strategy has been properly considered in the process, is frequently the best that an individual director can do.

The strategic plan itself is reviewed annually in most companies. This is a point of key involvement for the director. Management typically prepares an updated plan, which is frequently lengthy and complex, and explicitly or implicitly raises all the critical issues of the company. Review, study and preparation is a major job for even the most experienced director. It involves understanding how various company activities are reflected in shareholder value, and an ability to relate the various elements that influence or determine profitability, return on investment, the cost of capital, cash flows, and other financial elements. It also involves a knowledge and understanding of the environment within which the company is operating, and a sense of where elements of that environment are heading, and might impinge on the company. The ability to deal with such issues is manifestly a skill that is acquired over many years of business and life experience.

EVALUATING PEOPLE

It is impossible for company directors to avoid making judgments about people. A major part of the director's job is the evaluation of the chief executive officer and his or her performance. In addition, the director should be sizing up other senior managers who may be candidates to succeed the CEO. To do this well calls for experience, wisdom and judgment of the first order, and even where the director possesses such qualities, it is often possible to make serious misjudgments. It is very difficult, if not impossible, to judge the work of a CEO if you have not had important leadership responsibilities yourself. By the same token, personal knowledge of the difficulties involved in managing a company may make a director too understanding and tolerant when it comes to judging another CEO. There is little difficulty in cases where performance has been consistently bad or consistently good, but in most companies the situation is much less clear.

By the same token, the director is often called upon to exercise judgment regarding the ethical and moral behaviour of key individuals in the company. Without a strong sense of ethics and personal values, how is it possible for a director to make such judgments?

TECHNICAL ISSUES

Directors are often thrust into the centre of many specialized and technical issues, especially in the course of working on a committee. Serving on an audit committee, for example, frequently calls for an understanding of accounting practice, terminology, and the limitations inherent in the methods used to record and monitor company performance. Scientific knowledge or specialized engineering or technical skills may be necessary in judging strategic investment decisions. Pension committees deal with actuarial evaluations, knowledge of different pension systems, providing direction to money managers, and evaluating investment performance. Human resource committee members are frequently involved in complex performance evaluation and compensation issues.

STAYING IN TOUCH WITH SHAREHOLDERS

In all of this it is sometimes easy for a director to forget that he or she is there to represent the best interest of the shareholders, especially if that director is not a substantial shareholder. Many boards require directors to own shares in the company, and may make this a condition of appointment. An increasing number of boards pay part or all of the directors' fees in stock, and/or in stock options, in an attempt to link the board more directly to the shareholders' interest.[2] While ownership of shares may or may not motivate directors to work effectively in the interest of shareholders at large, there is little doubt that many shareholders are convinced that it does, judging from the views that are often heard at annual shareholders' meetings.

There are many other ways in which a director can maintain a sensitivity to the shareholder point of view. Clearly, direct contact with large, influential shareholders on a reasonably frequent basis helps. Staying current with leading business publications is a must, and exposure to the analysts and their published views on the company and its competitors can help.

TAKING A LEADERSHIP ROLE

After an introductory period on any board the director is usually assigned to one or more committees, and, as he or she gains familiarity with these, the director may be asked to become a committee chairman. These assignments can be very demanding, requiring leadership and initiative. There is usually a "pecking order" of committees, some less demanding and less critical to the board than others; as the director gains experience he or she moves up the ladder and takes on greater responsibility. This will involve greater contact with company staff, time spent between meetings reading and attending conferences or seminars, and taking on the job of managing the committee's work: planning meetings, agendas, presentations, presiding over discussions, formulating conclusions and recommendations and reporting to the board.

Occasionally, all of these and many other skills are called upon in dealing with special problems. Acquisitions, mergers, buyouts, regulatory and financial problems, many of them unanticipated, can challenge the limits of a director's ability.

HANDLING PROBLEMS WITH MANAGEMENT

It is usually impossible to avoid problems and issues, sometimes related to the most serious questions of performance, behaviour, policies and morality, related to top management. When, as is sometime the case, these centre on the CEO, the board can find itself in extremely troublesome situations. For example, one CEO in a recent human resource committee meeting adamantly demanded support on a very sticky point on the thinly-veiled threat of resignation. One director, upset at the CEO's attitude and what he had done, asked the CEO to leave the meeting and began to argue that this was an offer and opportunity that the board should not pass by. An hour later, after the flood-gates of pent-up frustration with the CEO had been aired for the first time, the human resource committee voted to recommend to the immediately-following board meeting that the CEO be taken up on his threat. Two hours later the CEO had been fired and the board became enmeshed in the very difficult problem of replacement. In two hours, with no notice, a very sudden and unexpected turn of events precipitated a major crisis upon which the board had immediately to decide and take action.

PROBLEMS IN THE BOARD

Another challenge with which directors must frequently deal is sub-optimality and trouble in the function of the board. Lack of really penetrating and informed dialogue, lack of sharp closure on issues, meetings running too long and with too little focused leadership, one or two directors who talk too much and say too little, inconvenient travel logistics, a lack of unity and cohesion among directors, and avoidance of facing up to issues are some of the frustrations and relatively common annoyances that many good directors have to put up with on many boards. Unfortunately some board problems become serious issues. Unsatisfactory directors and/or chairmen, too much tension and conflict between management and the board, management performance that is substandard, cliques in a board working at cross-purposes, management or director behaviour that is not acceptable, company problems that are out of control, committee management problems and so on. All such problems must be tracked, evaluated, and subjected to the director's prayer ("Grant me the serenity to accept the things I cannot change, courage to change the things I can, and the wisdom to know the difference") and then followed up with many different kinds of actions.

Occasionally directors are confronted by a wide variety of special problems that are demanding of immense ability and wisdom. Highly confidential personal problems, acquisitions, mergers, buyouts, regulatory, financial, and emergency problems, often unexpected and unpreventable, challenge the limits of a director's capacity to respond wisely. One way of beginning to think about competence requirements is to examine the functions and requirements of the job. From this brief overview of some typical tasks of directors we can conclude that the job requirements are extremely demanding, in fact sometimes impossibly so.

REQUIRED ROLE BEHAVIOUR

"A role is a set of expectations about how a person in a given position in a social system should act..."[1]

A board of directors is, among other things, a social system which may usefully be described by outlining the roles enacted by the people within it. These roles indicate the parts that people play and the relationships they take on as necessary to make any social system function adequately.

One approach to understanding the competencies necessary to be a good director is to examine the roles that a director is required to play. On the basis of the task requirements outlined above and wide observation of directors in action, the primary role requirements are as follows:

- trustee: guardian and steward of assets as an agent for shareholders
- consultant: provider of advice and counsel to management
- business analyst: size up, examination and diagnosis of businesses and their problems
- financial analyst: analysis of company from an investor's point of view
- general manager: responsibility for supervising the overall management of the firm
- meeting participant: contributor to formal group discussions of company's problems
- advocate: proposing and defending ideas, initiatives and policies
- dissenter: questioning and opposing as appropriate all unwise proposals
- referee: adjudicator of differences between or among conflicting ideas or positions
- cheerleader: supporter of good performers and wise proposals
- decision maker: taking a position in voting on proposed actions

- politician: using influence to support or oppose other directors and/or managers
- educator: teacher involved in activities to produce desirable changes in behavior and abilities of others
- ethicist: analyst of moral problems and advisor on what is right or wrong
- policeman: apprehending and stopping bad activities, initiatives or persons
- coach: personal and team advisor
- father-confessor: confidential relationship of trust and intimacy with others, especially the CEO
- investigator: running down and analyzing a variety of information, rumors, and innuendo from sources of widely-varying validity
- surgeon: cutting out and eliminating harmful ideas, initiatives and persons
- healer: bringing agreement, comfort and reconciliation to tension and conflict
- compromiser: seeking mutually acceptable middle ground in disagreements
- negotiator: working with conflicting individuals to find acceptable agreement
- individualist: taking and defending a tough-minded position as appropriate and alone if necessary
- student: being a good learner and "quick study" of new ideas, technical change, legal complexities and so on as necessary when new issues arise requiring understanding and judgment
- chairman: chairing the board or a committee requires group leadership functions of a wide variety

Competence for any director requires almost impossible versatility in role behavior and action. The strength and variety of a director's role repertoire is a prime indicator of competence.

THE ELEMENTS OF COMPETENCE

If competence is the capability to handle the problems that typically confront directors, and to play effectively the required roles, what are the basic elements of the competence required to be a director? We suggest that they fall into three categories: knowledge, attitudes, and abilities.

Knowledge

Knowledge is the conscious understanding and use of information, ideas, concepts, generalizations, and principles. The validity of these ideas and concepts derives mainly from observation, rational analysis, and scientific reasoning. For example, understanding the conceptual framework that links the determinants of shareholder value is knowledge that must be possessed by any qualified, competent, director. Other basic knowledge required of the director includes understanding the system of corporate governance, strategic management, the environment of business, organizational behaviour, control and information systems and so on.

Attitudes

Attitudes are the beliefs, predispositions, feelings, desires, or values that lead a person to behave in a particular way. The feeling, for example, that it is important for a director to take the initiative and responsibility for providing leadership, trusteeship, and counsel for management is an attitude without which a director could not be effective. Attitudes that are important for directors include valuing and respecting the private business system, respecting the skills and abilities required to manage organizations well, understanding and respecting the primacy of shareholders, being action-oriented, conscientious, demanding of performance and accomplishment, holding high ethical standards, and being demanding of oneself as well as others.

Ability

Ability refers to such qualities as skill, judgment and wisdom, effectively applied to issues encountered in practice. An example would be good performance in problem diagnosis, analysis, and decision making. Basic ability factors that are critical to director competence include wisdom, judgment and common sense, skill in human relations and financial analysis, ability to prioritize multiple and complex issues, ability to perform as a member of a team, contributing to collective decision making, ability to communicate clearly, and skill and understanding in the manifold matters that come before the board.

QUALIFICATIONS FOR THE DIRECTOR'S JOB

All of these qualities are seldom found in a single individual. Boards are collectivities, and for effective corporate performance what is important is for the board as a whole to possess these qualities. The board must therefore be composed of a group of individuals, none of whom may possess all the knowledge, attitudes and abilities that are required, but where, by combining the individual talents, the desired overall output is achieved. This is no different from the difficult task of blending the abilities of a group of athletes into an effective, winning team.

Nonetheless, as in sports, there is a basic level of knowledge, attitude and ability required of each director. Just as any competent hockey player must be able to skate, pass, shoot the puck, and check, so every competent director must be able to deal effectively with the common issues that come frequently to corporate boards. Over and above that basic level, individual directors will bring a wide range of special knowledge and ability to bear on the board's agenda. A board, to be effective, needs diversity of knowledge, attitudes and abilities in order to be able to handle the special situations and unusual issues that inevitably arise.

BASIC REQUIREMENTS

The first requirement for any corporate director is for the kind of elementary and systematic knowledge, attitudes, and abilities that are necessary for high standing in the completion of a good MBA program. This may not have been true for directors in the past; in our opinion, it is true for directors today.

This is *not* to say that we are suggesting an MBA as a minimum qualification for directors. The knowledge, attitudes and abilities that emerge from an MBA program can be gained in many other ways, including on-the-job experience; the means by which they may have been acquired are not important. But possession of those qualities is basic to competent performance by a director in the economic and political environment of today and will be more so in the future.

Specifically, this means exposure to, and a grasp of, the essential concepts of strategic management and business policy, organizational behaviour, marketing, finance, production and operations management, control and accounting, managerial economics, management communications, and the environment of business. Additional requirements would include the following (or some reasonable equivalent): middle management experience that demonstrates capability at the operational level in a functional area of business (finance, marketing, operations, etc.); general management experience demonstrating capability to run a business and coordinate all the functional areas; top management experience indicating mastery of "big picture" problems and overall leadership talents and accomplishments; understanding of and experience in corporate governance and board operations; and capacity for learning and growth.

These qualities can be acquired through some combination of formal training and experience. Increasing effort to improve director training and to make the job more professional, possibly through formal accreditation courses and certification, is an important step towards the improvement of corporate governance and the board system. While the Institute of Directors in the United Kingdom has perhaps advanced the most towards formal training for directors, there is as yet little available in either the United States or Canada. Attempts to implement accreditation raise serious questions involving the lack of agreed standards of practice, qualities, qualifications, and skills, as well as concerns about who would define and enforce these standards.

Combined with this minimum level of competence are a number of basic requirements of every director: time availability; personal credibility in terms of general reputation, high standards of behavior and values; breadth of interest and intelligence. These are difficult to measure, but are no less important in assessing the basic competence of any director to do the job required.

SPECIAL REQUIREMENTS

In addition to the basic competence requirements described above, there are the special needs of individual boards. An important element is the need for diversity of skills, backgrounds, and experience. The selection process for directors, as it has been practiced in many companies in past years, has tended to result in greater homogeneity, rather than diversity, in board composition. The old-style, informal, chairman/CEO-controlled system has in many cases led to boards composed of "people-like-us" — for the most part male, white, better-educated, regionally-concentrated directors, drawn heavily from the ranks of active or retired CEOs of noncompetitive companies.[3] The lack of diversity in the system has been obvious; it has exacerbated the problem of bland, "group-think" boards which have failed to challenge management on many of its critical assumptions, and it has resulted in strong resistance to proposals for change in the corporate governance system.

The special qualities and skills required obviously cover a tremendous range, and vary from company to company, depending on its strategy. Increasingly, as North American companies compete in the international economy, greater diversity of international experience and contacts is required. As companies respond to political and social change, there is a greater demand for gender and ethnic diversity on boards. And so it should be. But the need for diversity must be tempered with an equally-growing need for professional competence, without which no one should be entrusted with the significant responsibility of serving as a director of a corporation.

NOTES

1. Frederick J. McDonald, *Educational Psychology*, (San Francisco: Wadsworth Publishing Company, 1960).

2. See, for example, the results of annual surveys of board compensation conducted by The Conference Board, Korn Ferry, and Spencer Stuart, among others.

3. Surveys of Canadian corporate boards provide strong backing for this. See particularly two working papers prepared in the early 1990s for the National Centre for Management Research and Development: ''A Profile of Canadian Chairmen,'' by Paul Moynihan, and ''Managing the Board: A Survey of Chairmen of Canadian Corporations ''by Jonathon Kovacheff (NC 91-006-B).

Chapter 13

THE COMPETENT DIRECTOR: Selection and Training

TORMAX MANUFACTURING CORPORATION

The October meeting of the board of directors of Tormax Manufacturing Corporation had as agenda item 14, "Board Succession." The item came late in the meeting, and the chairman asked the management members present to absent themselves while it was discussed. "As you may know, gentlemen, one of our members, Frank Jones, has reached retirement age of 70," the chairman began. "Consequently, Frank will be leaving the board effective at the annual meeting in April. His retirement will leave the board at nine members, while our bylaws specify a minimum of 10. We need to discuss a replacement for Frank."

The board listened with keen interest. The outside members had been together for some time, and this was the first vacancy to occur in four years. During this period the board had become close, and was widely regarded as cohesive and effective. Company results had been outstanding.

In the discussion that followed, the chairman suggested the name of William Logan, chairman and CEO of one of the country's largest steel companies.

"Bill Logan, whom many of you know, will be stepping out from his chairman and CEO jobs within the next year under their early retirement rules. He is now 62. I'm on another board with him, and I have had several informal conversations with him over the last year or so. I believe he would be interested in joining us. He has already had approaches from a number of other companies, and he will no doubt have a lot more. But he knows a number of us and thinks highly of the company. I think he would say yes to an offer. I would like to know what the rest of you think."

The chairman's suggestions elicited a lively and enthusiastic response. Several members spoke warmly of Logan, including Frank Jones himself. Logan was a very high-profile businessman, active in a number of national and community business and charitable organizations. His company had a reputation as a leader in its industry and as a good corporate citizen, and it was apparent that Logan was well respected personally. After about ten minutes, the chairman closed off discussion with these comments: "All right, then. I take it that it is the sense of the meeting that I should approach Bill Logan with an offer to join our board at the next annual meeting. I'll do so in the next few weeks, and I'll let you know what happens." With that, the meeting broke up.

Bill Logan was later approached by the chairman and accepted. His name was included in the list of nominees to the board mailed out to shareholders with notice of the annual meeting and other documentation. The list of nominees proposed by the company was routinely approved without comment at the shareholders' meeting, and Bill Logan became a director of Tormax.

* * * * *

This process, or something similar, describes how many, if not most, directors are chosen. If, as many argue, corporate boards are not performing adequately, this selection process has resulted in the choice of the directors whose performance has been deemed unsatisfactory.

THE TYPICAL DIRECTOR SELECTION PROCESS IS FLAWED

How do people get to be directors of major corporations? The Tormax Manufacturing Corporation experience does not necessarily reflect the way in which all corporations choose their directors. Some companies have a nominating committee handle the process, develop a list of specifications, hire consultants and use rigorous search and screening processes, including personal interviews with candidates. But many others, like Tormax, use an *ad hoc* process built on an old boys' network, where the board has at best a kind of veto over candidates put forward by the chairman, with the tacit approval of any major shareholders. One of the unwritten rules governing this process is that an individual has to be invited to join a board. Campaigning or lobbying for a directorship is just not done. In fact, few things are so calculated to turn off a selection committee as a candidate who is seen as being too pushy. There are ways of having one's name injected into the process, but they are subtle, personal, and informal. Eagerness to serve is considered bad form.

What is wrong with the system used by Tormax? It is simple and straightforward, quick and inexpensive. It does much to ensure compatibility of the candidates, and uses the prior knowledge and contacts of the board in an effective way. While we concede some of the strengths of the system, we believe that it is at the root of larger problems, and although the procedure may have been useful in an earlier era of *laissez-faire* for business, it is no longer adequate for the pressures that have been building on corporations and their governance.

Many corporate boards have been widely characterized as ineffective, impotent and irrelevant. Most have been criticized as secretive, closed, narrow and inbred, removed from the realities of the society that surrounds them. Periodic catastrophic decisions have emanated from corporate boards composed of sterling, high-minded and intelligent businessmen and women selected by the above process. How can this be?

The directors of our largest corporations represent a unique and elite part of society. Despite decades of criticism and sporadic attempts at change, they remain predominantly male, middle-aged or older, WASP businessmen and professionals. They are distinctly higher-income, and by and large, well-educated and experienced gentlemen (seldom women!). Furthermore, in many companies, barring serious personal or professional problems, sale or collapse of the company, they hold their appointments under a kind of informal tenure that means they have the job until age 70. They are not overly well paid for their services as directors, but there are numerous perks, and it is, generally, a rather comfortable pew. Depending on the scope of the company's operations, with a relatively small group to draw on, directors usually know each other, often went to the same schools, live in the same neighbourhoods, belong to the same clubs, and frequently serve together on several boards. Not surprisingly, they share similar value systems, political beliefs, interests and activities.

The traditional methods of selecting directors tend to reinforce this picture and make change very difficult. But, as the world outside is and has been changing rapidly, corporations must change as well. They have not been doing this. Their structures, processes, and methods of governance produce a resistance to change and a preservation of the *status quo*. This increasing divergence between the rapidly-changing environment of business and the slow response of many business organizations is creating a crisis of governance, which is at once an opportunity for those that can grasp and meet the challenge, and a threat to the existence of those who cannot. This applies at least as much to corporate boards as it does to management itself. Corporate boards need to become more effective; as long as they are chosen by the kind of process followed by Tormax, most will not do so.

We do not underestimate the difficulty of change. Many, if not most, corporate boards are locked in a power-sharing arrangement and culture that is extraordinarily deep-rooted and complex. Effecting change is not a matter of appointing more outside directors, imposing onerous liabilities on directors or developing lengthy and punitive regulations. It is much more fundamental than that, and it starts and ends with the chairman.

STEPS TO BETTER DIRECTOR SELECTION

The most important single requirement for effecting change in boards is having a chairman who knows what he or she wants and is determined to get it. One key and important element in achieving this is a willingness to adopt a more proactive, planned, and rigorous director selection procedure. Director selection itself is part of a vital process of renewal and change; it begins with the need for a director, and it is not finished until the new director has been integrated as an effective contributor to a total team effort focused on shareholder value.

Achieving a better balanced board can be broken into four basic steps:

Planning Board Composition

The approach taken by Tormax and many other companies is personal, completely *ad hoc* and unplanned, with preservation of the chairman's personal power often as a prime motivator and hidden agenda. A few months before a director is due to retire, someone, usually the chairman, starts looking for a good individual, preferably one he or she knows. An individual who is "one of us," who knows the unwritten rules, who will not rock the boat, and who will fit in with the rest and add lustre to the board.

This approach ensures harmony but it does little, if anything, to add a different point of view. The board remains male, white, Anglo-Saxon, "establishment", and frequently insulated by power, wealth and association from major parts of society and the world outside. No confrontations, showdowns or even challenges here! The discomfort level is low to non-existent.

Some companies take a more rigorous approach and plan their board with strategic considerations and objectives in mind. Tormax is an international company, with major operations in other countries. Should there not be someone on the board who knows these other areas well and has contacts there? Similarly, many of Tormax's products are purchased and consumed by women; how well do a group of aging men understand the problems and viewpoints of this segment of their market? Tormax operates internationally, yet the board is composed almost entirely of Toronto-based businessmen. How well do they understand the viewpoint of other parts of the country, or other countries, and the problems of doing business in these regions?

Of course, specifications such as these are no substitute for an individual's worth and qualifications. Better ten really able male board members from Toronto than a board with barely competent representatives of regions, experience, or gender. But all talent does not reside in Toronto; competent, qualified candidates exist within these other categories if one takes the trouble to look; it is surely not out of the question to develop, over time, a board combining both competence *and* varying backgrounds and viewpoints.

Surely the place to start the planning process is by looking at the objectives, strategy, and operations of the company. From this, the specifications of an ideal board mix can be developed that will be unique to each company, and will serve as a guideline and starting point for the process of planning the selection of directors. Several boards on which we serve have undertaken this exercise as part of the management resource committee's mandate; the process has never failed to produce active involvement in a worthwhile and productive exercise.

By overlaying the profile of the present board on the profile of the ideal board, gaps that should be corrected can be identified. Looking at normal retirement dates for existing directors indicates a minimum or base timetable when changes can be made. If this timetable is too slow, candidates for early retirement may have to be identified from among the weaker contributing board members. Plans for the ideal board indicate the specifications to be sought in looking for replacements.

Developing Director Specifications

The operational requirements for being an effective director today are demanding and growing. The complexity of business and the strategic challenges facing corporations call for minimum directorship qualifications that are not readily met. Integrity and independence of thought are fundamental; without them, no director can meet the trusteeship requirements of the job. Moreover, today's corporate director cannot operate effectively without a good grasp of the realities of business operations, an understanding of the changes that are taking place in the business environment, and a facility with the language of financial statements, accounting concepts, systems of organization and the like. In addition, he or she must have time available — lots of time — and a willingness to commit it to the affairs of the company.

Such minimum qualifications do not come easily. They eliminate most of the population as candidates. But boards are not designed to be legislative or representative bodies, reflecting all aspects of society. They have onerous responsibilities; the livelihood of thousands of people, of entire communities, may hinge on their decisions. The fundamental skills and talent to analyze and come to grips with such issues must be in place.

The necessity for directors to possess such skills explains why most businesses take the easy route and appoint other CEOs or prominent businessmen to their boards; those people have, after all, by their present stature demonstrated prior competence on such issues. But this competence, while necessary, is often not sufficient. Over and above such minimum skills are other, less obvious, qualities: sensitivity to regional, ethnic or gender viewpoints; understanding the nature of the business and industries in which it competes, trends and developments in government regulatory agencies or other key institutions likely to affect the corporation's future. Also needed are specialized skills that are important to the kind of company or industry, leadership, life experience, judgment, knowledge of people, and ability to work as part of a team.

Planning board composition also implies planning succession. The age mix of a board is a significant consideration. Having several experienced and competent directors retire at or about the same time can result in a serious loss of the board's collective memory. Staggering ages and thus retirements, so that a balance of experience and freshness is preserved, should be a key goal of the planning process.

There is no single template for developing director specifications, but it starts with the corporation's objectives and strategy, and should embody a job description for directors that is particular to, and developed by, that organization, one that combines the generic requirements for good directorship with company-specific requirements that flow from its unique ownership pattern and strategy. The job description, coupled with the specifications necessary to carry it out effectively, is the pillar on which a director selection process is built.

Searching For, Screening and Selecting Candidates

The places to look for prospective directors will be dictated by the specifications that will have emerged from the planning stage. If the company has significant international interests, it makes sense to have someone on the board who is well "plugged into" the foreign countries involved. If the company is heading into real environmental problems, it will need to look for someone with expertise in that area. No longer will it be acceptable to pick someone whose main qualification is that the person happens to be on another board with the chairman, and who gets along well with him or her. A planned process of board development carries with it a commitment of energy, time and money to the search process. It may call for hiring consultants to help with the process, as people with the sort of specifications described are unlikely to result from contacts at the chairman's club, or to be found among the personal acquaintances of board members.

A number of executive search firms have recently begun to develop practices specializing in director searches. Some of them have international offices, and can draw on those resources if candidates are sought outside the country. Others specialize in recruitment of talented women. The appropriate consultant will be driven by the strategy of the firm and specifications sought in each case. Yet others can be employed to check out credentials and reputation, factors that may be important if the candidate is not personally known to the existing board.

Regardless of the resources used, the process will inevitably be more time consuming and expensive than the less formal methods of the past. Mistakes will still be made. But the effort is worth it. Several companies are still living with the embarrassment and disruption caused by ''big name'' directors whose egos and reputations turned out to be much larger than their competence and commitment. This could have been forestalled with adequate research. A director represents a significant, long-term commitment for a company, with costly potential for error; it is worth doing the search and selection job thoroughly and well.

In the process, the expectations of both parties must be clearly communicated and harmonized. Too often, busy CEOs are wooed onto other boards by promises that the job ''won't be too time-consuming, just six (or eight or whatever) meetings a year'' — and so on. Such statements ill serve either party. Better to start with frank and demanding expectations and be refused than to bring someone into a situation that calls for more than the person had been led to expect or is willing to give.

This is where the director's job description comes in. At the very least, the job description should be prepared and circulated to candidates, together with any standards of performance that may have been developed. Elaboration of expectations, including committee assignments and workloads, and an indication of preparation requirements, should be part of any interview. Where possible, the chairman should encourage candidates to talk to existing board members to capture some flavour of the board's operations.

Briefing and Training New Directors

With the selection, most boards tend to consider the process complete. The new director is introduced at the annual meeting and welcomed to the first board meeting thereafter. And that is the extent of orientation, briefing, and introduction. Some background papers and annual reports may have been sent, and the new director may have been a guest at a lunch with the chairman, but usually not much more. Most boards operate on the principle of dropping the director into the deep end of the pool and letting him or her learn to swim. This is manifestly ridiculous; the job should be more analogous to wading in from the shallow water with a lot of hand-holding. Even for new directors who have had considerable previous experience on boards — good or bad — there is much to learn before they can become effective contributors. Other directors, with the advantage of years of prior experience with the company, have a presence and speak at board meetings with an authority that can be quite intimidating. It takes time for new directors to sense what issues they can take a stand on and add value, how far they can go in pushing or querying before they become aware of the ''no-man's land'' where they are not expected to probe, or before they are prepared to challenge established members of the board.

New directors need to be brought up to speed as quickly as possible. The planning of this process is surely the responsibility of the chairman. Plans should be worked out for the director to visit company facilities, to meet key executives, and to become familiar with company products. Background history and data should be provided, along with any recent analysts' reports on the company.

Furthermore, briefing should be provided on the role of the board and what is expected of the director. Major shareholders should be introduced. Legal briefings should be held on matters such as personal liability and insurance, purchasing or selling company shares, and insider trading reports. Briefings on committee responsibilities and concerns should also be held. In short, the chairman must coach new directors to bring them to an effective level of contribution. Usually this is done inadequately or not at all.

THE NOMINATING COMMITTEE PLAYS A MAJOR ROLE

In the case of the Tormax Manufacturing Company, the process was guided by unwritten rules and essentially led by the chairman, working with the major shareholder. The board had a kind of veto over candidates proposed by the chairman, but directors knew full well that the chairman's nominee had been cleared with the major shareholder, and they were not expected to upset the process or disturb the power structure by suggesting other names or by raising major objections unless there was new information damaging to the candidates. This process is faulty, and should be made more formal, proactive, open, and rigorous. The basic issue is power and responsibility: a more formal and open process implies a greater sharing of that power among the members of the board.

The question of who is to manage this process is critical. The chairman obviously plays a key role. But where the chairman is also the CEO, the process breaks down. One of the key functions of the board is to monitor and reward or punish the CEO in the performance of his or her job of managing the business. Where the CEO has selected the directors, this board responsibility creates problems. With all the best intentions in the world, it would be a naive (and foolish) CEO who consciously chose directors who were likely to be critical or want some of his or her power. And the directors chosen by the chairman/CEO would think twice about being critical of the person who chose them as director, and who could remove them from that job. The result is, predictably, a lot of mutual back-scratching, or implicit cooperation.

If the chairman is not the CEO, these objections do not apply and the chairman can, and must, play a key leadership role in the director selection process. In many companies, the chairman is assisted by a nominating committee, on which he or she also would normally be a member. The major shareholder, if there is one, would also be represented. The balance of the membership should be independent directors.

The introduction of the independent nominating committee has been one of the most significant developments in corporate governance in recent decades. It has been designed to minimize the illogical and self-fulfilling characteristics of the CEO-led selection process, and to inject a greater degree of independence in the board itself. The committee plays a principal role in the first three stages of the four we have proposed, particularly when the chairman is also CEO.

Clearly, choosing directors will ordinarily involve any major shareholder. The directors, after all, are there to represent shareholders, and the major shareholder's wishes can and should be given substantial weight in the choice of new directors. But that is not the whole story; since the board's duty is to all shareholders, including the minority, the selection of new directors must also take into account the preparedness of the prospective director to influence or even to take a stand in opposition to the major shareholder. Nominations may come from the major shareholder, but other committee members must be free to nominate directors as well. And decisions should be made on the basis of the votes of individual committee members, of which the major shareholder may be just one. Some observers have suggested that the nominating committee should consist exclusively of independent directors, and that the major shareholder's role should be reduced to having a veto over candidates proposed by the committee.

Control over this process is obviously of great importance. In the long term, it determines the role, composition, and power of the board. Some commentators believe that the nominating committee is the key board committee and the key to sound corporate governance. We concur. The composition, mandate, and operation of the nominating committee should be subject to clear and open terms of reference and policies, and its members should be some of the most senior, experienced, and competent independent members of the board.

CONCLUSION

The selection of directors is critical to effective governance. If the process is handled well, a strong board will result and the corporation's long-term interest will be served. If the process is handled badly, as it too often is, the company ends up with a weak, insulated, and self-perpetuating board that leaves the corporation vulnerable to catastrophic decisions and losing strategies.

The process can be managed. Ideally it should be planned and proactive, flowing from the unique character and strategy of each company. It should result in a board that is right for that company at that point in history, and provide for continuity and reasonable stability in the process of renewal and growth.

Chapter 14

BOARD CULTURE: Generating Constructive Dissent

Every board has a culture resulting from the firm but unwritten rules dictating how directors should think, speak and behave, both in board meetings and in other contacts in the company. These implicit but long-established codes, absorbed almost automatically by observing and interacting with other board members, heavily influence everything a board does and how it does it.

This insiders' club rules range from the subtle — the appropriate tone and degree of deference directed at different personalities on the board, proper speaking order when the chairman asks for an opinion, or seating at the boardroom table, to the blunt — "I don't think you should bring this up", or "we just don't do things that way on this board". Established members of a board have learned these rules over time; new members learn them by listening and observation. Indeed many of the social rules (politeness, deference, respect) will have been learned much earlier in the director's upbringing, and less-than-rigorous director selection processes focused on a candidate's compatibility tend to reinforce the unstated rules of behaviour. Couple this with the pressures of the process of consensual decision-making and limited time for discussion, and the result is often a tendency to "group-think".

Culture, the board mold into which a director must fit in order to work comfortably with other board members, is a powerful factor in board effectiveness. Our purpose in this chapter is to examine different board cultures and consider the key element in the culture of effective boards — constructive director dissent.

BOARD CULTURE

Board culture embraces the set of established beliefs, values, attitudes, traditions, norms, rituals, role models and ways of thinking and acting that shape the way a board and its directors behave.

Beliefs are what directors think they know, understand and hold to be true. For example, ''companies are run by management, not by shareholders'', ''or governments have no place in private business'', or ''subsidizing an operation leads to inefficiency''. These are all important beliefs of many directors.

Values are priorities with respect to what is important and respected. ''Integrity is the most important quality of a director'', or ''directors should focus on shareholder value''.

Attitudes are preconceived opinions, prejudices or judgments that govern thinking and action: ''our competitors will do anything to take away one of our customers'' or ''unions have too much power''.

In our experience, there is remarkable homogeneity among directors in terms of their beliefs, values, and attitudes. This is hardly surprising, considering that the preponderance of directors are white, male, middle-aged or older, well-educated, well-to-do, went to the same schools, travel in the same social circles, play the same sports, belong to the same clubs, and share many of the same political beliefs.[1]

The norms, traditions, and rituals under which board business is conducted follow very similar patterns. It is customary for directors to wear conservative suits to meetings, to greet each other formally at the outset of the meeting, to sit at a particular place at the table, to get the approval of the chair before speaking. In the normal course of events, directors meet six or eight times a year on a regular schedule, and proceedings follow a regular pattern, approving minutes of the previous meeting and having the CEO or CFO report on the results of the intervening period, followed by reports from various board committees. Traditions are frequently respected: oil paintings of previous chairmen ring the room; the December meeting is usually preceded by a Christmas dinner to which spouses are invited; uniformed waiters often serve tea or coffee from elegant china at intervals during the meetings.

These are only some of the more evident trappings of culture at most corporate boards. More important subtle but powerful elements strongly influence the pattern of discussion and the manner in which decisions are reached. Ultimately, the culture becomes so ingrained that the pattern of behaviour is taken for granted and never examined critically.

We have postulated that board cultures can be broadly categorized as one of two types, the ''old'', representing the more traditional and passive board, and the ''new'' — professional, vigorous, challenging, dynamic and involved (Exhibit 14.1). In cases where the old culture prevails, it often controls the directors. In the new culture, it is the other way around: directors establish, form, control, and use the culture as a means to the end

Exhibit 14.1

THE OLD AND THE NEW BOARD CULTURES

	BEHAVIOR CODE **OLD**	**NEW**
Approach	Passive	Active
Function	Ratification	Leadership
Style	Reactive	Assertive
	CULTURE	
Beliefs	Directors are honoured guests, cheerleaders to support management	Directors are trustees, consultants, leadership agents for shareholders
Values	Prestige, ego, selfish, exclusiveness, shrewd politics, autocracy	Servant leadership professionalism, management excellence, democracy, collegiality
Attitudes	Follow the group, be compatible	Be responsible, take charge, dissent as appropriate
Norms	Guardedness, political correctness	Openness, problem oriented
Traditions	Formality, indirectness	Informality, directness
Rituals	Process, politics	Penetrating analysis, group discussion
Heroes	Powerful, wealthy, tough CEOs	Professional, modern leaders, managers, innovators, Alfred Sloan types
Role Models	Old fashioned, macho CEOs	Counsellors and coaches, turn-around specialists

of effective board operation. The old culture seems by comparison dysfunctional and stultifying, whereas the new culture is empowering and healthy. The old culture seems trapped in a vicious circle in which it is difficult, if not impossible, to get the other key success factors strong and working. When the new culture is strong, it leads almost automatically to improvement throughout the board's operation, and board discussions feature the kind of open, positive and constructive dissent that is the true added value of a good board.

CONSTRUCTIVE DISSENT IS THE DUTY OF DIRECTORS

For many chairmen and CEOs it is almost a matter of faith that the board is there to support management, and their boards are run on this presumption. Directors who challenge management in such a situation often meet with defensiveness, hostility, and incomprehension, and are viewed as under-informed nuisances, liabilities rather than assets.

It should be just the opposite. Constructive, timely dissent can be the most important duty of directors. What is the point of a board that exists only to support management? Such a board is not only redundant, it is dangerous, because it gives a veneer of credibility to management decisions that may or may not be justified. It is fundamental to corporate governance that management proposes and the board judges and disposes. In this system, without effective director dissent, management runs unchecked, resulting at best in less-than-optimal performance and frequently in disaster.

What is needed, in the words of one former CEO, "... is a change in the culture, an acceptance of ... [the] view that a good director is a pain in the ass — a guy who recognizes that he's not working to be the friend of the CEO, but to do what's right for the owners of the business."[2]

EXAMPLES OF DIRECTORS DISAGREEING

To illustrate let us describe a few cases that any experienced director will find familiar.

The board of Company A, a huge chemical company, included a widely-respected senior director who was noted for asking tough, penetrating questions that got to the heart of important issues. In a board meeting in which a presentation was being made seeking approval of a major investment for a new product, the senior director listened to a long, detailed description of the technology involved and related production, marketing, financial, and organizational plans. Eventually, after listening carefully to the ensuing discussion, he asked one question: "How many other competitors are going to get into this business?" Since no one really knew, the director asked that his question be recorded in the minutes for follow-up. At the next meeting the answer was given: "Several." After considerable discussion, the director spoke in this meeting for the first time, asking his next question: "If there are several other competitors, what do we bring to the business that will give us a distinctive competence and competitive advantage?" The resulting discussion revealed that the company was contemplating entering a business that promised to be impossibly competitive on a ''me-too'' basis, an answer that was unacceptable not only to him but also to other directors. His next question was: ''Why then should we get into this business?'' Answering it himself, he expressed a strong opinion that the investment should not be made. His argument carried the day. As it turned out, his dissent saved the company from a $200-million mistake.

* * * * *

Company B, a leading, independent public company, was caught in a worsening, worldwide competitive battle. Strongly urged by the management and the chairman, the board decided to recommend acceptance of an offer to merge with a dominant foreign competitor through a cashless stock swap, with its shares being priced at $28, their then market value. One veteran director disagreed. He argued that the stock was worth much more, that in making the decision in a seven-hour emergency meeting called on a Sunday, the board was acting precipitously, that directors were not asking enough questions about the effects of the deal on the company and were not actively soliciting better offers. After adamantly opposing and trying to block the deal orally and in writing at several subsequent board meetings, the director was denounced by the board, threatened with legal action and treated as a pariah. Not dissuaded, he went public, and in the delays in the legal process required by regulatory agencies he campaigned against the deal personally and in the media. Largely as a result of his efforts, a second competitor bid $30 per share. In response, the original bidder upped his offer to a preemptive $37, a gain of $250 million over the first offer.

Soon after the deal, the director was praised in the business press as the ''courageous lone voice of dissent'' who single-handedly defended shareholders' rights and saved the company from a board decision that would have sold control *en bloc* to a foreign owner at far below the company's real value. While he took great satisfaction in being vindicated, he was bitterly disappointed in his fellow directors, exhausted by the personal strain and stress, disillusioned by the experience, and exasperated at having to pay personal legal expenses of over $30,000.

* * * * *

Company C, controlled by a major shareholder, went through a much publicized failure, with subsequent public shareholder charges of wrongdoing and an investigation by a securities commission. The company secretary, a lawyer, prepared a brief defending the major shareholder on business judgment grounds, and stating that all directors had unanimously agreed with actions taken and statements released to the press. One director, who had vigorously opposed the decisions made and policies followed, protested to the company secretary that the brief should indicate his opposition. In his discussion the following heated exchange occurred:

Director: You know full-well that I argued long and hard that these things were wrong and never should have been done!

Secretary: Oh no you didn't. You never criticized or opposed any of these actions.

Director: That's not true! This is incredible! You were there! You know I did!

Secretary: No, as far as I'm concerned you didn't! Ever! There's the minute book. If you think you did, show me where in the record.

Since the director had made no written submission to the board and had not demanded that his dissents be recorded in the minutes, legally he was on very weak ground. Technically his dissents did not exist.

* * * * *

In Company D, after a long and difficult meeting, a senior vice-president and inside director close to retirement approached an outside director who had taken a tough stand against a major proposal being pushed by the chairman/CEO, and ostensibly backed by management. Taking the outside director aside, in a very low voice the senior vice-president made the following statement, "Thank you for all you are doing to help. We're lucky to have you. You would never believe what's going on here behind the scenes. Those of us who are insiders know this proposal is wrong, but our hands are tied. We can't say anything. We're all counting on you to keep up the good work."

* * * * *

DISSENT SHOULD BE MANAGED

Any experienced director will be familiar with these scenarios. They occur in many, if not most, boards. They involve clashes of opinion and power at the highest levels for the highest stakes. Almost invariably they are zero-sum games — somebody wins and somebody loses, often with serious consequences. Large egos are confronted and long memories persist. For obvious reasons, these confrontations are seldom made public except when the issues are disclosed in legal hearings or become so explosive they are picked up by the media. Obviously, from a public relations point of view, such revelations are anathema to the company. Informed dissent, however, remains important to the effective functioning of any board.

SKILLFUL CHAIRMEN SEEK CONSENSUS

Boards of directors operate on a consensual basis. Unanimity is the rule; votes are seldom recorded, and dissenting votes almost never. A skillful chairman guides the discussion to a point where he or she senses a consensus forming before calling for the question. If there are obvious dissenters or serious unanswered questions, the chairman will either continue discussion until differences have been resolved, or postpone discussion for a later meeting. Rarely will the chairman try to force a decision on a divided board unless it is a major matter and time is critical. Obviously, interpersonal skills of a high order are called for. Their lack on the part of the chairman can severely inhibit the process of board discussion and dissent.

To dissent means to disagree, but disagreement can be expressed on many different issues, in many different ways, and to many different degrees. For a director to dissent in the board context usually means to question, criticize, debate, or oppose a management-backed recommendation or action that implicitly or explicitly has CEO approval. To reach the board level such an issue will usually be strategically important to the company. Almost invariably such issues are considered and recommendations developed through an extensive and intensive organizational due process. As a result, management recommendations on proposed decisions, plans and policies are normally made only after careful management study, discussion and agreement, and the decision of the CEO to present the finished product to the board for approval. Consequently, for a director to disagree is a very serious matter, not to be undertaken lightly.

Ill-considered or frivolous dissent can be very disruptive to board functioning, and indeed to the company as a whole. Effective dissent is appropriate disagreement, selectively applied and powerful enough to challenge or change a recommended decision so as to improve the results and enhance shareholder value.

Effective director dissent is what is missing in high level councils when something goes dreadfully wrong. As such, it is the most important responsibility of any director. That is what directors are for — to bring judgment, breadth of viewpoint, standards, and perspective to the decisions that are made, balancing the focused and often technical perspective of management. That is the value-added by an effective board.

THE CONTEXT OF DIRECTOR DISSENT

The context of director dissent has two basic dimensions: (1) Dissent usually relates to issues arising in the process of strategic management, including moral and ethical standards, and (2) it takes place in the operational arena of the board of directors.

This usually takes place at the board meeting, where strategic issues are introduced, discussed and resolved for the record, the usual approach being for management to identify and raise problems, propose solutions and recommendations, review and discuss them with the board, and ask for formal approval. Typically, because board time is severely limited and there is much material to cover, there is scant discussion of issues until they reach the decision-making stage. By then, of course, management has done the research and fact-finding, analyzed the evidence, drawn conclusions, and made decisions pending board approval. As a result, management's position is generally firmly set, organizational positions have been taken, careers may be on the line, and the die tends to be cast. This makes in-depth review and discussion by the board somewhat redundant and dissent difficult and unwelcome. Occasionally, in cases where implementation has already begun, dissent is pointless. The timing of board intervention in the process is thus critical: too late, and it becomes very difficult for any individual, no matter how strong the argument, to alter the course of the corporate ship.

THE SUBJECTS OF DISSENT

While the problems of dissent are unique to any board, the topics tend to repeat and are commonly found across a variety of companies. The sensitive issues that most frequently trigger dissent among directors tend to fall in one or more of seven categories:

1. *Major decisions*: Important recommendations on vital subjects such as financial structure, investments, mergers, acquisitions, divestments, adding or dropping product lines, geographical expansion or contraction, organizational changes and other basic problems.

2. *Company public communications*: Official reports requiring directors'

due diligence and approval including prospectuses, proxy statements, reports to shareholders, public disclosures, and news releases.

3. *Unsatisfactory results*: Where budgets, profit plans and performance targets are not being met; when shareholder wealth is being eroded because return on investment on specific capital investments, organizational sub-units, or the company as a whole does not show a satisfactory margin over cost of capital. This is a signal often causing great director concern, spirited questioning, and pointed admonitions and recommendations.

4. *Strategy:* The master plan defining the scope and nature of the company, and how its purpose is to be achieved.

5. *Top management changes*: Hiring, firing, promotion, transfer, evaluation and compensation of key executives, especially the CEO and officers of the company.

6. *Policy changes*: Key changes in important policies such as pension and benefit plans, environmental management, employment, safety and health rules and regulations, compensation plans, conduct, ethics, and other basic operating rules.

7. *Company culture, processes, morality, ethics and values*: Sloppy analysis, "surprises", missed deadlines, signs of complacency, lack of competitiveness, failure to challenge the status quo, lack of vitality, slowness in needed turnarounds, improper behavior and relationships with customers, suppliers, governments and potential investors.

While this list is not exhaustive, it does include the topics that most frequently raise the red flag and cause directors to intervene with questions, expressions of disagreement and suggestions for change of one sort or another.

DEGREES AND TYPES OF DISSENT

There are many different manifestations and degrees of dissent (Exhibit 14.2). For example, Company A described earlier is a textbook example of the penetrating-question dissent. The approach taken by the dissenting director resembles the style of Henry Fonda, the dissenting juror in the classic film, *Twelve Angry Men*. In this story, the protagonist, a lone juror who believes that a man accused of murder is innocent, reverses the

Exhibit 14.2

DEGREE OF DISSENT

KEY FACTORS	LATENT	MILD	MODERATE	SERIOUS	TOTAL
Visible response and behaviour of director	Dissent not expressed verbally. Negative body language, aversion of eyes, disinterest.	Simple questioning with no follow-up. Concern mild.	Tough questions with follow-up. Concern significant.	Tough questions with answers pursued by tough cross-examination; misgivings stated. Opposition obvious. Abstain or vote against.	Convinced disagreement, argued hard and long. Opinion can't be changed. Opposition vociferous. Vote against. Resign, go public. War.
Surface message	I don't support this, but won't openly oppose it.	I see possible problems; you should be careful.	I think there are real problems; you should do more investigation because you may be making a mistake.	These are serious problems. I won't vote for this.	This is absolutely wrong. I am totally opposed. I will campaign and vote against it.
Potential benefits/ costs to director	Minimal	Indicates interest, concern. Participation acceptable, positive if not overdone.	When done occasionally for good reason, establishes wisdom, commitment and contribution, but if overdone perceived negatively, loose cannon, disruptive.	May be seen as tough, able and courageous in taking a position on difficult issues, but in dangerous territory with high risks if not correct.	May be seen as white knight, valuable leader, but relationships, influence and power may be ruined. High professional, legal, social, psychological risks and costs.
Potential benefits/ costs to company	Minimal	Keeps management aware that directors participate and try to contribute.	Stirs up valuable dialogue; may warn of unanticipated problems, but board cohesion and processes may be hurt.	May lead to changes, improvements of great value to company but management may lose face. Board unity and CEO leadership set back.	May prevent disastrous mistake, unwise plan or policy and serious loss, but threatens board unity. Effect on loser(s) may be termination, bad publicity almost certain.

convinced conclusions of the other 11 jurors through rational and civilized questions and analysis of the evidence. The end result is a sound decision agreed to by the various participants without loss of face. A very different model is the hostile clash described in Company B, where the dissenting director is isolated and goes public, resembling the pattern of Western films where the white hats and the black hats shoot it out for large stakes in a winner-takes-all battle.

Between these two dramatic extremes are many different degrees of dissent, which can be clustered in five levels as follows:

1. Latent Dissent

Dissent in its lowest or most neutral form is dormant — submerged and hidden. While for many reasons a dissenting view may not be volunteered, it would be a serious miscalculation to assume it does not exist or, worse yet, mistake it for approval. While such a dissenter may vote approval, suppressed doubt and potential opposition may be manifested at a later date on this or other issues.

2. Mild Dissent

The first manifest level of dissent is often expressed through a cool, low-stake, probing question. "I'm not sure I understand how this budget was put together. Could you tell us more about how the sales and cost figures were calculated?" While substantively simple, the underlying meaning of such a question can be ambiguous and hard to read. On the one hand the questioner might mean, "I'm a little uncertain on this and would like some assurance that you have really made a sound analysis," or on the other hand, "These figures don't make sense to me, but I don't want to be too critical until I check out you and your work." Answered with openness and good supporting information, the implied criticism of such a question can be overcome immediately. Answered with defensiveness, confusion, coverup and lack of information, the attitude behind the question soon hardens and rises to the next level.

3. Moderate Dissent

At this level, the director's criticism becomes more obvious. "I think this sales estimate is too high. Did you analyze the market, the new Asian competition and factor in the weakness of our marketing program?" Without adequate assurance, other directors also become concerned, climb on the bandwagon, and lend their weight to the growing opposition. However, in spite of their reservations, directors dissenting at this level will usually vote with the majority.

4. Serious Dissent

At this level, serious confrontation is inevitable. The focus may shift from information to people and process. "How was this budget put together?" (Why didn't you do a better job of fact finding and analysis? or, How did we get into this mess?); "Who did the work on this presentation?" (Who screwed up? or, Why didn't they know what they were doing?); "Why are you making this recommendation?" (Why didn't you stop this before it got to us?). At this level the board faces a serious problem and great skill is needed to help management or the questioning director to back off and save face. If not, disaster can be near as the problem escalates to its final stage.

5. Total Dissent

At this level, illustrated in the Company B case, there is an apparently irreconcilable, zero-sum game, win-or-lose confrontation. The company can declare war on the dissenting director, or try to freeze him or her out. The risks are so serious and the stakes so high that devastation of one side or the other is almost inevitable. Possible legal action or resignation of the director and potentially huge gains and losses for the company all come into play.

CHAIRMEN SHOULD BE SENSITIVE TO SIGNALS

Any intelligent and sensitive observer can perceive important signs of dissent long before it is obvious that questions are becoming pointed, cross-examination rough, the atmosphere tense, voices raised, and attack and defense serious. The key signals to look for are individual interests and attitude; body language; verbal, supportive intervention; position taking; manner and behaviour. Moreover, even in serious dialogue about open disagreements, the relatively guarded, civilized and professional culture and rules of permissible behavior usually prevail. As a result, reading the different surface and underlying meanings of the language of dissent is a skill requiring wisdom, experience and insight. When a director puts a superficially simple question to the CEO or chairman, it may have a much deeper meaning and more significant intent. As one director explained, "This chairman is so lacking in insight and sensitivity that when I press him about why results are off budget he doesn't understand that I am really telling him to smarten up, get off his butt, and start taking some real action to turn things around!''

REASONS FOR LACK OF DISSENT

If lack of dissent is so serious and widespread what are the reasons?

1. Board Culture Inhibits Dissent

The basic precepts of the widely prevalent ''old'' culture of the board demand conformity and obviously dampen, if not eliminate, dissent. The manner in which most board discussions take place is almost unfailingly polite and civilized. Directors have normally worked together for some years and usually intend to continue. They know and often like each other, come from similar backgrounds, and respect each other's skills and experience. They tend to share many basic values and often have close business and social ties. They operate on long-standing, unspoken assumptions and rules of behaviour that are seldom critically examined or discussed. Discussion relies on business jargon and terminology that could baffle laymen, but is completely understood by everyone in the room. Reflection, introspection, and soul-searching are rare. In their view, directors are present to share their experience and judgment, and are expected to ''get on with it,'' not wasting time in philosophizing. Directors are expected to have a view — not to express doubt or uncertainty. They typically bring a broad, long-term perspective to issues, downplaying company politics, job or career considerations. They hate surprises. This environment can be quite intimidating to a new, inexperienced director; the easy response lies in conformity with the majority view.

2. Many Directors are Incompetent and Unfit

If the essence of the board's task is to control and direct the firm in order to increase the value of its shareholders' investment, the critical value added is the judgment, knowledge, skills and attitudes required for prudent financial management. The key to creating shareholder wealth is the habitual pursuit of rational action following from present value analysis of all investments (forecast cash flows, discounted by the cost of capital) and the economic value-added of all operations (margin of return on investment over cost of capital). Many directors do not have the necessary education, training and experience in corporate finance to analyze, test, and pass judgment on investments and operations.

In addition, many directors lack the professional ability, self-confidence and courage to size up a business, analyze its problems and opportunities, understand the capabilities and limitations of its human resources, formulate appropriate action plans and then take an independent position defending their conclusions in top level councils — in other words to function capably in their role of consulting to management. In many corporate failures most directors simply did not understand the problems, let alone have the leadership ability to begin to solve them and initiate needed turnarounds.

Flaws in the process of selecting and ''training'' new directors, coupled with the absence of any rigorous evaluation of director performance, have resulted in many boards being heavily weighted with poor performers incapable of dealing with complex issues of corporate strategy, management performance, compensation and the like.

3. Few Chairmen and Directors Understand How to Manage the Board Process

Managing the board discussion and decision-making process is an art, not a science. It calls for not only a high degree of understanding and sensitivity from a competent chairman, but also perceptivity, sensitivity, discretion and skill on the part of individual directors. They must recognize their role in working together with others to reach a group conclusion that clearly serves the best interest of the company. Compromise is often required. It is the chairman's job to manage this process so that optimal results are achieved, not just on individual issues but over time. This is done through selection of competent board members, providing them with the necessary information, time and forum for expressing their views, drawing out their judgment, and guiding the process towards good decisions that the group is prepared to stand behind.

For the individual director, working effectively in such a process also requires important skills. Some of the more obvious problems are created by:

- Directors who do not do enough homework or have enough knowledge to attack with facts, logic, and conviction.
- Loose cannons who complain and cry wolf so often that no one takes them seriously.
- Ineffective, nonparticipators who lack credibility and influence.
- Lone wolves who do not build adequate group support to speak for a consensus and to make their points carry political weight.

- Instigators of self-serving power plays that are devoid of any real company benefits.
- Actions and tactics that are unprofessional and lacking in wisdom or integrity.
- Directors who do not understand the requirements of their own job, representing interests or constituencies other than those of the company as a whole and all its shareholders.
- Directors who insist on having their own way, are unwilling to work constructively towards a group decision, and, once a decision has been taken, refuse to close ranks and support the board decision.

4. Directors Often Lack the Necessary Information

The essence of board dissent is for directors to use their own perspective and judgment to discuss and reach positions, conclusions and recommendations that may differ from those of management. Since sound conclusions and recommendations must follow reasonably from good evidence and logical analysis, the key to being able to dissent effectively is having more, better, or different information than management, or doing a better job of analyzing what it means. This, of course, can raise a tremendous obstacle. Due to lack of time, restriction of sources and limitations of costs, directors generally get their information on specific issues from management. Moreover, they do not have the time or resources to match management's analysis. Directors' input may be sought too late in the process to allow them to do any further investigation. Frequently, managers under the control of autocratic chairmen or CEOs who are determined to have their own way may consciously or unconsciously deceive directors by reporting biased and incomplete information to back their own recommendations. Moreover, recently-publicized major governance problems indicate that, in many cases, directors are uninformed about subjects on which they almost certainly would have dissented if they had had the chance.

5. Dissent Involves Potentially Large Risks and Costs; Conformity Seldom Does

Dissent is usually based on uncertainty that arises from incomplete knowledge and debatable reasoning processes connecting evidence, analysis and conclusions. In confrontations involving conflicting points of view, if the director is right, management or other directors are wrong, and vice-versa. Dissent can therefore be a dangerous game in which ability, wisdom, logic, credibility, reputation, status and power are all on the line. It is hard to overestimate the potentially-huge personal costs incurred in terms of stress and social, economic and political losses. On the other hand, the personal rewards from effective dissent tend to be muted, intangible and long term. The board reward-punishment system encourages compliance and discourages dissent.

HOW TO ENCOURAGE CONSTRUCTIVE DISSENT

Without dissent, directors are redundant and irrelevant. Effective dissent should therefore not only be accepted as legitimate, but encouraged as necessary to the proper functioning of the board.

Through dissent the board benefits from better contributions and decisions, and, in the longer term, improved results and greater success. Major costs for the board as a group include the tension and stress of disagreement; confrontation and occasional unpleasantness (no matter how diplomatically handled); the worry and concern of facing up to uncertainty and difficult judgments and choices; and the worry of insights into the foibles and weaknesses of directors, managers and the organization. The costs of too little dissent — wrong decisions, drift, complacency, a non-contributing board — and of too much dissent — waste of time, confusion, gridlock, personal animosity, the negative atmosphere, discouragement, the undermining of management — can be equally serious. A reasonable balance should be the goal. Given the general consensus that many boards have failed to control and guide managers to achieve optimal results for shareholders, the only logical conclusion is that the balance of needed dissent has been lacking.

More directors should dissent more aggressively over performance, initiatives, decisions, and plans that need to be pushed back to management for rethinking and improvement, or, in some cases, abandonment. Dissent interventions also need to be more effective. They should be critical of unresolved problems and substandard work and performance. They should be constructive in getting to the heart of unresolved issues, suggesting better approaches and ideas, and active in stimulating demand, support, and reward for management improvements in creating shareholder value. Specific suggestions for all directors are:

- *Track the company's strategic agenda and dissent as early as possible in the issue development cycle.* The sooner dissent is registered, the more helpful and acceptable it is to management. If dissent is delayed until after minds are closed and decisions jelled, it is generally too late, and is resented.

- *Do your homework thoroughly.* The responsibility of a director is to control and guide the company by sizing up its businesses, understanding its problems and opportunities, and reviewing and assessing what management is doing and proposes to do. Excellence as a director demands insight and analysis, perspective on the issue agenda and priority of strategic problems, forecasting future scenarios on action agendas, and understanding the organizational network and process through which plans are implemented. Dissent effectiveness is based on demonstrated understanding, logic and judgment, without which criticism is credible neither to management nor to fellow directors.
- *Be sure that the degree and form of dissent is appropriate.* Depending on the importance of the problem and the context of the situation, widely differing degrees and kinds of dissent may be appropriate.
- *Beware of dissenting too little or too much.* Directors who seldom, if ever, dissent will be perceived as lightweights — rubber stamps — who will support almost anything the management does or proposes. Directors who dissent too often will be viewed as loose cannons — undisciplined, time wasters and a general pain.
- *Count the costs of dissenting or not dissenting and understand the risks involved.* If a high level of dissent is necessary, the company may declare war on the director with very serious consequences. However, better to take a stand and pay the price than duck the issue and pay much more later if disaster results.
- *Focus on evidence, analysis, conclusions, and recommendations and avoid personalities and politics.* Recognize and emphasize that dissent relates to sampling information, analyzing what the information means and perceiving the implications. Deciding what to do should always be last in the chain; issues about recommendations can best be resolved by first gaining agreement on the evidence and analysis.
- *Lobby for support.* The more dissent is supported by other directors, particularly those who are more influential, the stronger and more decisive it will be.
- *Minimize personal and political carryover baggage.* Once an issue is resolved, close ranks and get on with the job. Demonstrate goodwill

and cooperation with all, especially former opponents. Resist the natural inclination to remember, to be suspicious, to carry grudges and, if you lost, to get even.

- *Be responsible and courageous.* This sometimes means taking a tough position and resisting being intimidated, silenced or pushed around by management or other directors who do not understand or care. Many companies would have avoided debacles if they had directors who foresaw problems and paid the price to take a more vigorous stand against bad decisions.
- *Look beyond the surface manifestations of dissent.* Significant personal or interpersonal problems are often hidden below the surface. It is important to be able to read signs and signals that are not perceived by the casual observer. The art of dissent is obviously to get the maximum improvement for the minimum hassle. It is important to apply the appropriate kind and amount of pressure in the right way to achieve optimal results. Depending on the individuals and situation involved, this could be a one-on-one telephone call, lunch, letter or meeting of two or more to ask questions, request changes or threaten future action, or a more formal procedure of boardroom questioning, follow-up, and dialogue. Priorities, sequence and timing are also critically important. Judging by the number of directors who have run great risks or suffered serious costs by hanging on to their jobs in embarrassing circumstances, resignation is a dissent tactic not used nearly as often as it should be.
- *Be prepared to handle the potential legal problems of dissent.* The first legal issue in dissent is making sure it is correctly registered. This means (1) getting it on the record of minutes of meetings and (2) refusing to sign any legal document that has not, if necessary, been thoroughly checked and corrected. If dissent reaches a high level the major issue is knowing whether, when, and how to resign. At this stage independent legal counsel, even though expensive, bothersome and time-consuming, is necessary to avoid potentially serious procedural and judgment errors.

THE CHAIRMAN: KEY TO EFFECTIVE DISSENT

As in all other aspects of board operations, the chairman has the key role in managing the all-important function of dissent. Whether dissent is an unwanted problem (troublesome fault-finding by impertinent, uninformed directors who are trying to butt in on affairs that they should leave to management) or an invaluable opportunity (the priceless cautioning and counsel of committed, knowledgeable trustees and consultants that helps stimulate and motivate management to achieve success and avoid failure) depends largely on the chairman.

Master chairmen use dissent to advantage in getting at problems, improving management and improving cooperation. For example, one outstanding chairman we know has an almost routine reaction to questions, possible criticisms or objections. First he sincerely thanks the questioner, often commenting on the importance of the issue raised. Then he asks the CEO or presenting manager for an explanation that specifically addresses the concerns raised. When this has been delivered he asks the director for a comment or reply. If this suffices, he will move on. If not, judging by the concern of the questioner and the interest of the rest of the board, he will encourage dialogue and comments by others. If this leads to a clear consensus he will then move on. If not, he will refer the matter back to management for more investigation, review and a subsequent report, often asking the director and manager involved to meet to discuss any remaining issues. This chairman is noted for running good meetings: the culture is open and dissent is routine, professional, expected and legitimate; meetings cover routine quickly, and slow right down for discussion of questions.

One of the many interesting paradoxes of the chairman's job is that, notwithstanding the legitimacy and desirability of dissent, he or she should always work hard to make it unnecessary. The necessary and legitimate ways to minimize dissent are to manage so well that results are good and plans and proposals are sound and well-presented. Directors' questions and objections are anticipated by getting management to address them voluntarily, to ensure a culture that is open, informed, and sensitive to developing issues, to avoid complacency and defensiveness and to inform and involve directors on issues before opinions, decisions and plans have jelled and change involves loss of face.

The management of dissent is a primary problem and one of the most basic reasons why many boards have been less than effective in their governance function. Only if the importance of dissent is recognized and the management of dissent is handled positively can boards develop a culture that will enable them to function as they should.

NOTES

This chapter has been taken, with some changes, from our earlier article: ''Effective Director Dissent'', *Business Quarterly* (Summer, 1994), which won the Deloitte and Touche Award for best article of 1994. It was subsequently reprinted in *Significant Issues Facing Directors: 1996*, published by Directorship, Inc., and the Institute for Research on Boards of Directors, Inc., Greenwich, Ct., 1996.

1. This pattern of social homogeneity has been documented in numerous research studies, including those cited in the endnotes to Chapter 12.

2. John Hanley, retired CEO of Monsanto Chemical Co., quoted in ''Directors, Wake Up!'', by Myron Maguet, *Fortune*, June 15, 1992, p. 92.

Chapter 15

MANAGING THE BOARD'S WORK

WESTGLEN MINES

Frank Funston, chairman of Westglen Mines, opened the board's discussion on the agenda topic, "Committee Assignments".

"As you all know only too well, we're a small board, and we seem to want to keep it that way. The fact is, there's a lot of work to be done, and our small board means a big commitment in time and effort from each of you. Not only do we have a lot of board meetings, but each of you is serving on at least two board committees as well.

"I think our 'busy-ness' tends to bog us down at times, and we don't seem to be spending enough time and attention on key strategic matters. For example, exploration and business development are critical in our business. We spend a couple of million dollars a year looking for mining opportunities and acquisitions, but we don't have a lot to show for it, and we don't spend a lot of time in the board looking at these aspects of our business — we spend a lot more time on pensions and our funds' investment performance!

"While I don't want to create yet another committee of the board, it seems to me that we need to get a lot more focused attention on both exploration and on business development, both of which are so important to our strategic planning. I'm proposing that we create a board committee for this purpose, with Jack Taylor as its chairman. Jack has had a lot of experience in this sort of thing with his own company. The committee would meet with our vice-presidents of exploration and business development regularly, monitor what's going on, and direct their activities along the lines of our corporate strategic plan. I'd be interested in your reaction."

Bill Brooks listened carefully. He liked this board and the way it operated. Funston was a good chairman and ran the board well. There were only ten directors all told, including Funston and the CEO. They all got along well, worked hard, and seemed to enjoy the experience. Westglen, a medium-sized producer with holdings in several countries, had performed extremely well. With a strong balance sheet and consistently profitable results, the stock had doubled in price in the last two years, outstripping most of its competitors.

Still, Brooks was dubious about Funston's proposal for a new board committee. One of the good things about this board, he felt, was that everyone participated actively in resolving major strategic matters. Exploration and business development were the essence of strategy in Westglen. Hiving off responsibility to a committee meant less involvement by those not on the committee, creating an "in-group" of directors controlling large parts of the strategic agenda. This made good sense for the audit, pension, compensation, human resources, and environment functions, where there were already committees: these were important, often technical, and called for special interest and skills, but they weren't central to strategy in the same sense as exploration and development. The more he thought about it, the less he liked Funston's idea: Yes, these topics needed more board attention. But creating a special committee was not the way to go about it.

* * * * *

CRITICAL FACTORS IN PLANNING THE BOARD'S WORK

Last, but not necessarily least, of the six critical factors affecting board effectiveness is the job of managing the ongoing work of the board. This includes planning and implementing the changes needed to upgrade the board for maximum effectiveness, picking up all the administrative details and putting them together, making sure that things run smoothly.

Organizing the work of the board is always a major item in the chairman's position description, and a key item in his or her standards of performance. It is the chairman's job to develop an operating process that makes the most productive use of the directors' time and effort; good people will not long tolerate an inefficient process, and if the board is poorly run, frustration generally leads either to a director revolt, or resignations. Doing this part of the chairman's job well takes commitment, time and continuing effort, and can make a real difference. Doing it badly virtually dooms the board's efforts from the start. Among other things, the chairman must demonstrate a high level of personal commitment if he or she wants to inspire it in others.

The guiding principle is that common *expectations* of the job to be done must set the pattern for the board, regardless of current practice or past culture. Securing some understanding, if not agreement, among major shareholders, top management and directors around these expectations is a vital step, and helps define and smooth the way for subsequent actions. The chairman, in other words, must have a clear set of objectives and a strategy for the board, communicated to, understood by, and agreed to by the principal players. This may take some selling, but from agreement on these objectives, the chairman can begin to develop a plan for carrying them out.

The chairman interested in moving his or her board towards the goals of competence, energy and more independence from management — in other words to create what we have called a ''new-style'' board — must consider the following:

1. board structure; size, committees, and organization,
2. meetings; frequency, location, agenda,
3. managing internal information,
4. external communication and disclosure,
5. managing director and board performance,
6. compensation of directors,
7. succession planning and selecting new directors, and
8. shareholder relations.

SIZE, ORGANIZATION AND STRUCTURE OF THE BOARD

If the job to be done should determine the way the board operates, and if the objective of the job to be done is to revitalize the board, then the board should be relatively small. A committed director expects, if not demands, that he or she will have meaningful work to do: legal responsibilities and director liability problems require no less. Large boards may provide an element of representativeness to the process, but they do not provide effectiveness; in the trade-off, effectiveness should be most important. Large boards are, by definition, rubber-stamp boards; small boards dig in and do the work. Large boards diffuse the responsibility and accountability, weakening their ability to deal with management from a base of power and legitimacy. It is difficult, if not impossible, to build a dynamic, proactive, and committed board culture with any group of 15 or more. If representativeness is a major concern, it should be dealt with in other ways, such as creating advisory committees or boards.

In our experience, a board of 8 to 10 members is optimal in most cases. Much more, and the sheer arithmetic of topics to be discussed and time available rule out effective participation. Much less, and it becomes difficult to divide up the work of the board. The normal corporate board has at least three or four committees, and to be effective, committees should have at least three members. The chairman is usually an auditor at most committees, and the CEO is excluded. This leads to independent board members serving on at least two committees. If committees are functioning effectively, this is a heavy load, especially if one of the committee assignments involves a chairmanship. It can also be a heavy load for the board chairman.

Much of the work of the board is increasingly done in committee, freeing the full board to focus more time on items of overall strategic importance. Corporate laws require companies to have at least an audit committee, and the practice in most medium to large companies is to also have a committee dealing with compensation and human resource issues, and a committee dealing with pension and retirement matters. More recently, with increasing attention focused on corporate governance, companies have been setting up committees to cover board nominations and other governance matters. The growth in director liability for safety and environmental matters has also spawned a rapid increase in the creation of such committees.[1]

Coupled with the expansion in the number of board committees has been a parallel growth in their activities. Formerly-sleepy audit committees have become proactive and probing, grilling management and the auditors not only on the financial statements, but on such matters as accounting policies, adequacy of internal controls, internal auditing, hedging strategy, computer security, disaster planning, risk management, pension funding, and audit costs. Compensation and human resource committees have expanded their terms of reference to include succession planning, pay equity, anti-discrimination regulation, training and labour relations issues. Pension committees have become important profit or loss centres dealing with a variety of complex issues arising from actuarial valuations, accounting for surpluses and deficits in pension funding, changing demographics of the work force, tax laws, and investment performance. Committees dealing with emerging issues of the environment, governance, worker health and safety have greatly expanded the reach of board responsibilities and concerns. The time and expertise required of directors in dealing with their committee responsibilities has seen an exponential increase in recent years, posing significant problems for chairmen in organizing the growing and more complex work load required of the board.

MEETINGS

The frequency of board meetings can be critical. Crisis situations or critical decisions often require directors to drop everything, and meet frequently and on short notice. While serving on independent directors' committees negotiating "going-private" transactions, we have attended as many as 35 meetings of a committee in the space of one year! Otherwise, regularly-scheduled meetings can be set up on a cycle to handle the ongoing and predictable work of the board. The pattern varies considerably: some meet monthly, some bi-monthly, some quarterly. For most companies, monthly is too frequent; attendance suffers, and the directors tend to "micro-manage"; by the same token, quarterly meetings leave too much time between meetings, and directors tend to get out of touch. A schedule of bi-monthly meetings with the option of calling *ad hoc* meetings as required has worked best for many boards on which we have served.

The regular, ongoing work of the board involves operating and financial reviews, operating and capital budget approvals, approval of major expenditures, legal requirements, banking resolutions, reports of committees, release of results, and compensation approvals. Such standing items take up much board time, and can be allocated on a regular cycle to specific board meeting agendas as required. Strategic matters, including a review of the board's own performance, come up less frequently, and are often the subject of a special board retreat each year or two. Many companies have a policy of holding board meetings at different plant locations, or in other places where the company has significant groups of employees, customers or stakeholders, in order to develop better communication with directors and "show the flag".

Focusing a great deal of work at the committee level frees full-board meetings to deal with other issues. Time is the most precious resource of competent, committed directors, there are limits to how long they can spend on board matters, and it is important for the chairman to set priorities and control the agenda. The most important issues for the board as a whole have to do with the company's strategic management and decisions arising from it, including the adequacy of management. Unless the time of board meetings is managed carefully, these key issues tend to receive short shrift, squeezed out by the parade of routine, legally-required reports and backup presentations by management. The sheer mass of work can lead to longer board meetings, producing fatigue and impeding participation and discussion.

INFORMATION MANAGEMENT

The quality of decisions made by the board can only be as good as the quality of information provided to directors. Managing the quantity and quality of information is a vital element in the chairman's job description. There are three fundamental information problems.

First, information packages for boards focus on past financial results of operations — sales, costs, profits, assets, liabilities, and cash flow. What is needed is information on leading indicators — customer satisfaction, developing trends in markets, technological forecasts, new product development, competitors' intentions, employee attitudes and the like. When this kind of future-oriented information is not made available to boards, their strategic management function is largely nullified.

Second, because management generally controls the agenda and is the source of most information that is made available to the board, directors are often explicitly or implicitly misled and deceived. The chief financial officer of one company told us that "on key strategic issues over the last five years, our directors were given either no information, half the information needed, or misleading information". In such a case, small wonder that the monitoring, consulting and control aspects of the board's job are done poorly!

Third, in many companies the information package sent to directors before each meeting is often too thick, takes too long to read, is difficult to understand, leaves problems buried in the numbers, and is not pointed towards relevant action options. Information is presented in raw form, leaving the directors to discern the issues and meaning. It takes time and trouble on the part of those responsible for the board to sift through the data, sort out irrelevant material, and digest it in meaningful form for the board to deal with; many managers take the path of least resistance and, when in doubt, throw in everything but the kitchen sink, hiding behind the defense that "it's in there — you must not have read the material carefully enough." Most directors who lack the time or commitment to sort through it all and make their own analysis remain on the outside of active decision-making and consequently often develop cynical and critical attitudes toward management.

Unless understood and dealt with by the chairman, these basic problems in the form and content of the information process make it extremely difficult to control and guide the management of the company.

In many companies, electronic networks are increasingly being used to provide more comprehensive and timely information. With PC-based electronic mail and faxes, directors can readily receive a great deal of the information needed to do their jobs.

EXTERNAL COMMUNICATION AND DISCLOSURE

The board is the principal channel through which key information about the company is communicated to the outside world, including shareholders, potential shareholders, analysts, investment dealers, advisors, the media, regulators, and public interest groups.

All financial reports, including the company's annual report, proxy statements, annual information statements, required regulatory filings and any press releases related to financial results must normally be approved by the board prior to release. This can be a demanding and time-consuming task, sometimes so much so that the board has little time to address other, more critical, issues. Much of the work can be delegated to the audit committee, but the board as a whole remains responsible for the accuracy and completeness of information provided. How can this be done, when these filings and reports may involve several hundred pages of detailed numbers and other information about which a board member cannot reasonably be expected to be personally familiar? Many boards deal with this conundrum by auditing, not the details of the report, but the *process* by which the reports have been prepared and by whom, requiring those who have prepared the data to sign off as to the thoroughness of the process and the completeness and accuracy of the results.

Many other items, other than financial reports, come to the board for decisions and approval. The question almost inevitably arises: is this a disclosable event? At what point does it become so? What, if anything, are we required by law to report, and at what stage? And, more judgmental, what *should* we report to shareholders or potential shareholders so that they can make informed decisions concerning their investment in the company?

A classic issue is that of a proposed acquisition or merger that could dramatically affect a company's results: what should the board report publicly, and when? Early discussions may be highly tentative; reporting that discussions are under way could be most misleading to shareholders, and could "queer the deal". The general attitude of most boards, backed by legal advice, is to say nothing until the deal is concluded. But even here, there are difficult judgment calls. The deal may be concluded subject to a period of due diligence by both parties, or subject to regulatory approval, or some other condition. Waiting for such conditions to be fulfilled to announce the merger may be unfair to shareholders and investors, and provide a period for "leaks" of information and insider dealing.

Some boards go strictly by the book, reporting only what is required by law, which is itself often vague. Others take the position of "erring on the side of disclosure" — in other words: when in doubt, disclose. This is often one of the most difficult decisions facing the board member who is concerned about his or her fiduciary duty to shareholders, and liability for withholding relevant information.

MANAGING DIRECTOR AND BOARD PERFORMANCE

The management of the human resource which is a group of directors so as to enhance shareholder value is very much an art form, calling for a high degree of interpersonal and leadership skill on the part of the chairman. It is the chairman and his or her skill in management that determines whether the board is a collectivity composed of eight or ten or more individuals with only a passing commitment to the company, or an effective team working together in such a way that their contribution is greater than the sum of the individual parts.

A basic element in managing this job is the chairman's attitude and perspective. The successful chairman, in our experience, views the board as an asset and take as a personal challenge the opportunity to enhance and operate that asset effectively and efficiently. The chairman's perspective must be broad and long-term, not simply as chairing a series of meetings, but planning, building and maintaining an effective team over time to deal with the host of problems and issues that will inevitably arise.

One of the keys to improving board management is for chairmen to take the lead in applying to directors the time-tested basic elements of control — definition of the job and performance standards, measurement and evaluation of effectiveness, feedback and reinforcement (reward or punishment). Until chairmen begin to implement a performance appraisal process and require improvement from, or terminate, obviously unsatisfactory directors real improvement will not likely take place. The first step in beginning an evaluation system for directors is to develop a position description and standards of performance, as described in Chapter 11, Defining the Director's Job.

COMPENSATION OF DIRECTORS

Complicating the chairman's problem in recruitment and motivation of directors is the issue of director compensation. The fact is, as one director recently put it: "Director pay is much too low for the job that should be done, and much too high for what most directors do."

In the old-style board, pay tends to be a relatively low honorarium for perfunctory duties. The implicit bargain, based on long-standing tradition, is that the director is paid a modest retainer and meeting fee in exchange for the use of his or her name, attendance at meetings, and the performance of routine legal duties in relatively short, formal meetings that are long on ritual and short on any real direction of the company.

In the new style board, often with the leadership of the chairman, job standards are defined first, and routines and processes are set up to see that directors are paid fairly for value added and services rendered. Pay follows purpose. Systematic reviews are made of director compensation to ensure that directors' pay is periodically adjusted to reflect the opportunity costs of their time, fees for comparable professional services rendered and the market — the demand and supply for directors, as reflected by the fees paid by well-run companies competing for the best directors.

While there will always be many willing board candidates, the supply of competent candidates is not extensive, and able, experienced directors are much sought after. Their time is limited, and they normally have many other demands on it. If a company is going to attract, retain, and ensure excellent performance from such individuals, it is going to have to make sure that they are paid adequately for serving. Personal financial risk will have to be covered as far as possible by directors' liability insurance, corporate bylaws covering indemnification and, in extreme cases, trust funds to cover potential costs of possible liabilities. Travel and other out-of-pocket costs will have to be fully reimbursed, of course. But the most important consideration is that the director should receive total pay based either on the opportunity cost of his or her time, or the rates of other comparable professionals, such as top-ranking corporate lawyers, audit partners and consultants.

Should all directors be paid on the same basis? Because all directors share the same legal responsibility jointly and severally, it is very difficult to make a case for differential rates of directors' compensation, even where it is necessary to attract an outstanding individual who would not otherwise be available. It is important to maintain the integrity of the system, and that dictates paying each outside director on the same basis, differential amounts varying only with the time actually committed and responsibility undertaken, such as committee chairmanships. Deviating from this principle would destroy the sense of equal responsibility and teamwork among the members; special deals, consulting relationships and the like can be very divisive, and pose a conflict of interest.

Stock-based elements of the total compensation package have become much more important in recent years, and provide a means of rewarding directors for performance while aligning their interests more closely with other shareholders. Other more controversial noncash components, such as pensions, have also begun to appear in a few cases.

The increasing responsibilities and pressures on directors, coupled with a trend to more professionalism in directorship, mean that overall levels of director compensation will continue to rise. In our view that is a good thing. It is unquestionably better to err on the side of overpaying directors rather than underpaying, because paying at a reasonably high level sends a message to all that the expectations are high, and makes it easier for the chairman to demand and expect more from his board.

SUCCESSION PLANNING AND SELECTING NEW DIRECTORS

The qualifications required of a board member parallel the changes in the nature and magnitude of the work to be done on today's boards. Time and talent are critical. Growth in the time demands of the job, coupled with the need for flexibility in being able to "drop everything" when the situation demands it, means that active CEOs of other companies have to severely limit their commitments to other boards, reducing the supply of potential board members from the traditional major source. The same is true of many professionals like lawyers and consultants. Retired CEOs, politicians and academics remain a promising pool of talent, but there is little doubt that the substantial time demands of being a director limit the availability of qualified candidates and have encouraged a number of search firms to enter the field of director recruitment.

The demands for increasing expertise from directors continue to grow. The high-technology sector of business demands technical facility and comprehension in dealing with strategic matters; given the pace of technological change in virtually every business, directors who have retired from other jobs are likely to lag in their understanding and appreciation of the technical aspects of key decisions, aspects that are often vital to an appreciation of the problem and its solution. Technologically-illiterate board members are often incapable of evaluating product strategy and research and development investments, cannot understand the strategic options, and hand decision making over to management by default. The issue was starkly illustrated when, at the time of its fall from market grace, it was reported that none of the outside directors of IBM possessed a personal computer.

Expertise demands of other kinds have escalated. Literacy in the financial aspects of business is a *sine qua non* for competent directors, and this is not something that can be learned on the job. Recent debacles involving investments in complex derivatives have alerted many boards to their ignorance of such devices, and their consequent exposure and potential liability.

Today's director has to have at least basic understanding of a wide range of subjects. He or she must be literate not only in the relevant technology, finance, pensions, compensation, human resources, production techniques, internal controls, marketing, taxation, regulations, legislative developments and global trends, the director must also keep up with current developments, and understand how these all interact with each other in the business. And on top of it all, the director must be a shrewd observer of human nature, and a wise and independent counsellor.

Identifying and recruiting individuals with such qualifications for any board is manifestly no small task, and few candidates will pass the screen in every respect. Most will be lacking in knowledge of the company's operations, and those of its competitors — key elements in evaluating strategy. Bringing the director up to speed on these matters is a job for the chairman, through a program of initial orientation and regular updating.

SHAREHOLDER RELATIONS

The board of directors is elected to represent the interests of shareholders in the process of managing the company. Yet in many companies, directors have no regular or systematic contact with shareholders. Indeed, even when shares are readily available, many directors are not themselves significant shareholders. How can such directors purport to understand and serve the best interests of the owners of the business?

In many companies, particularly those that are widely held, individual members of management have responsibility for shareholder relations. Note that it is usually considered a management function, not one directly controlled by the board. And management often resists any attempt by board members to intervene in contacts with shareholders, except perfunctorily at the annual meeting, and then at a distance. As a result, directors are often insulated by management from the very people whose interest the board is supposed to represent. Control of the process should, instead, rest with the chairman, whose job it is to manage the shareholder relations process and open up systematic contact between the board and its constituents, the owners.

In companies that have a major shareholder, that individual is usually represented directly or indirectly on the board. He or she then is party to all the information available to board members, and in a position to participate directly in the decisions of the board. The presence on the board of the major shareholder can be very intimidating to the independent director, who knows that he or she is present at the pleasure of the shareholder, and can be removed at any time if the shareholder wishes. It also fosters an attitude that "it's the shareholder's company, and if he wants to go right when I think we should be going left, why should I challenge him?" The result is that on many controlled boards, the major shareholder takes over control and may dictate unwise policies and decisions; minority shareholders share in the suffering.

When a board's power is co-opted by a block in this way, its function of controlling and guiding is usurped, often with devastating results for all shareholders, including the minority. At one such board meeting, when the controlling shareholder complained that the rest of the board didn't seem to be taking his position into account in their discussion, an independent director replied:

> Look. You've been here and had all the information we have had, maybe more. You've heard all the arguments pro and con, and you've voiced your own views. I've heard you. My position is that you are more than able to look after your own interests. I'm here to represent the minority who don't have a voice in this discussion. I have a responsibility to all the shareholders, and I'm going to make my own decision on that basis. If you can't live with that, then you have my resignation.

The presence of large, long-term investors in the form of institutions has complicated the picture. Some institutions have taken an activist position towards board representation and communication of their views on the boards on which they sit.[2] Others have opted for a more passive point of view, publishing guidelines for good governance and voting their shares for or against management, but not seeking seats on boards. Others have remained almost entirely passive, abdicating their ownership rights. Most funds attempt to keep their holdings in any one company below a certain limit, often 20 percent, not wishing control. Regardless, the presence of such substantial shareholders provides both an opportunity and a challenge for the board of directors. The opportunity is to communicate directly with shareholders, explain what is going on, understand their point of view, and integrate their views into the process of decision-making. The challenge is to balance this input with others in such a way as to give the large shareholder no inside advantage over other, less powerful shareholders.

In sum, the task of managing the board is neither simple nor inconsequential. The idea that this could be done as a part of the job description of the CEO is, in our view, naive. If being a chairman is not a full-time job, it is certainly close to it. The days have long passed when the two jobs can be effectively combined in one person — not if they are both to be done well. And having them done well is central to the whole idea of corporate governance.

NOTES

1. This and other trends noted in this chapter have been reported in regular board surveys conducted by The Conference Board, Spencer Stuart, and others.

2. See, for example, D.S.R. Leighton and Kathryn Montgomery, "The Unseen Revolution is Here," *Business Quarterly* (Summer, 1993).

Chapter 16

TURNING AROUND A SICK BOARD

The shortcomings of boards of directors, with many widely-publicized governance failures pointing up the problems, have become understood and accepted by most leaders in the business community. To this point, the outpouring of news, commentary, research, and reports on corporate governance has been either largely descriptive or has consisted of simple generalities and structural guidelines without much practical advice on how to make them work in the tough, real world of high-level corporate power and politics. Among the ranks of business leaders there is much frustration with the plethora of governance remedies advanced in reports such as Cadbury (U.K.), Treadway (U.S.) and Dey (Canada). In their view there is an over-abundance of generalized and theoretical remedies that don't seem to apply to their specific circumstances.

The provision of experience-based, realistic recommendations and how to apply them to upgrade the effectiveness of corporate directors and boards is long overdue. In their absence, many troubled boards and directors will continue, with rising concern and frustration, to put in time going through costly, often-pointless rituals ratifying flawed decisions and reluctantly supporting managers whose performance is leading to huge opportunity costs for all concerned, particularly shareholders.

Our purpose in this chapter is to describe and explain how one company implemented practical actions that are tested, hands-on tools for improving board performance. We focus on the six key factors that determine whether boards succeed or fail in carrying out their mandate.These six key success factors (see Exhibit 16.1) are leadership, legitimacy and power, job definition, competence, culture and board management. While each factor is important in its own right, all are interrelated and reinforce each other. They work together in a way that multiplies their cumulative effect for good or bad. Where all six of these critical success factors are congruent, well-managed, strong and integrated, the result is an effective ''new-style'' board with competent directors actively participating in meetings that are penetrating, strategically focused, challenging and leading to good decisions which, effectively implemented, we believe will result in increasing shareholder value.

Now let's see how these ideas can be applied in practice. For this, we examine the case of the Bartram company, a disguised but actual situation.

THE CASE OF THE BARTRAM CORPORATION

Monday, February 6: The phone call came from a prominent businessman in Toronto: "I need some help. I'm on the board of the Bartram Corporation. We're having some real problems. For four or five years now the company has been sliding badly down hill. The board is very unhappy and frustrated. Poor leadership, endless bickering, and worsening business problems have several of us worried, not only about our reputations but also about potential liabilities. I've been asked to head a three-man task force to look at our corporate governance and come up with some recommendations. I've heard about some of the things you've been doing and I think you can be a tremendous help. Could we possibly get together some time in the next few days to talk this over?"

As he reached for his calendar, the consultant was thinking. He knew something about Bartram. Big in the retail business. An old, established family concern with stores in several leading cities. Family still involved, although the company had gone public many years earlier. There had been something in the press a few years ago about a possible takeover, headed off by a share exchange and standstill agreement with a "white knight". A pretty stodgy company, he thought — one of the pillars of the establishment. They'd tried some diversification in recent years into other retail-related businesses, but they had loaded themselves up with debt, and the results had been poor. The phone call pricked his interest for two reasons. Not only were the problems challenging, but he was confident he could help — he had developed a practical analytical framework and approach that helped to diagnose board problems and point out action needed for a turn-around.

A date several days hence was open. He made an appointment with the caller and hung up. Three days later he was on the plane to meet his contact. He had blocked out the following day to discuss problems and issues with the full governance committee.

In reviewing the situation, he confirmed that for several years the management problems, operating results, and share price of the Bartram Company had been going downhill. As a result, the directors, prestigious names from business and politics, had become increasingly demoralized, dissatisfied, fractious, and frustrated not only with management but even more so with their own inability to turn around the company's worsening governance problems, which were increasingly the topic of negative comments in the media.

Concerned that Bartram's condition was seriously deteriorating, the CEO was out of control, the board was dangerously ineffective, and potential personal risks were mounting, three of the most experienced directors had led a movement demanding that the chairman appoint a special governance committee with a broad mandate: "To review the board of directors and the governance of the corporation and to report back to the board their findings, conclusions, and recommendations."

Since there was a sense of urgency, sensitivities were extreme, and they were all committed to other full-time jobs, the committee members decided to hire a consultant to assist them in diagnosing the problems and advising on what to do.

Friday, February 10: The consultant and the governance committee met in a conference room at a downtown law office. The committee chairman, a personable and competent outside director, was joined on the committee by a nominee director from Genco, the "white knight" and largest single shareholder, and another outside director who was the chairman/CEO of a large company. After introductions they settled in to work.

Jack, the committee chairman, opened things up. "For the last two years things have been very difficult, unpleasant and counterproductive. The Genco directors and Ron Bartram, the president and CEO, are in a bitter feud. Genco has opposed diversification and is demanding that the company focus on a turnaround, selling most of the new divisions and getting back to basics. The family directors are at odds and divided. The independent directors, all appointed by the CEO or his father, look on in dismay because we don't know whether we should sell the acquired businesses and take our losses or hang in there and count on promised improvements in results.

"The CEO is acting irrationally at times. Recently he lost his temper and stamped out in the middle of a meeting because the Genco directors wanted to sell off one of the new divisions. Genco's people are very unhappy, claiming that they are greatly underrepresented on the board and no one is listening to them. The chairman has been trying to smooth things over, but it hasn't worked. Things have pretty much ground to a halt, and we're not dealing with important issues. Our results show it. We're overloaded with debt, the interest charges are crippling, and the banks and shareholders are getting itchy. That, in a nutshell, is why we're here. At the last meeting, the board voted to set up this committee to see if we can't break the logjam and get things back on track."

With the help of the other two committee members, the chairman continued to cover the relevant background information. For decades, they explained, Bartram had been a successful retailer with big stores in 18 major cities. Although the company had gone public many years earlier, and was a popular retail stock in many investment portfolios, the founding family collectively still owned 25 percent of the shares and, although they didn't always vote together, they dominated the board and management. About 16 years earlier, under the threat of a takeover, the company had sold from treasury, with a standstill agreement, 20 percent of the shares to Genco, a large diversified corporation. The rest of the shares were widely held by institutions and individuals. The long-serving CEO and president, Ron Bartram, a grandson of one of the founders, had succeeded his father. The non-executive chairman, aged 68, was a long-time family friend who still ran his own business. Under the heavy-handed dominance of the CEO, who feared that retailing prospects were bleak, the company had diversified aggressively into several other related businesses. Results had been poor, and over the last three years the share price had fallen from $43 to $26. Investors were unhappy and analysts were generally negative on the company's outlook. The consultant noted that committee members indicated great insight into the management, human and legal complexities of the situation. So much so that it was puzzling that their sensible views on the problems and needed remedies had been stifled and frustrated for so long.

Board members were divided as follows: Five family (including the CEO and the chairman), two Genco and ten independents. The independents included four lawyers, of whom two were heavily dependent on company business; three CEOs (two of whom were from major suppliers); two former politicians; and an academic.

The meeting continued for two hours as the consultant asked questions and worked out the terms of an assignment whereby he would discuss the situation in greater depth with each of the board members and key top managers and prepare a report to the committee with his findings and recommendations on possible changes to the way the board operated. The committee and the consultant would work together to prepare a report to the full board.

The next few weeks were busy ones for the consultant. He reviewed background data on the company, its varied activities and financial results. He interviewed personally each member of the board, with the understanding that comments would be used in a feed-back session but that anonymity would be respected and no one would be quoted directly. Although he did not work with a structured interview guide, his approach to all the interviews was similar, starting with a query as to how the director saw the state of affairs, what he or she saw as the basic problems and contributing factors, and seeking suggestions on what should be done and how. He had expected to hear negative reactions to the way the board and company were being run, but he was unprepared for the frankness, vehemence and the strong language of the respondents. For several directors the criticisms, emotions, frustration and bitterness were so pent-up that interviews scheduled for two hours went on for four or five or more. Things were indeed in bad shape, and there was a strong sense of urgency to take action.

Saturday, March 25: The consultant presented his report at a weekend meeting in a hotel conference room. All three committee members were there, and the discussion was lengthy and frank. There was little disagreement with the consultant's assessment of the situation and recommendations for action; much of the time was spent considering how to implement the actions.

The consultant had recommended the replacement of the CEO and president by the head of one of Bartram's most successful divisions. He had also recommended the enhancement of the chairman's job and replacement of the chairman by an independent director. A good deal of discussion centered around who should replace the chairman. In both cases, the manner in which the replacement was to be carried out was critical. The consultant also made a number of recommendations concerning the board's responsibilities, function, size and composition, committee structure, the timing and handling of meetings, the information package for directors, compensation, and other operational matters. By Sunday afternoon, the group had hammered out the outline of a committee report, to be presented at the next board meeting about two weeks hence. Meanwhile, the committee chairman undertook to meet personally with the CEO and president, the chairman and all directors individually to inform them of the committee's key conclusions and forewarn them of the recommendations that would be made to the board. The committee members were confident that, while there would be some vociferous opposition, the board would, in the end, support their report.

At the beginning of the board meeting held two weeks later, the CEO and president announced that he was resigning and would be leaving the board. The chairman also indicated his intention to resign as soon as there had been a transition to the new CEO and president. The board discussed and approved the appointment of the committee's choice as CEO and president, and these decisions were announced to the media, where they were front-page news. The chairman officially resigned at the following board meeting, and one of the independent directors, Frank Turley, was named to take his place.

The Chairman Takes Charge

One month later: Frank Turley's situation wasn't unique in business circles. Recent years had seen a number of ''palace coups'' as shareholders and directors attempted to reassert their power in corporate decision-making in deeply troubled companies. In many of these situations, a veteran director had been called upon to take over and provide leadership and direction in getting a business back on track.

As Frank Turley stretched out behind the desk in his new office on the top floor of Bartram's downtown, high-rise office tower, he reflected on the task ahead. He had accepted the board's offer somewhat reluctantly because he had plenty to do looking after his own business and two other demanding directorships. Still, he had been intimately involved with all the problems of Bartram's board, he liked the people, and he respected the company and its storied past. In addition, he had a good second-in-command in his own business and was in the process of passing on the reins to him. Since he was 62 and well off, he didn't by any means see the Bartram job as a long-term position.

He knew that it wasn't going to be easy. Things had been rough, and all the basic business problems still remained. He knew and respected the new CEO, Tom Ainsley, and had strongly favoured his appointment. They were both starting anew, as it were, and he felt Ainsley was competent to focus on the right strategic issues and lead the company back to profitability. Turley saw his job as being primarily to restore the board as an active and vigorous voice of the shareholders in the process of turning the company around. Where to start? And how to go about it?

The critical first step, appointing a competent, independent, nonexecutive chairman, was already in place. Turley felt confident that he could deal with the challenge. He had been on the board for ten years, and had observed the board's trials and tribulations at first hand. He had seen his predecessor try ineffectually to cope, and had some firm opinions on what needed to be done. The chairman's job required more time and effort than it had received; the relationship with the CEO needed to be better defined and more independent; the board needed to bite the bullet on some key decisions; the board itself needed some weeding out, and replacement of under-performers with a few highly competent and effective contributors; and the structure, processes and support systems for the board needed drastic improvement. The report of the governance task force had outlined most of these issues, and would be a valuable guide to him in trying to implement needed changes.

Step One: Upgrading Leadership

It was apparent to Turley that managing all of this on a continuing basis was going to be a big job, requiring a great deal of time and attention. His predecessor had really just turned up for meetings and taken the chair. He was pleasant enough and did his best, but had neither the time, interest nor commitment to dig in and attack all the aspects of managing a board, especially when confronted with an autocratic CEO and an unhappy minority shareholder with two seats on the board. He and Turley had two completely different ideas as to the job of a chairman and, indeed, of a board of directors.

Turley firmly believed in leadership by example. If he were to expect board members to work hard and effectively he was going to have to demonstrate his own commitment. Moreover, he had to focus on the major problems and issues and establish an effective due process for dealing with them.

Step Two: Increasing Legitimacy and Power

First, and most important, on Turley's list of things to do was to work out his relationship with the new CEO. The two of them would be sharing many responsibilities, and it was important that they understand clearly from the start just what each was responsible for individually, and where they would have to work together. Turley saw his mandate from the board as an activist one, much more so than his predecessor's. Since Ainsley was new to the CEO role, this was the ideal time for them to work out a different relationship than had existed before, one in which the chairman and the CEO would be essentially equal but different.

To do his part, Turley planned to spend roughly half his time on Bartram business. He wanted to be much more visible at head office and in visiting field sites, and he needed better communication with Ainsley and some of the major shareholders. It was important that Ainsley understood and agreed with this. One of the methods would be to develop a job description outlining the chairman's role and to encourage Ainsley to do the same for the CEO. The two men could then exchange job descriptions and sort out any differences. Turley was not a great believer in job descriptions, but in this case he felt that the process of preparing and sorting them out was critical; the end-product was not all that important.

His ultimate goal was to restore power and accountability to the board through leadership and performance and to establish a better balance between the shareholders and management. This, in his view, was what was needed to give potency to the shareholder's point of view. To do this he planned to meet regularly with Genco, major institutions and money managers, minority shareholders, investment analysts, and other groups, including family members, to report on progress, and to seek input and advice.

Step Three: Working on Job Definition

Turley had a whole list of things that he wanted to do with the board: revitalize its involvement and contribution; make the meetings more positive and productive; change the agenda to focus on strategic issues; get rid of some of the problem directors and bring in some new blood. But first, he needed to rethink the definition of the board's job. Agreement on what the board should be doing would clarify objectives and determine many of the steps to be taken.

The Bartram board, like most companies, had never had a job description. It was assumed that directors would know what they were there to do, and those who were new would quickly pick up the signals by observing the other board members at work. In Turley's view, they usually picked up the wrong signals. He couldn't recall a single occasion in his ten years on the board when there had been any discussion of a director's responsibilities or whether the board was fulfilling its mandate. He discussed the matter with the consultant and decided that with his help he would prepare a draft job description, and ask the board members to discuss it at an upcoming meeting. Together, they would try to work out something on which all could agree.

A draft job description was subsequently sent out to the directors and discussed at a regular board meeting. The discussion was lively, interesting, and enlightening. Several said that they had learned a great deal about being a director, and that there were responsibilities that they had never before appreciated.

Turley was delighted. He revised the draft to incorporate many of the comments, then recirculated it for board approval. He also undertook to add the ongoing responsibility for reviewing the job description, as well as other aspects of the board's role in corporate governance, to the mandate of the newly-created board nominating committee. And he planned to use the job description as a key document in approaching future board members, so they would know just what was expected of them.

Step Four: Improving Competence

The consultant's report had called for a drastic restructuring of the Bartram board, recommending that a core group of six or seven nonperformers be dropped. Turley thought he should go even further. He wanted a board of no more than ten, including himself and the CEO. He thought six of the existing directors should be retained, two of whom would have to be from Genco. He wanted to go outside to bring in two respected professionals who served on a number of large-company boards. Turley had seen these individuals operate on other boards and felt that they would add much needed talent and provide outstanding examples to the other directors. The fact that neither had any significant retail experience did not bother him. They would symbolize his "new-broom" professional approach to governance.

He also went to visit the chairman of Genco, who did not sit on the Bartram board, to check out his plans and see where they agreed. He recognized that he would not be able to accommodate all of Genco's requests, but suggested that if Genco would assign two of their best people to the Bartram board, and give them enough leeway to work for the best interests of all Bartram's shareholders, he could make the relationship work. Together they went over the names of possible Genco nominees and agreed on two.

That left the remaining four. It was not too difficult for Turley to narrow the list of existing Bartram directors and pick out the individuals he wanted. He was concerned first with competence and judgment, and then balance — a diversity of points of view, backgrounds, age, experience, geographical spread, and gender — coupled with the time and commitment required to serve effectively. He discussed the list with the CEO and several of the larger shareholders before coming to a final decision as to the names to be nominated at the annual meeting. The individuals were all approached directly by Turley, who discussed plans with them before asking their assent.

Step Five: Building a New Board Culture

In turning the board around, Turley knew that this board was seriously sick and that he had to do much more than just make a few superficial changes. Over the years he had formed some very definite opinions about the capabilities and personalities of his fellow board members; some were able, intelligent and knew what was going on; some were pleasant enough, but didn't have much to contribute; some were just plain incompetent and should not have been on the board. The trouble was that in the constant bickering and sniping between Ron Bartram and the Genco directors, most of the good people had been completely turned off and found excuses for not being more involved so they wouldn't be drawn into the controversy and unpleasantness. Meeting attendance was spotty; good dialogue at and between meetings was largely nonexistent. A number of the directors wanted to do more and would welcome any initiatives, Turley was convinced, but he would have to deal with the problem of what to do with the incompetent underperformers before he could make much headway.

Turley had served on another board that he felt could serve as a model for what the Bartram board could become. It was smaller, nine or ten members opposed to Bartram's 18. It met more frequently, and typically for shorter meetings than the all-day marathons that were typical at Bartram. The members were all completely committed, did their homework, and participated vigorously in discussion and debates about strategic issues. Coming from divergent backgrounds, each contributed special skills and experience. Although they did not always agree, and dissent was fairly frequent, in the end they seemed to be able to work out their differences and come together behind a line of action that would be best for the company. Mutual respect was evident, and a certain bond of friendship had grown among them. It was a joy to work within such a group, and Turley found himself looking forward to the meetings. Once a year, the board and their spouses took two or three days and visited one of the company's field operations, sometimes in distant parts of the world. He felt this had contributed significantly to the bonding of the group. Although it was hard to quantify, Turley felt that this board had made a significant difference to the company's results over time and had served the shareholders well.

This was what he hoped he could accomplish at Bartram. What a contrast with the fractionated, dispirited, bitter, and unproductive group of directors now in place!

Letting some of the directors go and reducing the size of the board would certainly help. But more was required. The breadth and diversity of skills on the new board would be important, and simply paring down the numbers wouldn't necessarily provide that. Moreover, the company had developed a bad reputation with shareholders and analysts, and Turley felt that he had to do something positive to restore confidence. Appointment of one or two well-respected professional directors would help accomplish that, and provide a higher standard for the remaining directors.

In addition Turley recognized that he would have to change the way the board operated. He would have to manage carefully the board agenda, cutting down sharply on the number of presentations and reports, and increasing the time for discussion. Relatively minor matters would be by-passed in favour of focusing on strategic issues. Meetings would be shorter and more frequent. More would be done in committees, which would have to be reorganized. The information flow to the board would have to be carefully controlled — better coverage of strategic issues, while at the same time cutting back on the bulk of paper sent to board members to prepare for meetings. A delicate balance was required, and this would take a good deal of his personal attention until it was attained. In this, as in everything else, his success in revitalizing the board would depend on how he handled the chairman's job; if he wanted others to give their best, and work hard and productively, he had to show the way. His example, and his skill in setting the tone and knitting together an effective team, would be crucial.

Step Six: Managing the Board

The kind of board envisioned by Turley would have to operate very differently from the present pattern. Active, involved directors — especially the two new outside members — would not put up with the inefficient way that Bartram's board had been operated. Getting the board's administrative house in order was a high priority.

Turley felt that the board should meet more frequently than the current quarterly pattern and that the meetings should be shorter and more focused. Turley wanted to start early, but finish by noon. The pattern of shorter, more frequent meetings meant some directors would have to travel more, but he believed the improvement would more than compensate. At the same time, he could schedule committee meetings to tie in with the board meeting dates so that the directors who had to travel could make efficient use of their time. Having committee meetings the day before the board meeting would also mean that the directors could meet together privately for dinner the evening before to discuss highly sensitive matters in a relaxed and off-the-record setting without management present.

Turley also wanted to make the committees work more effectively. The consultant had made a number of recommendations to this effect. His principal recommendation had been to create a nominating committee of the board, manned by independent directors, which would be responsible for overseeing board succession planning and developing a list of potential candidates for filling any board vacancies. This was an important responsibility, and Turley himself would be a member. The CEO would not be a member, but would be consulted by the committee in making up its list. The committee would also have the responsibility for recommending the proposed committee structure and membership to the board each year. A number of the Bartram committees had been chaired by the same person for many years, and Turley wanted to get the tradition of entrenchment out of the culture by having periodic rotation of both chairmen and members.

Turning to board agendas, Turley wanted to get away from the past pattern of day-long meetings crammed with lengthy reports and presentations by management, as well as the large amount of reading in preparation. He went over the presentations from the most recent meetings, and decided to pare them down to a brief update report from the CEO and equally brief reports from the standing committees as needed. Material sent out ahead of the meetings would be edited, nonessential items eliminated, and required reading time cut drastically to around an hour or two at the most. Much more time would be allocated to strategic issues and to discussion rather than presentation. Management would be encouraged to bring evolving strategic matters to the board at an early stage, before positions had hardened. He realized that a great deal of this was within his control and that it would take a while before the staff and committee chairmen became used to the new regimen.

As he got into the job the half-time estimate that he had made earlier was looking more and more suspect. Moreover, he was going to have to be paid at a rate that reflected that kind of commitment, as were the directors. Realizing that he wanted more involvement and work from directors he proposed to have their pay raised to a $20,000 retainer, $1,000 for meetings and $2,000 for committee chairmen, roughly double the old pay scale. His own pay as chairman on a half-time basis should, he believed, be around $200,000 to $250,000. He decided to assign the whole issue of compensation as a priority for the board's compensation committee.

In preparing for his first meeting with the new board, Turley went over with the corporate secretary the nature and timing of all the statutory requirements, and allocated them among the six board sessions so that they would not take up undue time at any one session. He also listed other matters that recurred on a regular basis — budget approval, audit approval, compensation and the like — and similarly spread these among the board sessions. He planned to spend part of each meeting on strategic matters; in some cases it might be relatively brief, and in others it would take most of the time available.

This way he was able to map out much of the year's agenda in advance and circulate it to the directors for their information. Once a year, the board would travel to one of the company's operating divisions for a two-day meeting, at which one half-day session would be devoted to a review of the board's functioning and ways to make it work better. Managers, key customers, suppliers and local government officials would be invited to a dinner with the board and their spouses.

* * * * *

While all boards and company situations are unique, many elements of the Bartram situation are common to other troubled companies with ineffective boards, and there is much to be learned from a detailed examination of this case. In our experience, improved effectiveness results from actions to strengthen and integrate all six key factors in the board value chain. These, we believe, are the major aspects of board leadership that can and should be addressed in the move toward the new empowered and effective board (Exhibit 16.1).

Bartram represents a case of a board in crisis, one that had been building up for years. When the crisis reached a head, drastic action was called for, and was taken. The system worked, albeit belatedly. There is a parallel here to GM, when the board took charge and replaced chairman/CEO Robert Stempel with an independent chairman and a new president/CEO. In both situations, the board's response came late in the game after prolonged delay had cost shareholders dearly, but the board did belatedly respond.

Governance crises like these emerge in the public arena infrequently, probably too infrequently. Many, if not most boards, muddle along most of the time at poor to mediocre levels of performance that never quite trigger a director revolt like those at Bartram or GM. Turning around an underperforming board is never easy: board cultures and patterns of behavior have developed over more than half a century, and attitudes and habits have often become deeply entrenched. Many directors have the view that challenging the existing pattern of operation is heresy, something usually propounded by impractical theorists and academics who have no real idea of the complexity of the system and how it works. The inertia in the system is substantial.

Yet there *are* excellent boards that do a superb job, year after year, for their shareholders, and which set a benchmark for others to follow. We know. We have had first-hand experience with some of them. Surely having an excellent, high-performing board is not beyond the realm of human capability!

It is our observation that substantial forward strides in governance have been made in recent years, as a difficult economy has exposed board weaknesses, and institutional investor and public attention has come to be focused on corporate underperformance and failure. Structural changes to boards and the way they are managed have helped, but in our view, shared by many colleagues in business, they have not gone nearly far enough.

In this and earlier chapters we have suggested ways of moving the discussion forward — towards practical, tested ways of turning poorly

Exhibit 16.1

THE SIX KEY LINKS IN THE BOARD VALUE CHAIN

Key Success/Failure Factors	Signs and Symptoms of Strengths
1. **Leadership.** Leadership independent from management which requires vision, foresight, sensitivity, energy, objectivity and steadfast commitment to the success of the company.	• Chairman is an effective catalyst of board talents, helps directors rise above themselves, makes the whole greater than the sum of the parts. • Chairman clearly manifests the knowledge, attitudes, skills and experience required for outstanding leadership. • Chairman's leadership causes board to perform fully and effectively. • Chairman sets an excellent example in terms of wisdom, behaviour, commitment and effectiveness. • Chairman gets the job done fully and competently. • Chairman does not suffer from character defects, personal inadequacies and/or blind spots that hamper effectiveness.
2. **Legitimacy and power.** The active support of the shareholders, and the recognition of the legal and moral authority that flows from that support—first to the board, and then to management and operating employees, who are all agents of the shareholders. Clear empowerment of the board to take charge and exert authority and accept responsibility for the success of the company in formulating and implementing a strategy that results in increasing shareholder value.	• Board clearly in charge, directing management. • Proper accountability chain of management to board and board to shareholders. • Shareholders respected, involved, informed, consulted, listened to. • Board performance satisfactory in terms of required results. • Demonstrated board leadership and value added. • Open, merit-based process for gaining and holding appointment. • Board has healthy degree of independence from management and/or major shareholders.

Exhibit 16.1 (*cont'd*)

THE SIX KEY LINKS IN THE BOARD VALUE CHAIN

Key Success/Failure Factors	Signs and Symptoms of Strengths
3. **Job definition.** Development and communication of a clear description of the board's purpose, functions, and tasks.	• Board has developed definitive job description for itself, the chairman and the CEO. • Board job definition effectively linked to company's situation, problems and strategic agenda. • Review and evaluation of individual and collective performance and effectiveness as related to job descriptions.
4. **Culture**. Creating the positive and necessary shared beliefs, norms, attitudes, values and expectations that will enable directors to do their job well.	• Frank, open, dynamic, committed, pragmatic, problem-oriented attitudes and approaches to board meetings. • Merit and contribution more important than position and politics. • Active, involved, take-charge approach. • Personalities and relational baggage from past minimized. • Loyalty to company and shareholders more important than loyalties to chairman and CEO. • Board lives in present, not past. • Humility and servant leadership attitudes prevail over egos, turf, and self-serving politics.

Exhibit 16.1 (*cont'd*)

THE SIX KEY LINKS IN THE BOARD VALUE CHAIN

Key Success/Failure Factors	Signs and Symptoms of Strengths
5. Competence. Building a board which has the required balance of integrity, knowledge, skills, attitudes, experience and other necessary qualifications.	• Clear realization that increasing shareholder value is the name of the game. • Good track record of growth in shareholder value resulting from leadership in effective governance. • Strong qualifications for directors individually and board collectively. • Dominance by outside, unrelated directors. • Strong dialogue, questioning and, where necessary, dissent expected from all directors. • Upgrading competence in contribution through turnover in board i.e. replacement of poor contributors by outstanding new directors.
6. Management. Outstanding planning and implementation of the administrative tasks, functions, and processes required for the board to be effective.	• The organization and structure—size, membership, committee structure and staff backup—of the board are all well planned and implemented. • The function and process—agenda, frequency of meetings, delegation and integration of committee work, communication and staff support—are fully and efficiently planned and implemented. • Good information management ensures that the right amount of the right kind of information is prepared, edited and distributed to directors in plenty of time for reading and study before meetings. Necessary reading time should ordinarily be limited to an hour or two. • Shareholder relations are adequately and properly developed and maintained. • Compensation is adequate to attract outstanding directors and motivate them to full commitment and performance. • Evaluation and upgrading of directors individually, and the board collectively, are built into board operating process.

performing boards around. We have seen the future and it can work — given the will and wit to make it happen.

Many outstanding directors know this, and understand the importance of making the system work better. If we as business leaders do not take the initiative, it will be done for us by outside forces who will dictate changes that a competent board should itself have made years earlier.

NOTE

The case described in this chapter actually happened. Certain facts have been disguised to protect the identity of individuals involved, and the section on Frank Turley (pp. 264-70) is only loosely based on reality. It represents our attempt to "get inside his head" and describe the stream of consciousness that a strong, independent chairman might have had in this situation. There is no way of knowing what actually did go through Turley's mind, but much can be inferred from subsequent actions. We make no claim that this is exactly what he actually did think or do.

Chapter 17

THE FUTURE OF CORPORATE GOVERNANCE

The basic premise of this study is that corporate governance and board systems are in a sweeping and dramatic process of transition from the old system — what they have been — to the new system — what they must become to be empowered and effective. Due to the impact of continuous, powerful forces of change, the board system of the 1950s has reacted and transformed itself almost unbelievably to that of the 1990s. There can be little question that this evolution must and will continue apace: coming changes in the board system of today promise to be even more dynamic and drastic than those of the past. In this never-ending process of transformation and improvement, the forces of rationality and progress will work to correct the many unsatisfactory features of the current practice of corporate governance. Our purpose in this chapter is to outline our view of the future of governance and the board system.

Our conclusion is that, despite significant improvements, the board system is still seriously underperforming at several levels, so much so that many boards are simply useless, if not worse. They are not, in reality, elected by, or represent, owners. They do not adequately understand the business well enough to intelligently control management. They don't really hire, evaluate, pay and, if necessary, fire the CEO. And they are not satisfactory stewards of shareholder value. To most corporate governance insiders these conclusions will not be controversial or surprising. For example, Myles Mace, a leading Harvard Business School professor, wrote these words in an award-winning article 25 years ago:

> The generally accepted roles of boards — selecting top executives, determining policy, measuring results, and asking discerning questions — have taken on the characteristics of a well-established myth, and there is a considerable gap between the

> myth and reality. I've found that in most companies, boards serve as a source of advice and counsel, *offer some sort of* discipline value*, and act in* crisis situations...
>
> ...I found...that boards *do not* perform three functions commonly considered their domain. First, the boards of most large companies do not establish objectives, strategies, and policies. In most companies, allocation of capital resources is accomplished through a management process of analysis resulting in recommendations to the board. Almost without exception, these recommendations go unchallenged by the board.
>
> A second role ascribed to boards is that of asking discerning questions. Again, I found that directors do not in fact do this. Many board members cited their lack of understanding of the problems presented by the president; thus to avoid looking like idiots, they refrain from questioning.
>
> Moreover, typical outside directors are selected by the president and thus do not ask questions inside or outside meetings. However, directors who own or represent the ownership of substantial shares of stock generally do. They are not selected by the president and therefore represent themselves and an interest more likely to be consistent with that of other shareholder.
>
> A third role usually attributed to directors is the selection of the president. Yet I found that in most companies, directors do this only under the crisis situations cited earlier.
>
> Boards do serve in an advisory role in the selection of a new president — in their capacity as a sort of corporate conscience. Rarely does a board of directors reject a candidate recommended by the president...[1]

Despite the progress noted in the last quarter-century, these words still ring true today.

The magnitude of reform required to empower boards and make them effective, and the difficulties involved in achieving this goal, should not be underestimated. Not the least of these difficulties is the inertia and self-satisfaction of many who are currently part of the system, the denial of any problem, the absence of any strong motives for change and the power to resist reform: the ''old-style'' board culture is deeply entrenched, and the defence of the *status quo* will be strong.

A number of alternative solutions exist, ranging from legislating boards out of existence to letting the market solve the problem. However, we believe there is no practical alternative to management oversight by a board system of some sort: the challenge is to make the board system work better. The existence of a number of well-functioning boards that do very effectively all that could be expected of them is testimony to the fact that the system *can* work. The challenge is whether we can transform a satisfactory standard that is currently practised by a few leaders into the norm for all industry. The key is to gain broad understanding of and agreement as to what these best-practice standards are, the benefits that accrue from adopting them, and the barriers that inhibit their adoption. From this starting point it is then possible in individual cases to manage the process of change from underperformance to having a high-performing board of directors.

THE BOARD'S EVOLVING ROLE

Boards exist primarily to enhance shareholder value. The principal value added by a board is to represent the shareholders' interest by bringing independent, critical, balanced judgment to play in the process of strategic management; to focus management on the rational pursuit of increasing shareholder value. Stripped to the core, this is its central role; if it fails in this task, it fails the shareholder. The board's role in strategy determination and implementation is thus critical in the management process.

Overseeing the development of strategy is a responsibility shared with top management. Where management is weak in strategic thinking but strong in operational skills, the board may have to play an active role in initiating and developing a strategic direction for the company; where management has strong strategic capability, the board's role can be more passive, overseeing and screening proposals and ensuring the avoidance of major mistakes. An independent, broadly-experienced and diverse board can bring perspective and judgment to many aspects of this process, providing a balance to management's more detailed and tactically-oriented plans and proposals.

Of equal importance is the board's responsibility to appoint, monitor, assist, pay and, if necessary, fire a CEO. Determining a strategic direction is of little value if the strategy is not competently carried out. But by the same token, hiring, and monitoring a CEO without the board having a clear sense of goals and strategic direction can be an exercise fraught with misunderstanding and frustration for both parties.

Of course, boards have other very important functions — overseeing the auditing of financial statements, ensuring regulatory compliance, reporting to shareholders, and the like. But, we have argued, these are all ultimately secondary to having a sound strategic direction and outstanding leadership to guide the company. The board's role in supervising strategic management cannot be delegated, and without active participation in the process, the board is failing in its job.

Awareness of the centrality of strategy in the board's job is growing,[2] partly a result of recent debates about corporate governance. As this definition of the board's role comes into sharper focus and is more clearly understood, the future evolution of corporate governance also becomes clear. The changes that are necessary, and that will doubtless be implemented in the years to come, grow from this critical understanding and acceptance of the board's strategic function. Today's leading-edge boards understand and focus on implementing their key role in strategic management. Without it they are defaulting on their duty to bring due diligence to their responsibility as directors.

Most of the elements of improved board practice that will become common in the 21st century are already in place in a handful of boards, and we are on the threshold of seeing the spread of these best practices to many more, hopefully the vast majority. Predicting the future of corporate governance in North America is not so much an exercise in crystal-ball gazing as identifying and extrapolating current powerful and continuing change forces and observing developing best practices that must be more widely adopted.

The main engines of change, all driven by the imperatives of the market and the enlightened self-interest of shareholders, directors and management as well as other stakeholders, include:

1. *Legal changes*, causing greater fear of both criminal and civil liabilities for directors' acts of commission and omission. For example, the wider application of class actions under the oppression remedy and direct environmental liabilities are relatively recent changes that compel increased attention from any informed director and board. Growing personal risks facing corporate directors make director competence,

proper care, informed judgment, and proper diligence in performance an absolute necessity.

2. *Shareholder activism*, led by investment institutions that are increasingly vigorous in asserting their ownership rights and in demanding more effective corporate governance, to the point of directly pressuring boards and managements to get their acts together, demanding seats on boards, and announcing well publicized "hit lists" of offending, poorly-performing companies.

3. *Increasingly severe global competition* and the complexity and magnitude of issues confronting companies, upping the ante of risk and potential decline and requiring a higher standard of performance from directors than has been true in the past.

4. *The world-wide upgrading of management experience and education* is increasing the level of ability required. The wide emergence, recognition, adoption and teaching of the concept of strategic management, a comprehensive basic system for monitoring, analyzing and diagnosing company problems and opportunities and formulating and implementing necessary solution and action, is substantially raising the state of the art. For any board to be weighed and found wanting in the application of effective strategic management will increasingly be evidence of non-performance of the directors' job.

5. *The widespread development and adoption of comprehensive and user-friendly management information systems* that can be easily made available to all directors, particulary those who are computer-literate, will eliminate the old excuse of directors lacking information or "being deceived by management." Rapidly-expanding technology and the technological illiteracy of most older directors seriously inhibit their usefulness in considering and debating strategic alternatives.

6. *The general politicization of society* is going to result in wider recognition, better analysis and higher standards of justice and ethics in regard to problems arising from conflicts of interest among shareholders, management, legitimate stakeholders and, of course, directors and boards. In particular, current concerns about the importance of shareholders and implicit or explicit claims on corporations will escalate.

These forces promise to cause sweeping and fundamental reforms and improvements in corporate governance and the board system. Demands for improved effectiveness and accountability will increase continuously in the future. Such future developments in the board system, already under way in many companies, can be categorized using our six-factor model of board effectiveness, outlined in chapter 8.

1. *Providing improved board leadership.* Understanding the critical role of the chairman, and the competence and time requirements of the job.

2. *Building legitimacy and power.* Active efforts made to build bridges to shareholders, to reform and make effective shareholder democracy, to empower and to restore the board to its proper and intended place in the system of governance.

3. *Clarifying and sharpening the job of the board.* Reorganizing the board to focus on its role in strategy formulation and implementation, oversight of performance and compensation of top management, reducing the size of the board, and making better use of committees to handle other aspects of its responsibilities.

4. *Raising the competence level of directors.* Defining the necessary qualifications, organizing a planned approach to director selection, evaluating the contribution of both the board and individual directors, and instituting educational and training initiatives for directors.

5. *Building a new board culture.* Creating a competent, active, committed cooperative board team with shared values, goals, and expectations, and in which constructive dissent is not only tolerated but encouraged.

6. *Improving the management of the board.* Better management of information, use of directors' time, committee assignments, compensation and the like.

PROVIDING BOARD LEADERSHIP

The individual whose job it is to lead in the transformation, upgrading and empowerment of the board is the chairman. Clearly, the role of the chairman will itself be reformed in the process. The growing demands of the job will mean the end of the existing pattern of a part-time, essentially "amateur" board chairman's job, whether handled as an add-on by the chief executive officer or by an independent director. The job of the chairman has become a serious business, with substantial time demands and a challenging job description. It has become a professional job in its own right, with commensurate authority and compensation. Selection of a chairman to lead the board is becoming as important as selecting a CEO and requires no less thorough a process, preferably managed by the nominating committee in close consultation with both the CEO and any large shareholders.

BUILDING LEGITIMACY AND POWER

The movement to restore the rights of ownership to shareholders, already under way, will undoubtedly continue, and boards will become increasingly accountable to shareholders for their decisions and actions.

The "unseen revolution" — the growth of mutual and pension funds, and their dominant role in the ownership of many companies — has been well documented. This revolution has been driven by demographic and social trends which show no sign of abatement. We should continue to see the growth of large institutional investors with a long-term point of view, and an even more rapid growth in the activism of these investors, including seeking board seats and requiring more current, frequent and comprehensive information from the companies in which they invest.

Paralleling this trend will undoubtedly be the continued movement towards liberalizing the process of corporate democracy. A few leading companies are already at the forefront in attempting to make the annual meeting a more meaningful, two-way means of communication between board and shareholders. Nominating and voting processes, particularly the use of proxies, are being opened up to rectify the long-standing bias in favor of management. Disclosure and reporting to shareholders, currently in an "overkill" situation for both management and most shareholders, will have to be streamlined and managed to make information more digestible and useful to investors. Convoluted and incomprehensible ownership patterns will be simplified in response to investor opposition. Demands for the legitimate election of directors are rising.

All these changes will increase the needed power and authority of the board in relationship to shareholders and management so that it can more effectively perform its legal duties.

CLARIFYING THE BOARD'S JOB

The impetus provided by increasingly active and committed shareholders will lead to the growing recognition of the concept that the board's major contribution is in overseeing the entire process of strategic management. Without a clear, strong and well-thought-through strategy, understood and accepted by shareholders, directors, and management alike, there is no adequate systematic basis for judging performance. The board's role in this process is critical: it is not to develop strategy on its own, nor is it to rubber-stamp a strategy developed by management. It is to be actively involved with management in the development of corporate strategy, and to take full responsibility for the strategy that emerges from this process. This also requires maintaining due diligence for the implementation of strategy through the board's audit, compensation, human resource, environment, and other committees, and the updating and amendment of the strategy as required.

The strong implication of the foregoing developments is that the work load on boards will continue to grow, and there will be pressure on each individual director to become an active participant in the process of strategy formulation and implementation. To do so will not only require a greater commitment of time, but a growing need for more diversified experience, knowledge, breadth of view, and understanding of the job required on the part of the directors individually and collectively. This suggests strongly a need for a more rational and planned director selection process, and continued opportunities for upgrading and updating directors' knowledge and skills.

RAISING THE COMPETENCE LEVEL OF DIRECTORS

Traditionally, most outside or "independent" directors have been chosen from the ranks of chief executive officers of other companies, with a smattering of lawyers, bankers, academics, retired politicians, and government bureaucrats. They have been preponderantly well-to-do, well-educated, white, and male. Not surprisingly, they tend to have similar interests, values, and political beliefs. The selection process, controlled by management or by a major shareholder, has reinforced the club-like atmosphere of many, if not most, public boards. Except in troubled situations, accountability has been absent and compensation correspondingly low.

The growing demands of the director's job, coupled with dramatically widened and increased personal liability, are substantially changing this picture. Many company boards are limiting the number of outside directorships that their CEOs can accept. Lawyers, bankers and other professionals who do business with the company are increasingly unacceptable as board members. Token directors can no longer be carried on the board. The time requirements, particularly the need to be able to "drop everything" on short notice when major issues arise, further restrict the availability of director-candidates. Growing complexity of board decision-making requires a higher standard of qualification generally. The result is a shrinking of the supply of qualified potential directors, and the increasing use of ''professional directors'' — knowledgeable hired guns who make directorship their profession, serving on a number of boards, and frequently helping transfer best practices from one to another. Many have retired from other jobs or occupations, and have the time to be able to deal with the demands of the active boards on which they sit.

As performance standards for directors and boards rise and are increasingly measured, it appears likely that greater use will be made of professional directors of this type. Further, better-planned selection of directors will undoubtedly help break down the ''club'' system and introduce greater diversity into boardrooms. Emphasis will shift from compatibility to competence and contribution.

BUILDING A NEW CULTURE OF PROFESSIONALISM AND TEAMWORK

The goal of board management in the future environment is to become effective in working together as a team of competent and empowered professionals — the emerging pattern of work demands it. Boards have seldom seen themselves as teams. Collective responsibility requires an approach built on the principles of competent participants engaging in open and vigorous debate, followed by consensual decision-making, closing of ranks, and group solidarity on decisions taken.

Strategic involvement implies a heavy work load on directors, more demanding qualifications, and a much greater time commitment and flexibility than has traditionally been the case. The board must be available to deal with complex issues on short notice. The difficulties implicit in a geographically-dispersed board are increasingly being mitigated if not eliminated by technology, in the form of telephone conferencing, video conferencing, facsimile, and the like — reducing the need for physical presence together in a boardroom and cutting down substantially on travel time and costs for directors. Encouraging and facilitating the transformation from the old culture — egocentricity, formality and ''don't-rock-the-boat'' — to the new — servant leadership, openness, dialogue and, as necessary, dissent — will become a top priority of all boards.

BETTER BOARD MANAGEMENT

The current trend, well identified in ongoing surveys, is towards smaller boards. This will undoubtedly continue; it is difficult to maintain an active, participative board of much more than 12 members, and many leading-edge boards today are even smaller. A balance must be struck between a board that is too small — overloading its members, and lacking breadth of perspective and viewpoint — and too large, where one quickly loses the contribution and sense of identification and commitment by individual directors.

The growing work load of the board will undoubtedly accelerate the growth in the use of committees to handle much of the work. Committees have long been used by boards for a variety of purposes. In many companies, executive or finance or special committees have been used not so much to spread the work of the board as to provide a forum whereby large or controlling shareholders could work directly with management without involving independent or unrelated directors. In this way, particularly thorny or financially significant issues could be dealt with, and a common solution agreed on, prior to discussing the matter with other directors.

The current trend is away from the use of such ''executive-type'' committees. Among other things, they tend to create ''two-tier'' boards, where some directors have a much greater access to information and influence on decisions than others. With larger boards, there may be a need for such a system; but with the growing emphasis on smaller, committed boards sharing collective responsibility (and individual liability), the focus is on having all key board decisions reviewed and dealt with by the entire board.

A second type of committee has been more common. These committees allow the board to do its due diligence in overseeing the implementation of strategy and fulfill its obligations in reporting to shareholders. The audit committee is probably the most common of these, along with committees to handle compensation, human resources, environment, pensions and the like. The work of these committees has become more significant in recent years, and will undoubtedly grow. In future, we foresee the development of strategic oversight committees charged with auditing the strategic management process — but not with the formulation of strategy itself, which remains a board responsibility.

A third class of committee has recently come into being. The nominating committee has been used by a number of boards to oversee the process of board renewal, with emphasis on the nomination and selection of new directors. In some cases, this committee or a governance committee has taken over responsibility for the review and oversight of the overall board governing process, including the board's own performance and accountability.

Many boards today have become captive to management, through management's control over the quantity and quality of information provided to the board on strategic issues. Board decisions can only be as good as the information on which they are based. Presentation of biased data and omission of key facts can decidedly skew board decisions.

Under the growing pressure for performance, boards today are increasingly taking control over their own information systems. Recognizing the need for broader, more timely and objective data, boards and board committees are insisting on the right to go beyond the data provided by management to supplement their information, including the use of electronic-based information systems. This makes sense: the kind of information required by a director is often quite different from that normally available to and provided by managers to the board. This can take the form of contracted outside sources and consultants, hired by and reporting directly to such board committees as compensation, environment, and audit. Or, it could be a consulting firm reporting on strategy options to the entire board. To make this independence a reality requires board control over its own budget, something which has seldom been the case in the past, but which will increasingly be so in future.

Existing director selection practices, based on an informal process and personal contacts, have been a major factor preserving the *status quo*. Increasingly, as the demands on directors grow, they are being replaced by planned succession processes and the use of professional search consultants. Rigorous selection criteria, growing from the individual company's needs and strategies, are replacing personal compatibility as the basis for nomination. And the administration of this process by a nominating committee, generally composed of independent directors, will go a long way to ensuring the selection of the most qualified individual for the job.

Joining a new board is a learning process for even the most experienced director. Gaining knowledge about the specific company, its history, its problems, its human resources, and its competitors is a necessary step for any incoming director. Few companies provide any systematic assistance in acquiring this sort of information, leaving it to the director and time to provide. More and more, enlightened chairmen and boards are planning orientation and briefing sessions for new directors in order to bring them up to speed as quickly as possible. And in some cases, existing directors are going back to school on subjects where dramatic changes have taken place, such as in the use of derivatives and hedging instruments and computer-based information systems. Developing and maintaining a high level of board competence will be a principal concern of the chairman in the board of the future.

Coupled with these developments will be a growing concern with evaluating the performance of the board and its individual members. A growing number of companies are taking initiatives in this direction, both through internally-administered questionnaires and through the use of external consultants. A principal objective is to identify both barriers to performance and persistent nonperformers, and to provide a more systematic basis for removing them, a burden which will fall primarily on the chairman, with assistance from the nominating committee.

A LOOK AHEAD

The issues of corporate governance, brought to the fore by the mergers, acquisitions, raids and takeovers of the 1980s and the corporate catastrophes of the early 1990s, are not going to go away. Corporate Canada has become acutely aware of the weaknesses that have built up in the system, and the importance of reformatting and getting governance right. Once learned, the lesson is unlikely to be forgotten.

That said, the governance issues of the 21st century will not be those of the 20th. Although attention swung much too late to the governing structure of our corporations, we are now launched into an era of substantial and marked improvement in governance. The early stages of this process, typified by the Cadbury, Treadway, and Dey reports, identified basic structural problems, and attempted to develop principles by which corporations should be governed. Although legalistic and mechanical, they helped identify many of the issues that needed resolution. An understanding of the subtleties and dynamics of the board-shareholder-management relationship was not their long suit, however, and the reports tended to be weak on implementation. We have attempted to take this process into a further stage, one based on intimate knowledge of the governance system and which lays out a practical, results-oriented route map for those who believe in making capitalism, and its governance, work.

NOTES

1. Myles L. Mace, "The President and the Board of Directors," *Harvard Business Review* (March-April, 1972). Mace was ahead of his time: much of what he wrote 25 years ago remains valid today.

2. See Chapter 7.